MERIDIAN

*Crossing Aesthetics*

Werner Hamacher

*Editor*

Edited by Simon Sparks

*Stanford University Press*

*Stanford, California*

*2006*

# MULTIPLE ARTS

*The Muses II*

Jean-Luc Nancy

Stanford University Press
Stanford, California

Printed in the United States of America
on acid-free, archival-quality paper

Library of Congress Cataloging-in-Publication Data

Nancy, Jean-Luc.
[Selections. English. 2006]
Multiple arts : the muses II / Jean-Luc Nancy ;
edited by Simon Sparks.
p.   cm. — (Meridian)
Includes bibliographical references.
ISBN 0-8047-3953-6 (hardcover : alk. paper)
ISBN 0-8047-3954-4 (pbk. : alk. paper)
1. Aesthetics.   2. Arts—Philosophy.
I. Sparks, Simon, 1970–   II. Title.
III. Series: Meridian (Stanford, Calif.)

B2430.N362E5 2006
700'.1—dc22
2005013559

# Contents

PART II: ART

# Acknowledgments

I would like to thank all those involved in the preparation of this volume. First, the other translators: Miguel de Beistegui, Jonathan Derbyshire, James Gilbert-Walsh, Sara Guyer, Leslie Hill, Hector Kollias, and Damon McCarthy, not merely for agreeing to undertake the almost impossible task of translating some of Nancy's least translatable essays, but for their graciousness in the face of my often excessive editorial intrusions. In particular, I would like to thank Miguel de Beistegui and Leslie Hill for their readiness to offer instant clarification on numerous points. Next, I wish to thank those artists who have generously allowed their works to be reproduced here: Lucile Bertrand, Susanna Fritscher, Guerrero, On Kawara, Soun-Gui Kim, François Martin, and Henri Etienne-Martin. Equally, I thank the galleries and institutions who have kindly granted permission to reproduce works in their possession: the Kunsthistorisches Museum, Vienna, and the Musée des Offices, Florence. I am grateful as well to the publishers of the first versions of the texts published in this volume; their names are listed in the sources section.

I owe an unpayable debt of gratitude to Helen Tartar, the most careful and patient of editors, to say nothing of the most committed, for her extraordinary help, patience, and encouragement over the course of this project.

My thanks, finally, to Jean-Luc Nancy, for writing the texts included here, and for his continual support, not merely in the preparation of this volume but in all things.

Simon Sparks

# PART I

# Literature

# § 1   Making Poetry

If we understand or, in one way or another, accede to a dawning of sense, we do so poetically. This is not to say that any kind of poetry constitutes a means or medium of access. It means—and this is almost exactly the opposite—that poetry cannot be defined except by such access, and that poetry occurs only when such access occurs.

This is why the word "poetry" refers indiscriminately to a type of language, a particular artistic genre, and a quality that may be present elsewhere, and indeed may be absent from works of this type or genre altogether. According to *Littré*, "poetry," used absolutely, signifies "those qualities that characterize good verse, and may be found elsewhere than in verse. . . . Poetic intensity and depth, even in prose writing. Plato is full of poetry." On this account, poetry is the indeterminate unity of a set of qualities that are not restricted to the kind of writing called "poetry" and can be described only by applying the adjective "poetic" to terms such as depth, intensity, daring, feeling, and so on.

*Littré* also states that, in its figurative sense, "poetry refers to everything that is elevated or moving in a work of art, or the character or beauty of a person, and even a product of nature." In this way, as soon as it is taken out of the literary context, the word "poetry" takes on a solely figurative meaning, albeit one that is merely an extension of the absolute sense, that is, the indeterminate unity of qualities that may be characterized generically by the terms "elevated" and "moving." Poetry as such is therefore always properly identical with itself, whether we are dealing with a piece of writing or a natural object, yet at the same time it is always only a figure of that properness, which is indeterminable according to any proper, properly proper sense. "Poetry" does not exactly have a sense; rather it has the sense of an access to a sense that is each time absent, and postponed until later. The sense of "poetry" is a sense that is always still to be made.

Poetry is in essence something more and something other than poetry itself. Or, to put it another way: poetry itself may indeed be found where there is no poetry at all. It can even be the reverse or the refusal of poetry, and of all poetry. Poetry does not coincide with itself: perhaps this non-coincidence, this essential improperness or impropriety, is properly what makes poetry what it is.

Poetry, then, may be deemed what it is only insofar as it is (at the very least) capable of negating itself, in the sense of renouncing, denying, or abolishing itself. By negating itself, poetry denies that the access to sense may be equated with any given mode of expression or figuration. It denies that what is "elevated" may be brought within reach, and that it may be possible to overcome the distance between us and what moves us (which is of course why it moves us at all).

Poetry, then, is the negativity by which access makes itself what it is—that which has to yield, and for that reason first refuses and withdraws. Access is difficult—but this is not a contingent quality; it means that difficulty is what makes access occur. Something that is difficult is something that resists our efforts to make something of it, and this is properly what makes poetry occur. Poetry is difficult, and hard to please. But because this is what it does to us, poetry seems too easy, and this is why it has long been treated as something frivolous. There is more to this than mere appearance. Poetry is at ease with the difficult, the absolutely difficult. With ease, difficulty yields. This does not mean it can be brushed to one side. It means that this is indeed poetry, presented for what it is, and that we are engaged within it. Suddenly, easily, we are in access, that is, in absolute difficulty, both "elevated" and "moving."

The difference between the negativity of poetry and that of its double, the discourse of the dialectic, at this point becomes apparent. The negativity of the dialectic, according to the logic of identity, puts to work the refusal of access as the truth of access. But it makes it not only into an extreme form of difficulty but also into an ever-present, regulatory promise of resolution and thus of an extreme form of easiness. Poetry for its part is not the slightest bit interested in problems: making things difficult is what it does.

(All the same, this difference cannot be resolved in terms of a distinction between poetry and philosophy, since poetry refuses to be confined to a single mode of discourse: "Plato" himself can be "full of poetry." Philosophy *versus* poetry does not constitute an opposition. Each of the two makes difficulties for the other. Together, they are difficulty itself: the difficulty of making sense.)

It follows that poetry is negativity, too, in the sense that it negates, in the access to sense, what would otherwise turn access into a moment of passage, either a way or a path, and that it affirms access as a presence, or an invasion. Suddenly (easily), being or truth, heart or reason yields its sense, and difficulty is there, holding us in its grip.

Correlatively, poetry denies that such access may be determined as one among others, or one relative to others. Philosophy accepts that poetry is another path (and at times, too, religion). Even Descartes can write that "within us are the seeds of truth: philosophers extract them through reason, while poets pull them out through the imagination, making them gleam with greater splendor" (I am quoting from memory). Poetry in return accepts nothing of the sort. It asserts the absolute and exclusive, immediately present, concrete and, as such, unexchangeable character of access. (Since poetry does not belong to the order of problems, there is no diversity of solutions either.)

It therefore affirms access, according to the rule not of precision (which is always susceptible to rearrangement, infinite approximation, and tiny adjustments) but of exactitude. It is finished, over; the infinite is here and now.

In this way, the history of poetry is the history of poetry's persistent refusal to allow itself to be identified with any given poetic mode or genre—not in order to invent one that would be more precise than all the others, or to dissolve them into prose, functioning as their ultimate truth, but in order ceaselessly to determine another, new exactitude. This is always necessary, every time anew, for the infinite is here and now an infinite number of times. Poetry is the *praxis* of the eternal return of the same: the same difficulty, difficulty itself [*la même difficulté, la difficulté même*].

In this sense, the "infinite poetry" of the Romantics is as determinate a presentation as the highly wrought texts of Mallarmé, Pound's *opus incertum*, or Bataille's hatred of poetry. This does not mean that these presentations are all interchangeable, nor does it imply that they are like so many figurations of a single self-identical, unfigurable idea of Poetry, or that struggles between different "genres," "schools," or "ideas" of poetry should therefore be seen as pointless. It does mean, however, that such differences are all there is: access occurs each and every time only once, and it has always to be done again, not because it may be said to be imperfect, but on the contrary because, when it is (when it yields), it is each time perfect. Eternal return and the sharing of voices.

Poetry teaches nothing other than such perfection.

To this extent, poetic negativity is also the rigorously determinate positing of the unity and exclusive uniqueness of access, its absolutely simple truth: the poem, or verse. (It could also be called: strophe, stanza, phrase, word, or song.)

The poem or verse is all one: the poem is a single whole of which each part is a poem, that is a completed act of "making," and verse is a part of a whole that is still verse, that is to say, a turning, a versing or reversing, of sense.

The poem or verse refers to the elocutionary unity of an exactitude. Such elocution is intransitive: it does not appeal to sense as a prior content; it does not communicate any sense, but makes it, being exactly and literally truth.

It thus utters nothing other than what serves as language, at one and the same time both its structure and responsibility, which is to articulate sense, bearing in mind that there is sense only by virtue of articulation. But poetry articulates sense, exactly, absolutely (and does not provide an approximation, an image, or an evocation).

That articulation is not solely verbal, and that language extends infinitely beyond language, this is something quite different—or just the same: "poetry" refers to "everything that is elevated and moving." In language or elsewhere, poetry does not produce meanings; it makes a thing and the "elevated" and "moving" into an objective, concrete, and exactly determinate identity.

Exactitude is integral completion: *ex-actum*, that which is done, acted to the limit. Poetry is the integral action of the disposition to sense. Each and every time it occurs, it is an exaction of sense. Exaction is the action of demanding a thing owed, then of demanding more than what is owed. What is owed by language is sense. But sense is more than all that may be owed. Sense is not a debt; it is not something to be demanded; and it is possible to make do without it. It is possible to live without poetry. It is always possible to ask, "Wherefore poets ... ?" Sense is a surplus, an excess, the excess of being in relation to being itself. The question is how to accede to this excess, to yield or cede to it.

This, too, is why "poetry" says more than what "poetry" wants to say. More precisely—or, better, more exactly: "poetry" says the more-than-saying as such and insofar as it structures saying. "Poetry" says the saying-more of a more-than-saying. And consequently also says the no-more-saying-it. But say it, sing it too, or beat it, chant it, thump it out.

The particular semantic field of the word "poetry," its perpetual exaction and exaggeration, its way of oversaying is a congenital feature. Plato (him again, poetry's ancient challenger) points out that "poiesis" is a word that was made in order to take the part for the whole: the solely metric production of chanted words for all productive actions in general. The former thereby exhausts the essence and excellence of the latter. The whole of *making* is concentrated into the making of the poem, as if the poem made everything that it is possible to make. *Littré* (him again, the poet of the "Ode to Light") gathers up this concentration as follows: "*poem*," he says, "from *poiein*, to make: the thing made *par excellence.*"

Why should poetry be the excellence of the thing made? Because nothing can be more accomplished than the access to sense. If it is at all, it is characterized entirely by its absolute exactitude, or else it is not (not even approximately). It is, whenever it is, perfect, and more than perfect, pluperfect. When access occurs, it is clear that it had always been there, and that similarly it will always return (even were one, oneself, to know nothing of this: but one has to assume that at each moment someone, somewhere, is acceding). The poem draws access from an immemorial past, which owes nothing to the reminiscence of some ideality, but is the exact existence, here and now, of the infinite, its eternal return.

The thing made is finished, finite. Its finishing is the perfect actuality of infinite sense. This is why poetry is represented as being more original than the distinction between poetry and prose, between different genres or modes of the art of making, that is, of art, taken absolutely. "Poetry" means: the first making, or making insofar as it is always first, each time an original act.

What is making? To posit within being. There is nothing more to making than positing as its end. But the end that started out being a goal now turns into its end in the form of its negation, and making is unmade as it reaches perfection. But what is unmade is identical with what is posited, perfected, more than perfected, pluperfect. Making accomplishes both something and itself each time. Its end is its finish: it thereby posits itself as infinite, each time infinitely beyond its own work.

The poem is the thing made of making in itself.

This selfsame thing that is both abolished and posited is the access to sense. Access is unmade as passage, process, aim, and path, as approach and approximation. It is posited as exactitude and as disposition, as presentation.

This is why the poem or verse is a sense that is abolished as intention (a wanting-to-say) and posited as finishing: turning back not on its own will but on its phrasing. Making no longer a problem, but access. Not to be commented upon, but to be recited. Poetry is not written in order to be learned by heart; but reciting something by heart is what makes each recited phrase into at least the suspicion of a poem. Mechanical finishing gives access to the infinity of sense. There is no antinomy here between mechanical legality and the legislation of freedom, but the first is what releases the second.

Presentation must be made; sense must be made, and perfected. This does not mean: produced, operated, realized, created, enacted, or engendered. It means none of all that, exactly; at least nothing that is not, before all else, what *making* wants to say: what *making* makes language do, when it perfects it in its being, which is the access to sense. When saying is making, and making saying, in the same way that one says "making love," which is making nothing, but making an access be. Making or letting: simply posing, deposing exactly.

There is no making (no technical operation or art, no gesture, no work) that is not shot through, more or less covertly, with this movement of deposing.

Poetry is to make everything speak—and to depose, in return, all speaking in things, with itself like a thing made and more than perfected.

Verses learned in childhood:

> Es schläft ein Lied in allen Dingen
> Die da träumen fort und fort
> Und die Welt hebt an zu singen
> Triffst Du nur das Zauberwort.

> There sleeps a song in every thing
> Which there lies dreaming on and on
> And the world will rise up to sing
> If you just happen upon the magic word.

This weighty, age-old business of poetry, which lies so heavily upon us and entangles us, resists our boredom and profound disgust for all poetical lies, affectations, and sublimities—even if it does not interest us, it forces us to halt, necessarily. Today just as much as in the age of Horace, Scève, Eichendorff, Eliot or Ponge, albeit in a different way. It was once said that after Auschwitz poetry was impossible, but then, conversely, that it was necessary after Auschwitz; but it was precisely of poetry that it seemed necessary to say the one then the other. The exigency of the access to sense—its exaction, its exorbitant demand—cannot cease forcing us to halt: discourse and history, knowledge and philosophy, action and law.

Let there be no more talk about the ethics or aesthetics of poetry. The making denoted as "poetry" comes well before, in the immemorial pluperfect. It lies lurking like a wild beast, tensed like a spring, and thus in act, already.

*Translated by Leslie Hill*

# § 2   Taking Account of Poetry

*1. The first chapter of* The Muses *acknowledges as a given the post-Romantic dispersion between the different arts. What happened to the poetic absolute that was once synonymous with the literary absolute? Why did poetry lose its status, irreversibly, as a unifier of the arts? In what way is this not something we should deplore?*

Is it the case that I "acknowledge as a given the post-Romantic dispersion between the different arts"? I must have expressed myself badly and not explained myself sufficiently. Romanticism displays a will to art in the singular, and in an absolute sense (which, by the way, does not mean there is no sign of something similar before—perhaps even long before—the Romantics). Anyway, that is what Romanticism displays—and that should also remind us, by the same token, that before the Romantics, the arts (which at the time were unified under the plural name "les beaux arts" or "fine arts," which itself was still distinct from the term "belles-lettres" or "letters," and which, by virtue of the implicit distinction it made, still believed in arts that were not fine, irrespective of whether they were free or mercenary), so, the arts, then, had relatively distinct modes of being. That was the situation before, which is not to say that something of the concept of "art" was not already present earlier, at least implicitly.

As far as afterward is concerned, I need to go into some detail. In this instance, the "dispersion" between the different arts is linked to their ceaseless gathering together under the aegis of "art" in the singular, working no longer as a federative principle but as a retrospective, unitary one. Underlying everything was a violent tension—all in the name of "art"—

between two poles: fragmentation on the one hand, and unitary hypostasis on the other. What is worth noting is the extent to which, increasingly, this hypostasis found its referent, its shifter, in the plastic arts rather than in poetry. For the Romantics, however, "poetry" was the absolute name. Under the name of "art," something was able to assert its freedom from religious, political, and philosophical tutelage, while also being hypostatized as a proper, self-referential, self-legitimating essence, thereby becoming quite distended in itself, less because of "dispersion" proper, than because of the mixing of genres and types, which resulted in confusion, interference, and an indefinite watering down of its effects.

But there is little doubt that poetry bore the main brunt of the process. Poetry, in this context, was simply the Romantic name for Art; so one could say that modern art is what happens when those "artistic practices" that had lost the proper name of their common identity, that is, "poetry," gathered together around a lifeless word, which was: "art." Why was this? Perhaps because poetry, for the Romantics, as for Kant and others before him, signified the organ of the infinite. The organ of the infinite was supposed to be what put to work (in the strong sense of the word "work") a kind of absolute transcendence beyond all determination. Romanticism was the liquidation (at least this is what it aspired to) of determination, as if some generalized anxiety had taken hold of society, which saw itself plunging into determination.

Poetry became the self-transcending of language, the self-transcending of sense—conceived as sense itself. This explains its tense, nervous, riven confrontation with philosophy. (Unless of course it was philosophy that sparked things off; but how can we tell, without rehearsing a whole lengthy historical process reaching back not just to the Romantics, and not just to the Renaissance, but surely to Plato, in order to make out what was at stake from the outset in the chiasmus and intimate conflict between poetry and philosophy? I do not want to venture any further here, and could not anyway, but writing that detailed history, parts of which admittedly already exist in fragmentary form, could be viewed today as a necessary task.) The other arts tried to protect themselves (but they were beset by the same vertigo, even as they struggled against it) by deploying all kinds of "formal" devices—"formal" in the sense that they refused to allow sense to leak away, and sought to apply a bandage to the hemorrhage. To say more, one would have to retrace the thoroughly modern tale of the big and the small in art: of large forms and little forms, great art and minimal art, the heroic approach and the arts-and-crafts approach, and so on. By such means, the "arts" could give the impression of being unaffected by the kind of internal dissolution or loss of identity by *overidentification* that overtook poetry.

This said, let me make one remark: you seem to think that it would be timely today to accept poetry's loss of privilege as a given. You speak as if the "hatred of poetry" (the expression, as you know, is from Bataille) had not already been under way for many years, since Rimbaud, Valéry, then Bataille and Artaud, and others too. This makes me wonder whether we should not be asking, today, given this long-standing suicidal or self-denunciatory situation, why the poetical, so to speak, if not indeed poetry itself, is widely held in the greatest suspicion. So much so that I am almost tempted to ask whether this suspicion in its turn should not itself be viewed with utmost suspicion. I do not mean we should abolish it, but we should know what is hiding behind it. What if, in fact, what lay behind it was a desire to rediscover "true" poetry? I will come back to this in a moment in my answer to Question 3.

2. *At the heart of this irreducible plurality of the arts, poetry enjoys the formidable privilege of being thought the most artistic of literary practices and the most arbitrary of artistic practices. (Compared to plastic artists, composers, or architects, poets often give the impression of being amateurs.) How might this ambiguous status be affirmed, in a rigorous manner that remains true to the demands of the present?*

I cannot answer this question, first of all because I find it hard to understand the terms of your first sentence, in particular the phrase "the most arbitrary of artistic practices." I rather would have thought that—if it has to be put in such terms—these days "arbitrariness" is already pretty widespread, not only because of the diversity of the arts themselves but also, more generally, because of current definitions of artistic "genres," the mixing, transgression, hybridization with which they are affected, and last of all the category of "art" itself. It seems to me that the question should rather be approached in that perspective. But I am in no position to answer what is being asked of me here, since I have nothing to prescribe as far as poetry is concerned. All I can say, at the very most, is that poetry surely cannot dispense with its relationship with philosophy, which is intimate, complex, conflictual, seductive, and manipulative all at the same time—on both sides and in both directions at once. Once again, we shall have to face up to this. At any event, a philosopher can hardly avoid being affected, one could even say riven, by a kind of need for poetry, which arises from the most urgent part of his or her practice, free of any exaltation or any "poeticizing" temptation. That does not mean poetry should—how shall I put it—take on board the whole of metaphysics. In any case, it is not a matter of "great subjects" or "profound thoughts," at least not merely and not simply. It is rather a matter of what, in respect of the relationship with language (or with being-in-language), is common to philosophy and poetry—that is, common to both and shared by them, even as it divides them from each other within the terms of that very community. I cannot say much more than this for the moment; in any case, what is at issue here is not so much arbitrariness as necessity.

3. *Contradicting in advance all previous versions, the early Romantics announced that the "idea of poetry" would be "prose" (according to the phrase Philippe Lacoue-Labarthe is fond of quoting). Does not this prediction still hold today? Poetry's fondness for part-objects and its formal fetishism periodically take it to the limit: by doing so, do they not prompt it to attempt a kind of self-transcendence, a sort of "prosaicization"?*

Not only does the Romantic prediction about "prose" still hold true today, but there is no doubt that, more than ever before, we are subject to its injunction or, if you prefer, faced with its prompt (as one might say in computer terms, "at the POE.TRY/> prompt, type in cd PRO/SE"). This whole business haunts us, literally, and there are numerous clues or pieces of evidence to this effect. It is here, though, that I would like to go back to what I had in mind under Question 1.

There is one straightforward doubt that to my mind ought to be removed, which is this: by laying claim to prose, all one is doing is laying claim to "the idea of poetry" as the Romantics' formula indeed has it. On that basis, there are manifestly a large number of precise and subtle things to be said, which some Romantics did say (the sober Romantics, as opposed to the sentimental and pseudo-mystical Romantics), which Benjamin said, too, and which today are being said, in very diverse and at times irreducibly contrasting ways, in texts by Lacoue-Labarthe, Badiou, Derrida, Agamben, Deguy, Bailly, and Alféri, as well as others, no doubt, that I have yet to come across. When all is said and done, the fact remains that what is at issue in all of this is "poetry." Things were much clearer with the Romantics, and you can add for instance to the phrase you were quoting a moment ago the statement from Novalis (which is cited by Benjamin in his *Concept of Art Criticism in German Romanticism*), "Poetry is prose among the arts." (We could talk about this in more detail later if you wish, but for the moment what I want to emphasize is that the "prose" at issue here is "true" poetry, or the truth of poetry.) What one can see today, I think, in many different formulations, as well as in your own question, is that a slippage is taking place, in such a way that prose has come to be seen as the "other" of poetry, meaning no doubt its realization, albeit its alienation or exteriorization (what Hegel refers to as *Entfrem-dung*). You yourself call it "a kind of self-transcendence." We need to think about the use of this dialectical term. For the moment all I am asking, in this whole affair, is that we should restore to poetry the particular emphasis that belongs to it and is still attached to it, instead of giving the impression that everything is tipping over into "prosaicization," which might lead one to believe that "prosaicism" is not far from the horizon, whereas you yourself (together with the others I have mentioned) are careful to avoid any such term!

What I want to say quite simply is this: even though it is abundantly clear that we neither can nor want to have anything more to do with the poetical, with poeticization, with grandiloquent fervor, with sickly-sweet suggestiveness, and all those things Bataille meant when he spoke of "the nauseous temptation of poetry," not to mention every sort of academicism—whether a Romantic, symbolist, Mallarmean, surrealist, or "postmodern" one—which are all now dead and buried, even though all that is abundantly clear, then, it is not at all evident what lies behind the demand for prose.

For the Romantics, once again, things were clearer: "prose" on the one hand was "sobriety" (let us leave that to one side for a moment; it is a huge undertaking, which, again, people today are more or less agreed upon—though without it always being entirely clear what precisely the agreement is); on the other hand "prose" was also a name for that dissolution or fluidification of genres for which the paradigm, from their point of view, was the novel. Admittedly, what the "novel" meant for them is not exactly the same as what it means for us. At one end of the spectrum, it had to do with a modern reworking of the epic (or the epic reworking of modernity), whereas at the other it was just a name with which to identify a problem, that of poetry's infinite "self-transcendence." The fact remains that we no longer even have the name as either a support or an index. Unless I am very much mistaken, the novel is now behind us, and it has not represented this idea of "prose" for quite some time. (Or else the name is deliberately used against itself, as when some writers call "novel" something that has nothing to do with that "genre"—and these decisions, too, should be examined.)

All this leads to the fact that "the idea of poetry" is more insistent than ever *as such*, if I can put it this way, that is, as an idea of poetry; but it also leads to the fact that in spite of everything, whether we like it or not, "poetry" is the word that we need to come to terms with, grapple with, or perhaps even fight against, but which, ineluctably, imperatively, we must take account of.

This is my view: that we cannot avoid taking account of poetry. In other words, we must take account of poetry. Poetry must be taken into account in everything we do and everything we think we must do, in our arguments, our thinking, our prose, and our "art" in general. Whatever lies behind the word, and even supposing it all turns out to be time-limited, finished, used up, or simply erased, the word itself still remains. There remains a word that has to be taken into account because it requires its due. We can get rid of the "poetical," the "poem," the "poet" without much loss (perhaps). But there is nothing we can do with "poetry," in all the indeterminacy of its meaning and despite this indeterminacy. It sits there, and refuses to go away, even when we challenge it, cast suspicion on it, or detest it.

4. *Might it be said that this transcendence is bound, yet again, to poetry's relationship with the other arts? More particularly, that it is bound to a new way of conceiving the technology of poetry?* The Muses *criticizes on grounds of principle the oppositions and reservations in which, in relation to the arts, the thinking of technology is mired. What particular effort may be said to be required on the part of poetry for these to be overcome?*

Let me take advantage of my previous point to move on to your fourth question. I shall endeavor to answer by continuing as follows:

If poetry insists and resists—it resists everything to some extent, and this is arguably also why poets often "give the impression of being amateurs," as you rightly say—the insistence of poetry extends to the humblest, poorest, most vulnerable of forms, including some that, in literary terms, are truly destitute, as well as the sickliest or stupidest liking for half-esoteric and half-sentimental pap (it is not very different in some ways from what happens when people are reduced to vagrancy), but it extends that far—and so far down the scale—because it insists, because it demands something, something that I really believe is irreducible to the petty-bourgeois fallout of the very worst kind of Romantic poetry (the "adolescent poet" genre or, going even further back, the clunking doggerel that is such an object of ridicule in Molière), something that does not belong to any "subculture," or even to "culture" at all—so if poetry insists and resists, it is in a way that goes beyond derisory manifestations like these and has other reasons. (Obviously, how the widespread phenomenon of poetic vulgarity is itself related to the apparent proximity of poetic techniques with one another, which differ in this respect from the techniques of the other arts, is something that needs analyzing, but I will not pursue it here.)

So what are the reasons for poetry's resistance? I see at least two types of movement. On the one hand, there is a resistance to discourse. But this is not a resistance to concepts, reason, judgment, logic, or demonstration. It is a resistance to the "bad infinity" (in Hegelian terms) of exhausted discourse, of discourse subject to infinite exhaustion—which is necessary in its own terms but is still exhausting. Indeed it exhausts itself, if I can put it this way, by following the paranoid injunction to constitute truth in the act of constituting itself, of coming to terms with itself and being absorbed back into itself in the process of its own self-constitution and self-understanding.

Let me give an example, because I think one is appropriate. Without wanting to be the slightest bit disrespectful toward Husserl, let me quote the conclusion, or at least the words that stand in for the conclusion (and therefore fail to conclude the text, which is unfinished) of the *Crisis of European Sciences and Transcendental Phenomenology*. It runs as follows:

> Reason is precisely that which man *qua* man, in his innermost being, is aiming for, that which alone can satisfy him, make him "blessed"; that reason allows for no differentiation into "theoretical," "practical," "aesthetic," or whatever; that being human is teleological being and an ought-to-be, and that this teleology holds sway in each and every activity and project of an ego; that through self-understanding in all this it can know the apodictic *telos*; and that this knowing, the ultimate self-understanding, has no other form than self-

understanding according to a priori principles as self-understanding in the form of philosophy.[1]

I think you can guess what I want to suggest. This discourse, which is indefinitely developable (and which Fink indeed planned to develop), says everything except what it "ultimately" speaks of, which is the *form* of philosophy. Or rather it says it; it makes it a subject of discourse; but at the same time it also turns into an indefinite de-formation or indefinite postponement of it (you will have noted too, in passing, the appeal to "aesthetic" reason, which should not be "differentiated" ... )This is what "poetry" resists. It can accept everything that is said here (let's not quibble for the moment about what is said in this particular instance and the way it is said), but it cannot accept that the "form" in question can envelop or enclose itself and "form itself," so to speak, on the basis of its own denial. When I say "poetry cannot accept this," this is not to say that poetry is an external authority to which the right and the power of any such refusal might be attributed. It is rather that this refusal itself is poetry, and even if "poetry" remains or appears, at this particular moment, to be completely indeterminate, then at least the word is determined by this refusal and as its very gesture.

(Let me add that in the third question I do not really know what you mean by "poetry's fondness for part-objects," but if the point is that what's involved is something that is not the "infinite object" of discourse, in that case I would say that there is no "object" that is *not* a "part-object," but that "part" here does not refer to any separation that has the value of a lack. On the contrary, it is the very distinction, or detachment—without anything lurking in the background—by virtue of which there may be "objects" in general.)

Second, what resists with poetry—and without any doubt this is closely linked to what I was arguing previously—is that which, in or within language, announces or keeps more than language. This is not any "super-language" or "overlanguage," but the articulation that precedes language "in" itself (and that might equally be termed "affection," "praxis," or "ethos," rather than "enunciation" in the proper sense of the term) and no doubt functions as something akin to "rhythm," "cadence," "caesura," or "syncope" ("spacing," "pulsating") and, at the same time, has the quality of what I would term, so as not to call it "figuration," an outline [*dessin*]: sense as outline, no longer within the continuum of sense, sense standing out, in this sense, and not as an object of discourse. It is sense, if you will, as *inflexion* (as in the inflexion of a voice, or a tone, whether being raised, lowered, or sustained; and in the sense of inflection as a backward turn instead of a straight line, a kind of folding rather than syntax, and so on). This is insistent even in songs and nursery rhymes, and of course even in discourse, in rhetorical or prosodic ways that are more or less in evidence. I would go as far as to say (though I have little liking for this particular vocabulary) that it insists in the "unconscious," and as the "unconscious" that language is (which is to say something entirely different, as you will have realized, from Lacan's claim that "the unconscious is structured *like* a language").

This insistence is, however, neither childish nor popular in the sense that it may be thought to verge on poetic infantilism or populism. (Admittedly it is also true that something of what makes the notion of the "people" so problematic, so difficult, and so remote for us today is evidently buried here, together with something of the necessarily popular existence of language.) "Popular" in this context means: not dominated, not regulated, not normalized.

If the "technology" of poetry, as you call it, refers to the different ways in which there is recourse to language as "outline" (distinct from its use as a vehicle for information, which exists so to speak outside language), if it refers to the entirety of those inversions by which "sense demands sound back" (in Valéry's phrase) or, alternatively, to the whole range of different kinds of thickening, densification, or hardening that affect the "sign" as such—and not its status as "sign-of" something—and also the whole of the equiprimordiality of language signs, their coalescing and interweaving, the structure that embeds them inside one another, both as a whole and singly, the whole machinery of assonance, and everything that shows that language is not one particular technique but technicity itself *as such*, or the symbolic technicity that is nothing other than technicity itself (as is clear from Stiegler's account of Leroi-Gourhan in *Technics and Time I*), if the technology of poetry refers to a whole set of linguistic devices (which are of course variable and diachronic, albeit arguably structured in synchronic cross sections, as for example—and perhaps this is more than merely an example—the whole set of possible variations on the *refrain*, which is itself a synchronic cross section ... ) in order to refer to itself in its quality as *techne*—yes, then, indeed, it is hardly surprising that the generalized technological display of the "arts"—which is also a turning back upon the sense of their name, *ars*, and that massive drift affecting the general sense of a word that was supposed to be subject to the authority of the aesthetic—it is hardly surprising that this exhibition should not be accompanied by a disqualifying of major "art" and a rediscovery—itself a major event—of its own technicity. Prosody, poetic meter, the canonical determinations of form, poetic "license," as well as lexical or syntactic freedom, "real sonority" (Hegel), all these things insist within us, they cluster together, so to speak, in Celan's *auseinandergeschrieben*—and beyond. I obviously do not mean that the ode or the sonnet, the hexameter or the caesura, is waiting for us on our immediate horizon; but I do mean that the tension of which they were the outcome is back—never having gone away, never having been capable of going away.

In that case let me add something else: once poetry is approached from this "technical" angle, which certainly is not at all a particular angle, it is entirely possible that poetry finds itself acting out on its own behalf the whole scene of the differences between the arts. There is no such thing as "poetry in general," any more than in reality there is a thing called "art in general," since art on the contrary exists by virtue of the differences between the arts. Poetry, however, occurs each time within the differences between what used to be described, years ago, as its diverse genres and forms, within these differences that themselves combine with differences between languages, and with the further difference that poetry, precisely, puts into play within each language. There are indeed only "poems," as we were once all told in primary school. Of course, I do not at all therefore want to abandon any questioning of the being or essence of poetry; but I do want to say that the plurality of different kinds of poetry is integral to that essence.

At the same time, let me also introduce one further consideration. In accordance with poetry's absolute "law of resistance," the idea or motif of poetry also resists being a general index for a certain quality or property shared by *all* the arts (including practices deemed to be nonartistic, technical, or scientific behaviors or procedures, and so on). We are all only too ready to speak of the "poetic nature" of a painting, a piece of music, a film, a space shuttle, a wedding, or a burial. ... No doubt, most of the time, the habit is a vague, sloppy, even dubious one. "Poetry" is the major signifier for what is indefinable, unnameable, and so on. "Poetry" always comprises a more or less surreptitious appeal to silent effusiveness. But, all in all, is it not precisely on this question of *silence* that we should know what we are in fact talking about, so to speak?

On the one hand, there is the silence that precisely constitutes all arts at the limit of discursive meaning, and shares out their roles according to the law of incommunicability between their "sensible" modes of existence. On the other hand, there is also the silence—it is of course the same—by which poetry in the strict sense is held in reserve, refusing all discourse, while also at the same time constituting poetry as one of the arts and as something differentiated from itself. Should we not ask ourselves whether the current inflation or implosion of poetry does not have—for very precise philosophical reasons (look at the whole history of the "sublime")—something to do with an overdetermination of silence: silence understood as a way not of *being silent* but of *imposing silence*, a "silencing" and a "falling silent," that is, not as the sovereign, silent margin of language but as a "self-transcendence," leading to effusiveness, exaltation, and, in a word, absolute chatter (all the while chattering on about silence, too) with which seemingly "poetry" has at last become synonymous?

I would like to say more about "mutism," were it not that the notion itself is determined as a lack of speech. I no more want to talk about the lack of language than I do about the taciturn restraint of a superlanguage. What is at issue is the need to address silence as an exact cut across the horizon of language, an outline traced at the margin of language and by that token at the margin of all the different art forms, dividing up and sharing out among all of them, insofar as they are incommensurable with one another, a *being silent*—or, if you prefer, a *silence of being*—of which the arts all "give account," so to speak, precisely in the sense that they do not speak about it, do not speak to each other either, and cannot in any sense be totalized or synthesized within a common language. Poetry, in these circumstances, is exactly the place where the different arts come together *insofar as they divide each other up and divide from each other*, and thereby divide poetry up along with themselves.

Let me put it yet another way. Poetry could be said to give in language an account of what, as art and the difference between the arts, acts as the margin and cut of language. It follows that poetry cannot but appear in a major, privileged position, as an art of language and as the poetic dimension of all arts (we cannot in this perspective simply dispense with the whole of tradition, or indeed with Romanticism). But it also follows that this major position does not give rise to any "federative" function or one that is "expressive" of the totality of art: it articulates the measure—both as delimitation and as distinct mode—that shares them out *auseinander*, that is, together but with each remaining separate from the others. (My indirect point of reference here is the motif of "measure" introduced by Heidegger on the basis of his reading of Hölderlin, which for that very reason demands detailed commentary.) This measure is itself the measure of sense, which is also what is intended as the essence and *sensible* finality of the arts, of each one taken on its own and of poetry itself. How sense is measured: that is what is at issue, and it implies simultaneously, each inside the other, both an ontology of sense and a technology of the arts.

What I have termed here the "resistance" of poetry could be described, all in all, as language's resistance to its own infinity (or its indefiniteness, according to the exact meaning one chooses to give to the "infinite"). It is resistance to the measurelessness that language is by itself—and, consequently, resistance as it is inscribed within language, but on—or as—its other side or underside. One could also say that the indefinite expansion of language, its constitutive chatter, belongs to the order of endless approximation; its other side is exactitude without remainder.[2] This other side is inscribed within language itself; it, too, is constitutive of language, and this is also the reason why poetry's resistance can just as easily end in silence (which is "exact" only by default) as become caught in the trap of chatter and measurelessness.

This is also why the resistance of poetry is more marked, but also more difficult, when (rightly or wrongly) an age is especially aware of being consigned to chatter, as is the case with our own. (Inversely, in a period when language was strictly controlled and exact, poetry went into decline: there is more "poetry" in the whole of Rousseau or Diderot than in Delille or Chénier.)

I will stop there. There are too many things to say all at once. Let us come back to all of this another day.

*Translated by Leslie Hill*

# § 3    Around the Notion of
## Literary Communism

## Introduction by Philippe Mesnard

Originally, these introductory remarks had an addressee. I drafted them
with the intention of asking Jean-Luc Nancy about a few of the ideas or
themes most prominent in his work. From this already substantial body
of work, comprising, at the time of writing, almost twenty books, I chose
to narrow the focus to two volumes. The first, *The Inoperative Community*, is a commentary on the notion of "community" taking Bataille's
work as its starting point.[1] In it, Nancy reflects upon the notion of communism while maintaining a close proximity to Heidegger (I won't attempt to summarize this book here). The second, *Compearance*, subtitled
*A Politics to Come*, includes both an essay by Jean-Christophe Bailly, "The
Isthmus," and Nancy's own text "Compearance: From the Existence of
'Communism' to the Community of 'Existence.'"[2]

Not only does each of these works take literature into account (and
how could they possibly avoid doing so?), they also initiate an engagement between literature and philosophy, inscribing themselves within a
tradition whose most distinguished representatives would be the German
Romantics. From this engagement comes a properly political concern, albeit one that seems to grasp the political only in terms of what calls it
into question.

I wanted to examine these notions and the vocabulary from which they
arise as well as the movement of thinking that accompanies them and the
grammar (philosophical? literary?) that arranges or adjusts them.

Jean-Luc Nancy, toward the end of "Compearance," you highlight the ambiguity inherent to what you term figuration: "in order to exclude, exclusion has to designate: it names, it identifies, it figures."[3] Immediately following this, however, you say that figuration "cannot itself simply be condemned," and raise the following questions: "How are we to exclude without figuring? And how are we to figure without excluding?"[4] Now, these two notions—exclusion without figuration, figuration without exclusion—are "two sides of the same limit," and you formulate accordingly the following proposition: "If 'politics' is 'management' . . . then it is so as the management of this unmanageable limit."[5] Now, is not the task of modern literature to disclose this limit of which you are speaking here? Ought not literature to reveal this limit of politics as what is inaccessible to it and thereby unmanageable? In showing that politics is unable to manage this limit, does not modern literature thereby pose, at least indirectly or independently of its content, the question of the value of politics? Perhaps this is what is meant by what are almost the last words of *The Inoperative Community*'s "Literary Communism": "'Literary communism' indicates at least this: that community, in its infinite resistance to everything that would complete it (in every possible sense of the term), signifies an irrepressible political necessity, and that this necessity in turn demands something of 'literature,' the inscription of our infinite resistance."[6] In showing this political limit, however, a limit that is also the limit of politics, in inscribing this resistance and in being an integral part of it, does not literature condemn itself thereby to a life wholly outside politics, to resistance or hostility to it?

How could we envisage, from a specifically political point of view, a delimitation of the space that we call literature? Is this space one of mere provocation alone? You write that "'literary communism' is so named in order to provoke."[7] Is it not rather dangerous, however, both for politics and for literature, for this to be merely a matter of provocation?

Pro-vocation: etymologically speaking, "to call out." Literature maintains a privileged relation with what has no place, with what does not take place as such, namely the Outside. In imagining what is excluded, does literature testify *on behalf* of those who have neither political representation nor political voice? Or is literature seriously mistaken about itself when it lays claim to sovereignty or to avant-garde speech, when it is thought under or, indeed, as the sign of revolution? Does literature not have (or does it not at least *also* have) a regulative function that chimes perfectly with the question of testimony (whether the testimony in question is that of the Horror or that of social misery), but that is no less an eminently cultural function?

—P. M.

~

## Around the Notion of Literary Communism

Having read your questions, I want to try to respond to the broader picture that they paint, rather than to their individual formulations. In what follows, allow me the improvisational movement of a response.

What is political about literature is not its representation of society (regardless of whether or not this representation is a critical one, and regardless, too, of the fact that, in a sense, no representation can ever be deprived of critical function), but that part of it that helps cement the social bond. Indeed, a critical representation can develop in a decidedly nonliterary way, sociologically, for instance. Or in a properly political way.

In saying this, I am also claiming that there is, from the outset, a properly political gesture that ought not to be confused with its literary counterpart. The political gesture aims at the redistribution of power, at breaking with a dominant order. Its condition of possibility is both a bond and the shattering of that bond. It assumes thus that there *is* a social bond and so a fundamental universal equality. Its goal, however, is not the establishment of such a bond (its fastening, let us say), but the exercise of equal power or of equality as power. What I am calling "the fastening of the bond [*le nouage du lien*]" is not a continuation of the political but something that falls on either side of it. It is not the principle or end of politics—or, if it is, then only in the paradoxical manner that implies a discontinuity and a difference in level between principles and ends on the one hand and power on the other. Politics happens wherever that bond is lacking as a principle or as an end. It happens in separation, therefore; indeed, one might say that it happens *as* separation and so happens in the name of displacing and overcoming an altogether different sort of separation: that of domination. Politics as nonseparation would be the idealistic projection common to an entire tradition (Rousseau, Marx, and so on, perhaps even Aristotle; or, more accurately, *a certain* Rousseau, *a certain* Marx, and so on). Here, the bond is thought as a subject-process able to complete itself by appropriating every sphere of existence and every actor on its stage.

As such, our modern tradition has exploited and projected away the grand image of the Athenian theater assumed both by politics and by literature (the assembled city gazing enrapt at its own myths in the various spectacles orchestrated by the city itself and its constitution, etc.). Without wanting to establish a historical truth contrary to this projection, I should note that the theater in Athens was wholly distinct from the assembly, from the institutions and play of political forces. The manner in which the Athenian people were the "people of the theater" was not immediately and identically that in which they were the "people of the city." It is certainly rather odd that so many still cling to a nostalgic celebration of this supposed communion of community in a supposed communion of politics and art. Yet this persistent belief has some significance for the reciprocal implication of this communitarian or communal ideal—this *communional* ideal, we could say—and the ideal of a reciprocal relation between politics and literature.

~

Now, the bond in question, far from being a communion, is one that fastens but does not complete (one that accomplishes nothing but a knot that preserves separation—and that also contains the possibility of inequality and domination). Incompletion [*inaccomplissement*] is the very condition of politics. Fastening is the very condition of literature. The two imply one another without ever infusing or transcending one another. If, on the contrary, we were to project a completion of this bond, we would end up with the Romantic projection of a "poetic republic" or with the Rousseauian projection of a subjectivization of community (and it is hardly by chance that the latter excludes literature and art from community, itself a superior "art"—witness the idea of the "civic festival," for example).

All of which does not prevent the two orders from implicating one another or prevent the fastening as such—literature in its modern (non-mythical) sense—from being strictly contemporary with modern (non-theological) politics. Nonetheless, the manner in which the two orders implicate one another is a curiously disjunctive or differential one.

Such considerations are still programmatic, of course. They require a rigorous distinction between "fastening" and "completion"; that is, they require a prior examination of what I have tried to term the "in-common" in order to distinguish it from "community" as the projection of completion. If there were community (as principle and end), there would be neither politics nor literature (for either one would absorb everything, the subject in the citizen or the citizen in the subject). Such is the idea of community as *work* and as its own work (community in the sense, then, of communism, fascism, National Socialism, and national aestheticism), to which I have tried to oppose a concept of an "inoperative" or "unworking" community, that is, community as essentially incomplete. "Politics" and "literature," therefore, would be the flip sides of the "inoperative" or the "unworkable," two sides necessarily disjointed or differential since neither one would complete itself in or through the other. At the same time, however, these two sides face one another, each one referring to the other as a limit rather than as a principle-and-end. Here, there is doubtless something essential for democracy, something that, as a negative symbolism, leaves behind the symbolism of the completed bond (as proposed by Claude Lefort under a more Lacanian schema) and suggests, rather, what Jacques Rancière terms "an in-constant community, suspended on the contingency and resolution of its act."[8]

With this, I am looking to displace something that, in a few of my published texts, might well give the impression of the deducibility or continuous derivation of a politics from the fastening of the bond. In a sense, there is politics because of this fastening. This fastening, however, is unequal in itself, the "fundamental" equality that it reveals being essentially unequal, able to constitute neither a "ground" nor an "end." Moreover, this equality is open to domination, that is, to unjustified, unsubsumed inequality (inequality drawn back to the theological register). The modern, nontheological condition is the disclosure of the "in-common" as a tension and differentiation between the fastening of the bond and the equality of the subjects of that bond. Now, these subjects happen only through the fastening of the bond and so according to an inequality that contradicts the bond itself. This contradiction is in no way a dialectical one; it is irresolvable in terms of a subject-process. It requires political intervention. Politics has to sever the inequality of this knot, just as literature cannot cease fastening it. Literature is political, then, in a paradoxical sense that both conjoins and separates in the same space. (And again, I think it is important to point out that this modern space is one in which neither "literature" nor "politics" is an accidental "invention," contemporary and connected; rather, this double modality of the in-common is sustained in all onto-theo-logical communities.)

~

At this point, I want to turn to what, under these conditions and with all of these caveats, situates literature *within the limits* of politics.

What properly *fastens*, whether by way of representation or not, is writing. This word, however, need not be charged with negative, needlessly sophisticated resonances, nor with the esoteric allure that has become oh so fashionable in certain circles. (This trend, moreover, always amounts to an abusive essentialization of writing, to giving writing the value of what does not fasten but completes, giving it thereby an immediately political import and stability: writing is supposed to be "politically active" in and of itself, just as politics is supposed to be an "inscription," all on the basis of a stable, fusional, or organic community—another version, then, of the myth of Athenian theater). Instead, then, this word "writing" needs to be brought back to its simple and necessary truth—an origin that can be sought directly in the work of Benjamin, Adorno, Bataille, Blanchot, Derrida, and Foucault. This body of work arises from reflections that were and are indissociably political *and* literary (and it is hardly by chance that its background is the problematic of what is usually termed *littérature engagée*). These thinkers, along with various others, have tried to think under the idea of "writing" the movement of saying that exceeds every sense, a movement without which sense itself would be neither *engagé* nor advanced.

Such a thinking is entirely necessary and thus cardinal for an epoch characterized by the seemingly endless multiplication of significations and of indifference toward them (which is also to say an epoch characterized by the end of the theologico-political). It offers precisely the reverse of nihilism: to the insignificance on which nihilism ruminates, it opposes *signification* as such. That is to say, it discloses not a sense but the birth of sense, the birth to sense, both within and beyond signification. The opposition here is not an external one. Nihilism—the end of metaphysics—is not "opposed" or "denounced" but shot through, significance drawing itself thus from out of insignificance itself in much the same way as that "layer of unrefined sense" to which Merleau-Ponty refers in relation to art (and the emergence of literature can be understood only within the context of the modern emergence of art).[9]

The first mark of significance is its singularity. There is no such thing as significance in general; or, more accurately, general significance, the absolute generality of the element of "making sense" in which and *as* which we are in the world (or in which and as which the world itself *is*), lies in its infinite singularity. Significance is *the singular* event of the emergence of sense. A general generality is always a signification, a constituted representation. The generality here, however, is the generative character of sense, its generosity: the gap, the opening, the step or the being-to that constitutes in itself a making or taking sense. This happens only as a singular event—and, reciprocally, that aspect of an event that constitutes the truth of the event (its "event-hood," its happening) is the opening of and to sense. "Writing" in its modern sense designates the event of sense and sense as event.

~

In a more aesthetic context, we might call this "style." In yet another context, a more psychological and moral one, we might call this "voice." Writing is merely the most austere and necessary name for the same thing—divested of aesthetic pleasure and the mysteries of interiority. Writing is style without ornament and voice without resonance, if I may put it like that. It exposes only the movement of clearing in each: a difficult and uncertain clearing, a movement that begins continually anew (a movement, that is, both continually rebeginning and continually withdrawing), clearing a path of sense through the jungle of nonsense.

Or, rather—and this is really what ought to concern us here—the only sense proper to writing's movement is that of the *address* of sense. In this address, sense is extended from one to the other or, more accurately, from one to all others, extended, put forth, or exposed to the fastened knot of a "communication." If the signification being communicated to me is not communicated by, in, and *as* the movement through which it makes sense for someone, then it is not communicated to me. It makes no bond; at best, it delivers information. And yet, it is always delivered *to* singular sense. The bond is reciprocal; sense, however, taken absolutely, is necessarily reciprocal or it is nothing at all. It does not comprise, for example, a sheaf of theological, moral, and political statements as contained in, say, *The Divine Comedy*. In this respect, such a poem has no "great message." Dante's *writing*, however—his voice, his style—exposes this collection of significations as a concern for sense. And this is why, perhaps, the opening of the poem draws attention to "the difficulty of saying." And with this in mind, we might risk the following formulation: sense does not entail that something be signified; rather, it entails the difficulty of saying.

The communication of sense, or the sense of sense, its sense as what binds, can be only the communication of a worry and a difficulty. This situation is not necessarily a dramatic one; rather, it means that sense has sense only as an act of communication or sharing that is precisely *not* the transfer of information. In fact, the only true transfer of information is the one between computer memory banks. Between ourselves, the merest passage of information is itself an act of sharing; at the very least, such information has the *sense* of coming from one to another and so of becoming, beyond any signification that it might contain, the movement of both in or toward sense, the sense of each and of their "being in common" (where the "in" designates the dimension of sense and not the substantiality of a community).

Nothing in the world is more wholly shared than sense, which consists, quite precisely, of its sharing alone. But this sharing is not an equal distribution among the various individual positions of an already established setup. Rather it is sharing's proper difference in the repetition of its transmission.

Not so very long ago, there was a tendency on the part of a certain structuralism to say (or for us to *want* a certain structuralism to say) that sense is an illusion exhausted, with no real consequence, in the combination of significations. What this fails to recognize, however, is that this "with no real consequence" is not itself consequence but constitutes the *significance* of all possible significations, of all making sense as such, and that this is itself possible only if sense is involved as *address* and as *fastening*, within, through, and beyond any signifying event.

∿

It is no accident that one major and continuous experience of the modern world is the experience that "everything has already been said, and it is too late to change that now" (La Bruyère). Yet while this experience would appear to be challenged or suppressed by a thinking of originality, it is nonetheless intimately bound up with it. Elias Canetti grasped something of this, writing, "It is important to repeat all great thinking by ignoring the fact that it has already been done."[10] What is central here is the fact that the repetition is able to be a repetition—and not, say, a reproduction—only by virtue of the difference introduced by the singular act of making sense, a difference that itself gives rise to this act of making sense and so to its writing and its address. As such, then, what is repeated where "great thinking" is concerned is not its signification but what is precisely *not* signified in it (or, put differently, "what still remains unthought").

This difference, however, is external neither to "great thinking" nor to signification. The repeated utterance of a sense involves no extrinsic variation in tone or situation. Rather, what is each time at stake is the total reengagement of sense, of what exceeds signification, and of this excess itself as address (addressed to the other, which probably goes without saying, but in a very precise sense: it is, in me, the other of the address who makes me come to sense; it is as its addressee, in other words, and not as its putative producer that I am the "subject" of sense—precisely what is meant by writing).

Furthermore, we should not put our faith in a finite stock of significations from which a variety of statements might be constructed. In a way, it is doubtless possible to say that the order of signification is finite. In saying this, however, we are not speaking of the end of an explorative process; rather, the order of signification *is* this process itself and has been so from the very beginning of this world of sense that we call the "West" and about which it would be no exaggeration to say that the celebrated second chorus of the *Antigone* already "says everything." What this chorus speaks of, however, over and above the marvels and evils of *techne*, over and above the uncertainty of our destinies, is the *deinotaton*, the "most troubling," the "most extraordinary" that man is. It speaks, that is, of the infinite peculiarity of sense. Literature is the repetition of this nomination and, in this sense, begins with the Greeks; indeed, it begins with the interruption of myth and as the voice of this interruption.

∽

Literature says that we are sense and does so unreservedly since there is no longer any sense that could be given (and trotted out), merely the gift of making sense (of addressing) (the desire to or the gift of the desire to make sense). The West anticipated an aspect of this in the invention of hermeneutics, that is, in the treatment of sacred texts as inexhaustible reservoirs of sense. Yet hermeneutics is still in thrall to and under the watchful eye of an unassailable core of pure, already-given sense, however "mysterious" this may be. Christianity, however, as the interpretation of mystery itself as *logos*, draws hermeneutics irreversibly beyond itself: the ever-renewed reservoir of significations is converted into infinite insignificance.

Likewise, there was a time when politics, as the interpretation and articulation of the various senses of the "good life," appeared bound up with a number of different significations. Politics *itself* was literature in that it implied the latter's narration(s), its gestures, its song, its staging.

(This succession of "times" or "eras" and the historical method presupposed by it is somewhat deceptive, far too straightforward a representation. It is always possible that, in every regime of representation—mythic, religious, etc.—the true praxis of sense, that is, the most original *ethics*, will always consist in distinguishing sense (matters of gesture, conduct, style) from signification (objects of belief, of commitment). It is far less certain, however, that we could ever divide history into an age of belief and an age of nonbelief. The scope of this question, though, is far too broad to be addressed here.)

The event of modernity (to speak in a historical idiom) is the exposure of making sense as such, an exposure divested of representations, as political as it is literary. In this sense, we might well chance our arm and say that the French Revolution and then Marx's exploits tended toward the reduction of all representation, a tendency that would culminate in the address of a making-sense-in-common delivered over to itself as end without end. Doubtless this is one sense of the word "people," its most difficult sense and the one that most exceeds signification, the one that sums up the novelty and the aporia of modern politics (or even one that comprises the true sense of the slogan "Liberty Equality Fraternity"). Yet what comes to be disclosed in this modern event and in this sense of "people" is the dehiscence and differentiation of politician and literature, the differentiation to the point of rupture between sense as what admits of representation and sense as fastening and as address.

~

As such it is entirely possible that, facing one another from opposite sides of the "people," we have, in this excess of sense, simultaneously discovered and abandoned a bloodless literature and an equally bloodless politics: a literature apparently bloodless because of its commitment to representing an infinite fastening that is unable to provide any completed figure of the people; a politics apparently bloodless because of its commitment to managing a domination whose subversion is unable to establish any figure of the people. And this is why both appear locked in the perpetual exchange of one and the same reproach, the inability to furnish a figure. I say that this is how the situation *appears* to us because we do not yet know how to decipher it properly. We do not know how to decipher what discloses the limit across which this literature and this politics ought never to move (one cannot become the fiction of the other—a formulation that, recalling Philippe Lacoue-Labarthe's *The Fiction of the Political,* is quite possibly that of fascism or totalitarianism.)[11] At this limit, we feel the modern need for an absence of figure, that is, an absence of the completion of the bond. And we need to acknowledge accordingly an irreducible heterogeneity between the sort of fastening that does not complete and the separation that is the space of domination and subversion. We need to grasp the two together without conflating them (precisely what is invited by the sirens of mythology, fundamentalism and essentialism, by the religious and/or populist politics which are, not surprisingly, in full swing today). I realize that this wholly negative need actually proposes nothing, indicates no literary or political positivity. And yet, I do not think that we should strive to maintain a pure and simple absence of figure, which would be the mere reversal of a presence and in this way a negative theology (which is still a theology). This means that we must reinvent, through and through, what a "figure" is (figure of a "people," or "people" as "figure"); and in order to do this we must first ponder this: there are at least two functions, that of fastening (which does not complete) and that of separation (which also does not complete). That these functions would be turned toward each other does not mean that they have a common end—a common figure or fiction whereby the gap between literature and politics, between sense and equality, would be overcome. Henceforth, we know that the closure of this gap is identically the closure of sense and of equality in a work of death. But inversely, the gap does not suppress the face to face.

I am well aware of the difficulty—indeed, the opacity—of my attempted response or of my preludes to a real response. I have wanted to say here, above all else, that the project I have sketched (in *The Inoperative Community* and in one section of "Compearance") in order to indicate in "literature" the truth of "politics" now appears to me to require serious revision and amendment. This does not seem to me to invalidate my initial analyses concerning the "essence" of being-in-common. Nevertheless, this project does approach something that must be denounced: the renewal of a myth of community (a renewal contrary to my intended theme, being-in-common).

What I have tried to say is this: there is, or there has been, a double project or fiction of politics in literature and of literature in politics. This double projection has been taken as the truth of both, of the one by way of the other and of the one in the other. This is, in a way, a truth (illusion) common to Romanticism and communism—basically, fascism, if we want to see in this apotropaic term an irresistible temptation toward the completion of community as signification (and thus, a refusal to confront being-in-common as the element of unachievable sense). "Fascism" names the politicization of literature and the literization of politics, leading both of them, together, toward the figural effectuation of the "people" (the theological-political purely and simply "secularized" or "immanentized"). "Democracy" comes to name not a "good" effectuation of the same "people" under the "legal State," but the tension maintained by the "people" at its proper figural effectuation. And this tension draws along with it the tension maintained, at the limit, between "literature" and "politics."

But our awareness of this double projection's fascist impasse does not mean that the two orders, literature and politics, are purely foreign and closed to one another. On the contrary, and in conformity with the absolutely contemporary character of these two orders (whether we take them from the birth of the West, or from the explanation that gives to these two words their irreversible modern senses; which is also to say, and not by chance, senses that are impossible to fix and are *approached only indefinitely*), this awareness brings to light a heterogeneity of the functions of being-in-common: the function of fastening and the function of separating and subverting. The function of sense and the function of equality. Heterogeneous *and* indexed to one anther. Freedom is in some way their chiasmus. And perhaps fraternity names the illusion that this chiasmus is being resolved—either that or it indicates something, the one to the other. Freedom is in a way the chiasma of the one and the other. (Fraternity perhaps names the illusory resolution of this chiasma—or perhaps it indicates something still unsuspected). But this still remains to be thought.

*Translated by James Gilbert-Walsh*

# § 4   He Says

He comes, introduces himself, and says:

I used to speak another language. As a child, not yet speaking, I used to speak a different language. The Latin for "child" means "one who does not speak." This is what linguistics tells us. But this only proves that Latin, this dead language, still speaks silently, obstinately, in the language that I am speaking. And in Latin itself, Greek speaks, and in Greek, how many more languages, known or unknown? In a language, there are always other languages that speak; none of them is alone in speaking, and it's impossible to get right behind any language. There is no child.

I used to speak another language, and this language still speaks, no doubt, in the language that you had me speak. You couldn't hear it, you couldn't understand it. Don't imagine for a second, as I know you might, that it was a language made up of screams, sobs, and mimicries, or of an obscure series of murmurs. It wasn't a child's language, nor was it a language in its infancy. I never mumbled. Others mumbled and stuttered, hoping to adapt their language to that of a child. You weren't that way, you didn't feign the infancy of a language. No doubt you knew that there was no such thing. My language was as old and as well constructed as yours, as all languages, living or dead. There is no language that is badly constructed, no elementary language.

You couldn't understand me, nor I could understand myself. This was not because we did not know, or because we had not learned. It was older than any apprenticeship. My language had nothing to say. Yet everything that needed to be said, everything that could be said, or indeed everything that could be left unsaid, it could, like all languages, utter with precision. It articulated it, allowed every single one of its jointures to play, isolated every single one of its syllables, always observing a just measure in moving from one to the other. It was an uninterrupted rhythm. It was not learned, and it cannot be learned. For that, we would need to indicate its beginning, an order in which to begin the rhythm. But there is no order; it does not begin; it begins anywhere, in any language.

Why did you teach me your language? I already knew about its rhythm, and I didn't need ...

He says nothing. Perhaps he wishes to leave. He moves. He says:

I have nothing to say. I cannot be upset with you.

He becomes quiet, then starts again:

I have nothing to say. You wanted to hear me speak. You needed it. It is only when we are spoken to that we know that we exist. The look does not have this power. The look cuts through and loses itself in the distance, along the surface of the body that is being looked at. Neither the gaze nor the touch can really be addressed. I used to look at you, used to touch you, but that was nothing; you didn't exist; I had to speak to you. And so I needed to speak in order to speak to you, and in order for you to exist.

But ...

He does not know whether he is going to say it.

Yet why did you need to exist? It was necessity. What I mean is, it would not have been inconceivable that you didn't. You could have not existed, you could have ...

The truth is, there was already nothing else to be done. You were there, and you wanted me to speak to you. I could have not been born, but I had been. And I spoke a language you could not hear, that I could not hear myself. Everything that could be told, and everything that could be passed over in silence, it uttered, word for word, relentlessly. I would imitate a language that I had been taught without ever having learned a single one, and I would imitate them all. But I wouldn't speak to anyone. You, you didn't know a single language. You didn't teach me anything. Nobody teaches the child to speak. Language is always more motherly to the child than is his own mother; it is always a language that exceeds the mother, an other mother [*une langue outre-mère*].

He laughs and says: it was blue; I was blue. *Er lacht, und sagt: Ich war blau; Ich war ganz im Blau. I was singing the blue note.*

I used not to speak. You opened my mouth; you forced my mouth open; you wanted to hear me; you demanded to hear me; I was no longer allowed to keep silent; I was no longer allowed to scream; you opened and closed my mouth rhythmically; the old rhythm was still there; you're not the one who invented it, but you would follow it to handle my lips, and my tongue between your teeth. You spoke to me and I spoke to you, but you spoke to me first, and therefore the words belong to you; I am not speaking to you; I have nothing to say to you, but you force me to speak; I tell you everything that can be said, and also everything that can be left unsaid. You do not teach me anything, but you make me speak a new language, and also always another one that speaks in it and that, in turn, you force to speak, moving my lips and my tongue between my teeth, and your tongue between my teeth.

*Translated by Miguel de Beistegui*

# § 5   Vox Clamans in Deserto

*As the scene opens, a dog is barking in the distance, alone in the silence. A cow is lowing. The dog will bark again two or three times during course of the piece. Another animal, a donkey, for example, will perhaps wander across the stage.*

*The stage is bare, brightly lit and resonant.*

*Two characters appear. They have very different voices, both male, but one is deep and sober, the other light, airy, a little hoarse.*

—I thought I heard a voice, so I came on over. Was it you?

—I don't know. It might have been; I seem to remember talking to myself. But there was a dog barking. Maybe that was what you heard?

—I'm hardly likely to have confused the two!

—Why not? The cries of a dog or of other animals aren't just noises. Every animal has a recognizable voice all its own.

—Do you mean that it's their way of talking?

—No! That's something completely different. Voice has nothing to do with speech. Yes, there's no speech without voice, but there *is* such a thing as voice without speech. And not just for animals, but for us as well. There's voice before speech. Because I know you, I recognized your voice as you were coming toward me, long before I could make out what you were actually saying.

—Of course, voice is the resonant side of speech, whereas discourse, or sense, is its spiritual side.

—You could almost find something similar in Saussure, if he'd ever spoken about voice, which he didn't. You could almost find it in his distinctions among the constitutive elements of speech. But then that's precisely what leads him to exclude phonation or vocality from his study of languages and, at the end of the day, from his study of language. Didn't he once say

*[We hear Saussure's voice, delivering his Geneva lecture course:]*

the vocal organs are as external to speech as the electronic appliances that transmit Morse code are to that alphabet; and phonation, that is, the performance of acoustic images, has no effect on the system itself.

—You're not too happy with that analysis, are you?

—No, I'm not, and what's more I'm convinced that Saussure himself couldn't have been entirely happy with it either. He was too attentive, in spite of everything, to the indissociable unity of what he called the "material substance of words" and to what he termed "the system of signs."

—Do you mean that voice is part of language?

—It's certainly not part of language in Saussure's sense of the term, any more than it could be said to belong properly to speech: that's precisely why it shouldn't be confused with "phonation" (what a perfectly ghastly word!) since phonation is nothing but "performance," as Saussure pointed out. Voice isn't a performance; it's something else, something that comes about prior to the distinction between an available language and the spoken performance of a word ...

—Before the whole of language, then!

—If you like, and in the strictest sense of the term, that's doubtless true. But what I want you to understand—and what I am sure Saussure himself was close to understanding—is that voice, which is something quite different from phonation, belongs to language *precisely because* it's both prior to and in some way external to it. It's like an intimate prelude to language, yet foreign to language itself.

—I like that. So, tell me a bit more about this intimately foreign prelude.

—Happily, so long as you listen to what I have to say, to me and to a few others. This one, for example; can you hear him all right?

*[Paul Valéry steps forward. He speaks in an extremely hushed voice, almost a murmur. Eventually his words become distinct enough to hear:]*

... voice, a heightened state, tonic, tensed, consisting only of pure energy, free, incredibly powerful, plastic ... what is essential here is the fluid itself ... voice—the evolution of a free energy ...

—I can hear him perfectly well, but I'm not sure that I understand. Why do you want me to listen to him, rather than explaining yourself?

—Because we need to hear each voice. They're all different. We all explain things differently, in our own voices. Did you know that vocal sounds are just about as singular as it gets, even more impossible to confuse than fingerprints, which are themselves unique?

*[Pulling on a mask of Roland Barthes, he says:]*

The human voice is in fact a privileged (eidetic) site of difference ...

—It's not enough simply to speak about voice. We still need to know in what voice we're going to do so. What voice should we use to speak about voice? Here, listen to this one:

*[Enter Jean-Jacques Rousseau, who declares:]*

Man has three kinds of voices: the spoken or articulated voice, the singing or melodious voice, and the pathetic or accentuated voice, which serves as the language of the passions.

—If I understand what he's saying, and what you were saying just a moment ago, it's not just that we all have our own voices, but that all of us have several possible voices. But voice itself, the vocality of voice, its essential voiceness, if you like, oughtn't to be confused with any of these different voices. Voice itself would be what neither speaks nor sings nor vocalizes passion, even though it can play all these roles, and even though it can become your voice or mine, this character's or another's. But I still don't quite understand what sort of thing it is.

—It's voice itself—and it's not clear that it *is* a single thing. It's the voice in which we can't actually speak because it's a prelude to speech, a speech *infans* that's heard outside all speech, even in the act of speaking itself; yes, it's infinitely more archaic than the act of speaking, but there's no speech that's not heard through a voice.

—So voice, in its archaic character, would be the true actuality of speech, which, in turn, is itself the being of language ...

—It's not that voice is the actuality of speech; it's only ever a voice, yours or mine, talking or singing, different each time. Voice is always shared; in a sense, it's sharing itself. A voice begins with the entrenchment of a singular being. Later, with its speech, that being will remake its ties to the world, give sense to its own entrenchment. But before anything else, with its voice, that being declaims a pure distancing, one that makes no sense at all.

—Every voice cries out in the desert, like the voice of the prophet. And it's in the desert of deserted existence, prey both to lack *and* to absence, that voice first makes itself heard. Listen, then, to what a woman says, a mother:

*[Projected on a screen, the face of Julia Kristeva says these words:]*

The voice responds to the missing breast, or is triggered off as soon as the path to sleep seems to fill with voids the tension and attention of waking hours. The vocal cords stretch and vibrate in order to fill the emptiness of the mouth and the digestive tract (a response to hunger) and the breakdown of the nervous system in the face of sleep ... The voice will take over from the void ... Muscular, gastric, and sphincter contractions reject, sometimes at the same time, air, food, waste. The voice springs from this rejection of air and nutritive or excremental matter; so as to be vocal, the first sonorous emissions not only have their origins in the glottis but are the audible mark of a complex phenomenon of muscular and rhythmic contractions that is a rejection implicating the whole body.

—I'm not about to contest that. That's not really a voice I'd want to challenge ...

—But do you really think that a voice could ever be challenged? I think that I'd want to suggest that voice or, rather, the infinite sharing of voices is the site or the element of affirmation multiplied ad infinitum, and that there's no room for negation there. There's no dialectic of voices, just the dialectic of and in language.

—But that sphere of voices isn't replete or unified ...

—No, it's not. It's made up of the spacing or the distancing of voices. And each one's different, each one's formed by a break, by an opening, a tract, a pipe, a larynx, a throat, and a mouth, run through by this nothing, this emission, this forcing out of voice. The voice cries out in the desert because voice itself *is* the desert that unfolds at the very heart of the body, beyond words. That's what voice confirms or affirms—and not in the straightforward sense of its being the counterpart of a negation. A desert: each time, each voice, a singular desert.

—I'm sure you're right. But I'd want to say, without challenging that sense of rejection, that one could propose an entirely different way of understanding what emerges with the cries of infancy. And it would also be an entirely different way of understanding the *vox in deserto*: as *vox clamans* rather than *vox clamantis*. Voice wouldn't respond to the void, as the last speaker was saying, but would expose it, turn it toward the outside. Voice would be less the rejection than the ejection or the throw of an infinitely open void at the heart of singular being, at the heart of this abandoned being. What it would expose would be not a lack per se but a failure on the part of plenitude or presence that isn't actually a failing, since it's what constitutes what's proper to existence, what opens an always already open existence to what lies outside it. Voice would show that a being that exists like that isn't a subject but an existence opened and run through by this throw, an existence thrown into the world. My voice is what, before anything else, throws me into the world. If you'll take what I'm saying with the appropriate grain of salt, I'd probably want to say that there's something irrevocably ecstatic about the voice.

—Are you thinking about song?

—Of course! How could I not be? But I'm not talking about lyric raptures. The one who sings—and the one who listens to the song—are the ones who are most assuredly, most simply, but also most vertiginously, outside of themselves. Listen:

*[He starts a tape player. We hear the words of the Queen of the Night and then the king's madness scene from* Nabucco.*]*

—The one who's singing is, for the duration of the song, not a subject.

—But why do you keep saying that there's no subject when it comes to voice? Surely there has to be a subject in order for there to be a voice, and, if I've understood you correctly, there has to be a subject for each singular voice. I'd say that voice, contrary to what you seem to be saying, is the irrefutable mark of the presence of a subject. Its imprint, as you put it. And that's what needs to be understood by a writer's voice: his or her style, his or her own, inimitable mark.

—I'll grant you that notion of the voice's imprint or indelible signature. But what's of concern here is knowing, before the impression of any imprint, what, in the tracing, opening, and emission of the voice, what is most properly vocal. You see, the subject is capable of containing and supporting its own contradiction ...

—I can hear Hegel's voice ... !

—True, true. I thought you might. But Hegel, like so many of the greats, had more than one voice ...

—So a great voice would always be more than a single voice? Is that why Plato, Aristotle, Galileo, Descartes, Heidegger so often wrote dialogues?

—Perhaps. But dialogue or no dialogue, there's still a polyphony at the heart of every voice. Why? Well, the voice isn't a thing but the way in which something—someone—takes its—their—distance from itself and allows that distance to resonate. Voice doesn't just emerge from an opening but is open in itself, open onto itself. Voice leads onto the voice within it. A voice immediately reveals itself to be a polyphony ...

—Fine, but I'd like to come back to Hegel. You've forgotten him.

—That's true, I had. But that actually makes us all the better placed to hear one of his other voices: the voice in which he speak about voice. For Hegel, voice comes before the subject. Voice precedes it, which means, of course, that they involve one another. I'll even grant you that voice paves the way for the subject. But it's still not the voice of the subject.

—If I'm following you correctly, wouldn't we have to say that it *is* the voice of the subject—precisely because it's what paves the way for it—but that that voice itself doesn't have a subject? I still don't know why, though. And you still haven't helped me to hear Hegel's different voices.

—The first of those voices is the voice of the subject. It states, in the imperturbable tones that you recognized, that being and truth consist in supporting their own internal contradictions. The subject is the one whose self-relation involves its own negation, and it's this that confers on it the infinite unity of an inexhaustible self-presence—even in its absence; and for our purposes, that's the same as saying even in its silence. With voice, we're not talking about a silence that could make sense or an absence on the part of the subject that's making itself heard. As I said, it's an affirmation, not a negation. Voice isn't a contradiction to be endured, first established and then overthrown, overcome. It's separate not just from contradiction but from unity itself. And that's why we have to hear Hegel's other voice, the other inflection that he uses in order to speak about voice. Listen:

*[Hegel, talking with Schelling and Hölderlin, who also utter some of the following sentences, without it ever being a real conversation:]*

Voice begins with sound. Sound is a *state of trembling*, an act of oscillation between the consistency of a body and the negation of its cohesion. It is like a dialectical movement that, unable to complete itself, remains a mere palpitation ... The soul is already present in the resonant trembling of an inanimate body, this mechanical repository of the soul ... But voice is first and foremost the act of a trembling freely in itself ... In this trembling there lies the soul, this actuality of ideality that constitutes a determined *existence* ... The identity of the being—the concrete presence of the Idea itself—always begins with a trembling. Hence, the child in its mother's womb, this child that is neither autonomous nor a subject, is traversed by a trembling brought about by the originary sharing of the maternal substance ... It is not an audible voice, but it still has to resound in the mother's insides. It is the gabbling vocalization of access to being ... The soul is the singular existence that trembles as it comes to presence, the singular existence whose trembling is its presentation ... It is the *singular* subject, not the infinite unity of subjectivity, but its singularity alone ... This singular soul takes on a form or a figure, rendering it a work of art ... a work of art that trembles ... So far as man is concerned, this work of art is human *physiognomy*, upright, possessed of hands, mouth, voice, laughter, sighs, tears ... all bathed in a spiritual tone that immediately shows the body to be the exteriority of a higher nature. This tone introduces a light, indeterminate, inexpressible modification, although it is actually no more than an indeterminate and imperfect sign for the universal of the Idea that presents itself thereby. This tone is not language. Perhaps it paves the way for language. It is the inexpressible modification, the modification of the soul that trembles, that cries and sighs and laughs ... the spirit that trembles in showing itself without yet having appropriated its own spiritual substance.

[Exeunt *the three characters. We hear the beginning of Schubert's "Gretchen am Spinnrade" being sung very softly:*]

*Mein Ruhe ist hin, mein Herz ist schwer,*

*Ich finde, Ich finde sie nimmer mehr ...*

—I admit I'm taken. But your Hegel wasn't alone. There were three of them speaking.

—Indeed there were. But it was him, I promise you, either him or the voice of an epoch ...

—Would I be right in saying that the modulation about which they were speaking, that spiritual modulation spread over the whole body, would basically be the voice of voice, the sound or the tone in which what would otherwise tremble in the open throat resonates properly? This tone or sound—whether of man or of an animal, of this or that particular man or animal, the always general sound of a vibrating singular difference—

would give voice its particular inflection, while voice itself would make the trembling of this tone audible ... Each one would be the voice of the other: a voice that isn't a voice but the tone of the soul spread out over the body, its outpouring bringing it to life. A voice, then, that would be the voice of this existence, thrust out through its mouth and its throat.

—Yes, I think that you could put that way. So you understand, then, that there's no subject here. A voice has its voice outside of itself and doesn't harbor its own contradiction; in any case, it doesn't sustain that sort of contradiction but casts it before itself. It's not self-present, merely a presentation out, as it were, a trembling offered up to the outside, the beat of an opening—once again, a desert, spread out and exposed, the air shimmering in the heat. The desert of the voice crying out in the desert—no subject, no infinite unity, always moving outward, no self-presence, no self-consciousness either.

—That reminds me of something someone once said—and I'm quoting from memory: man, unlike animals, has no voice; he has only language and signification as a way of filling up the space left by this missing voice, and as a way, too, of pushing his way toward this absent voice ...

—That was Giorgio Agamben. He said that voice was the limit of signification, not as a simple sound deprived of sense but as a "pure indication of an event of language."

*[Agamben, on the side of the stage, quickly adds:]*

And this voice that, signifying nothing, signifies signification itself, coincides with the most universal aspect of signification, with being.

—And I remember someone else saying

*[a child's voice, offstage:]*

sense is abandoned to sharing, to the difference between voices. It is not a given prior to or outside of our voices. Sense gives itself, abandons itself. And there is perhaps no other sense to sense than this generosity.

—This sense of sense is like the voice of voice, merely an opening, the trembling of an opening in the dispatch or the emission of something that's destined to be heard—and no more. Destined never to come back ...

—But it still resonates in itself ...

—Yes it does, but without ever coming back, without ever again taking itself up in order to be repeated and in order to hear itself ...

—But the voice that hears itself can do so only by keeping silent. Derrida's shown this, as you know.

—Of course. And that's why the voice that can't keep silent, why the voice that is a voice, never hears itself. It doesn't have the silence that it would need in order to release a sense beyond sound. And that's another way in which it doesn't harbor its own contradiction. It doesn't have this silence; it merely resonates, outside, in the desert. It doesn't—or doesn't really—hear itself but can always make itself heard. It is always addressed to the other. Here, since you were quoting him a moment ago, listen:

*[Derrida, speaking into a portable microphone held in front of him by a young woman:]*

When the voice trembles ... it makes itself heard *because* the point of utterance is not fixed ... pure differential vibration ... a *jouissance* that would be the *jouissance* of a plenitude without vibration, without difference, seems to me to be the myth of both metaphysics and death ... In living, plural, differential joy, the other is called ...

—But if that's the case, the other wouldn't be called by anything, not even by his or her own name. Does voice alone, saying nothing, still call?

—To say that it says nothing doesn't mean that it doesn't name or that it doesn't pave the way for the name. The voice that calls, the voice that *is* a call, without actually articulating any language, opens the other's name, opens the other to his or her name, to my own voice thrown toward them.

—But if there's no language then there aren't any names. Without language, there's nothing that could secure this call.

—You're right, but the voice summons the other only where, as other, he or she can come. To the desert alone, then.

—But who comes into the desert other than the nomads who cross it?

—But that's precisely the point. Voice calls the other a nomad, summons the other to a nomadic existence. It throws the other a nomadic name, a name that precedes his or her own. A name that calls the other outside, that in turn calls the other to give voice. Voice calls the other to come out into his or her own voice. Here, listen:

*[A desert nomad unveils his face and reads from Deleuze:]*

Music is first and foremost a deterritorialization of voice, which moves further and further away from language ... Voice is a long way before the face, far ahead ... To tool a voice is the first musical step ... Voice has itself to reach the point of a becoming-woman or a becoming-child. This is the extraordinary content of music ... The musical voice is itself just such a becoming-child; at the same time, however, the child becomes vocal, purely vocal ...

—The other is summoned at the point where there is neither subject nor signification. This is what I want to call the desert of *jouissance* or of joy. Arid, maybe, but never desolate. Neither desolate nor consoled, beyond either laughter or tears.

—But wouldn't you agree—and you seemed to do so at one point—that it's with tears that voice first slips out?

—That's true; that's the birth of tragedy. But what comes before this is the delivery of voice, and that's something that's not yet tragic. Its tears and cries know nothing of either tragedy or comedy.

—But does that have to mean that they know nothing of the way in which they slip out? Nothing of their own effusion? Of a body that opens and exhales, of a soul stretching itself?

—Yes, it's an open extension—*partes extra partes*—that vibrates—*partes contra partes*. It doesn't speak but calls on the other to speak. Voice calls on the other to speak, to laugh, or to cry. I wouldn't speak if my voice, which isn't me and which isn't in me, even though it's absolutely proper to me, didn't call on me, didn't call on me to speak, to laugh, or to cry, didn't evoke that other in me that can just that.

*[Montaigne, sitting at his desk, writing:]*

—Valéry said *[pulling a book from his pocket, he reads]*: "*language* issues from *voice* rather than voice from *language* ... "

—And presumably that's also why he could say that "voice defines pure poetry."

—So poetry wouldn't speak?

—Yes it speaks, but it speaks only with that speech that doesn't produce a language, with that speech that, on the contrary, issues from voice, a language being born. Voice is the precession of language, the imminence of language in the desert in which the soul is still alone.

—You're saying that it forced the other's hand!

—Of course. That's why the soul is always alone; not isolated, however, but with the other, within calling distance of the other, and alone as regards discourse, operations, occupations ...

—So would the other summoned by the soul still be the soul?

—It would. It's the soul itself that voice calls forth in the other. That's how it leads the voice to the subject [*fraye la voix au sujet*]. Yet rather than allowing it to settle there, it steers it in another direction. It doesn't call on the soul to hear itself or to hear another's speech. It calls it, yes, but that simply means that it makes it tremble, causes it to stir. It's the soul that stirs the other in the soul. And that, well, that's voice.

*Translated by Simon Sparks*

# § 6   Paean for Aphrodite

O divine one, sing to me the foam, the fringe, and the spray of waves on the wine-colored sea, and sing, too, the foam of the love that has just washed the lips, and sing, too, the foam that stays on the lips of the singer, the finished song, the scattered myth.

—Another song? That's impossible. You said it: the voices have faded.

—That's true, but it's why I say: sing to me what remains.

—But nothing remains.

—That's true also. But I say to you: sing nothing to me, foam or froth.

—That's too easy.

—Admit that it's too difficult, as well you know.

—No, I don't.

—Then don't sing. Just froth.

~

Aphrodite, born of the foam: this is what is meant by her name, *Aphrodite aphrogeneia*, according to the so-called "popular" etymology recorded by Plato in the *Cratylus*. No one believed it, of course, and Plato tells it with a smile. But Aphrodite is "the one who likes to smile," or "the one who smiles gladly." Whence, perhaps, the name of the blind singer, *Aphrodite philomeides*.

(Hesiod calls her *philommedes*, "lover of the rod." Which word hides the other? Which one makes the other smile?)

The plains of the sea smile on you, *tibi rident aequora ponti*. Lucretius says this as well, at the beginning of his poem: you alone govern the nature of things, *rerum naturam sola gubernas*.

The government of things begins with the *etymon*'s smile: a smile of the true and of the original. Nothing derisory or parodic, just a smile. There are numerous pretenders to the *etymon* here: we find the lord and the *fruit*, the tyrant and the *Phrygian*, the Etruscan and the Semite, the Aegean and everything that begins by vanishing, by merging, on voyage after voyage, with the churning contours and depths of the sea, this sea between so many lands.

Her name is also used with another epithet or nickname: *anadyomenus*, surging from the depths, reemerging, or, more properly, plunging from on high, a penetration that is like an elevation. The goddess inverts the sense of the profound. In her, sinking surfaces, sinking *is* surfacing; it rises and takes off with the foam, at the foot of the rock of Paphos in Cyprus. It's not Aphrodite who emerges from the abyss, but the abyss that rises in her.

And what else could it be, if the government of things resides with her, if, through her, things make their primordial entrance, *rerum primordia*, *semina rerum*, if, in her, lie the elements of everything that exists, all the atoms, seminal and dis-seminal gravity? Atomic Aphrodite.

(Do you understand the words that you are using? Don't you know that for us they are words of war and misfortune?)

There is no hidden god. Here, the divine is precisely what is not hidden, what has not absconded, and what is not secret. The depths rise to the surface, multiplied. This is not the subject matter of mysteries, theologies, or indeed of philosophies. *Aphros* is of the clouds (in Sanskrit, *abhra*), but a cloud that obscures nothing and dissimulates nothing. It is also the clarity of the sky, touched by the sea. It is the clarity of the sky washed by the foam.

This point of maximum clarity, a cloud of sky and water, is the place where the gods are stripped bare, the point at which there are no longer any gods.

Undoubtedly, the *etymon* of "foam" is the same as that of "obscure." Here, however, the *etymon* is inverted, at the same time as the depths. *Anetymology*: sense does not lie at the root, subtending and in advance; it lies right on the surface, pushing it skyward.

Aphrodite is naked to all the gods.

The surface does not rest on the bottom: it is the bottom that appears, the bottom that surfaces. The foamy surface is birth itself, it is the goddess who is born and who is divine only in being born in this way, on the crest and rim of each wave, and in each of the hollows into which the foam spills and spreads.

The birds of the air celebrate you and your coming, o divine one. *Aeriae volucres te, diva, tuumque significant initum.*

Moreover, this dawning of the abyss places nothing above the foam. Aphrodite is not profound, but neither is she a beacon [*un phare*] or a phallus, standing proudly on the sea and touching the sky. Penetration does not light up the sea and scan it; it merely soaks it, makes it foamy. It is the sea distilling its marine essence. Aphrodite disappoints straining, thrusting love. She is the disappointment of knowledge and does not buttress the heaven of Ideas. She touches only the foam; she *is* the touching of the foam.

All of which does not mean that the phallus is suppressed. No more than it means that this involves castration. This isn't Ouranos's scene, and the foam is no more sperm than it is each fluid and liquor of love.

*This* is the scene of Ouranos, however: Aphrodite born of the sea running with her own blood. Diogenes of Apollonia calls sperm *aphros haimatos*, blood's foam. *Exaphroun*: blood becomes foam, aphro-hemorrhage, alchemy, *menstrum universale*. It is the effervescence of the sky in the water, the sea fused with the sun. It is not a scene of mutilation.

And then there is the scene of Atys, in which the phallus is cut on behalf of Cybele, the Great Goddess, from Ida, the grandmother of Syria. But this cut of foam dissolves stone and bronze blade alike, and there is no sacrifice. The waves wash the mountain, and nothing is removed when one sex passes by the other.

*Philommedes, philomeides,* always irresolute. The scene is always different. It is the scene of this metamorphosis in which each difference stamps the other with the mark of its difference. Each enters the other beyond the other and itself, without returning or disappearing. Never identifiable yet always distinct, the truth in a soul and a body.

Aphrodite offers the phallus with the foam. It is presented in her worship with a grain of salt. Neither myth nor knowledge can grasp anything of this offering. A phallus not only soaked but itself the soaking; foam, nothing but salty foam. The first idols of the Great Goddess of Cyprus are of indeterminate sex. On occasion Aphrodite herself becomes Aphroditos. Rather than the couple phallus/excision, this would be the doublet *mons pubis* / penis, our common hermaphrodite, which no *etymon* subtends.

Twice Aphrodite: female, male, without mixture or confusion. Divided, multiplied, divided at the origin, lacking all common measure. The differential calculus of the unlimited limit of a double touching. From top to bottom and from the bottom up, the sexual organ, cutting name, fends off Aphrodite with a feint that mutilates nothing. The one and the other, foam intact—the charm and the chance of tact.

~

The name "Aphrodite" is far from being the only name, indeed the only divine name, whose provenance is so tortuous and disputed. But it is perhaps the only name of which a smiling *etymon* says this precisely: the pitching, rolling, and swelling of the waves, movement upon movement, the incessant backwash, the lapping, the wake. Marine Aphrodite, navigator, *pontia, euploia, Aphrodite.*

(Paean, your strophes are useless: you're giving us a froth of words, a fizzy wine, but the party's over. The music's now just a memory, and the infinite melody is lost in the mist. We're overwhelmed, nauseated by your froth. It's time to be silent.)

To the gleaming foam corresponds the brilliance of the star: Ashtorith, mother of the Baals; planet Venus, coming and going; Innana of Sumeria, Asthart, Ishtar of Babylon or of Nineva, who speaks with the Great Wave of the Sea; Hathor of Egypt, the cow with lyres for horns, who carries the Sun; Esther the Jewess, bathed for an entire year in myrrh for a king whose anger she wards off. Aphrodite, goddess of errancy, from one people to another, from festival to festival, name to name, under the errant signs of the sky: *caeli subter latentia signa.* Goddess of that for which there is no god.

Morning and evening star, Hesperus and Lucifer, shepherd's star, rising and setting in one place and then another, coming and going in the arms of Dionysus, Hermes, Adonis, or Atys, the mother of Harmony, of Eros and Anteros, of Deimos and Phobos, of Aeneas and Hermaphrodite. And naked before Paris, silently promising him Helen, by his silence. Grandmother and daughter all at once, Homer, Flaubert, Freud, and Offenbach.

Paean, hymn of hymns, "you are beautiful my beloved." This was sung in Jerusalem, in honor of Ishtar and Tammouz-Adonis. Later, despite Jeremiah's anger, Astarte was presented with a cake in the form of a naked goddess. Was not King Sargon of Accad put out to sea like Moses and then taken in by Ishtar?

Aphrodite, pantheon of the waves, pandemonium of the foam; a *pleroma* sheltering no gnosis, lacking all intimate knowledge of deliverance.

(Like us?

—Yes, like us.

—No more deliverance, no more salvation or belief.

—What's more, no more reasons to rejoice, any more than to regret.)

∼

Neither knowledge nor wisdom, but beauty. Plato will reunite, with all the élan of Eros, Ourania, and Pandemos. Beauty passes from bodies to souls. But how do souls, in order to be beautiful, cease passing through bodies? Aphrodite is the passage. The cortege comes and goes, between the two temples of Ourania—the one with the statue of Phidias, the other of Alcamenus—and the temple at Pandemos, in which Solon set up a brothel.

(Strabo says that all the Babylonian women, obeying some divine precept, got together with strangers in the temple of Aphrodite, in the middle of the throng. The money given by the strangers was put at the disposal of the goddess.)

Ourania is exclusively masculine, while Pandemos precedes the two sexes. At least that's how Plato has it. But what does Eros do if not put the one in the other, in every possible way? And how could Aphrodite divide the sexes? She is merely their apportioning, between one and the other. Aphrodite is one in two, not two in one. Not "bisexual" but one in two sexes, and in such a way that there cannot be one without two (ultimately, there cannot be one at all). No sex is one, unique. Nor is Aphrodite one. *Aphrodite androgunos.* Naked, always, for all the gods, for both of them.

Plato keeps her at a distance. He prefers Eros, whom he takes to be the offspring—born the same day as Aphrodite—of a pair of hardworking concepts. Industrious love, *Eros philosophos*: twin brother of the foam, withdrawn into the dryness of thought. The dry, solid ground on which one can build the hard way, for the long haul.

But Plato-the-friend-of-Ideas is not finished with the sex-who-is-without-Idea. He is searching for a philosophical Aphrodite, whom he finds in the shape of Diotima. We don't know who she is, whether she's a fiction, the recollection of a Pythagorean, or Zeus's priestess. What matters is that she utters the knowledge of beauty. But does it have to be a wise and beautiful woman who replaces Aphrodite? Who will know just how beautiful Diotima is? Hölderlin went mad for want of this knowledge.

Diotima hides behind Socrates, whose ugliness protects the Beautiful itself. However, Plato loves the beautiful—loves it more than he can say. Thus Diotima, the only woman-Plato, Socrates in makeup, crowds in on our memories in her very absence.

But why does the beautiful never let us go? When everything is ugly, all that remains of it is a memory. Why is the beautiful immemorial and without history? Why does Plato crave beautiful talk?

(Paean, beautiful thought, sing no more; silence the flautists and tell me the law of "this powerful Aphrodite whose rebelliousness is praised so." *Ataktos Aphrodite*, what is her order, rule, and measure without measure? Tell me, if you can, the saying of such a thought. Give me this naked sentence, aphasic Aphrodite.)

∼

Aphrodite: her name emerges from a froth of words, from their foam. A perfectly proper sense, woven in figures and soaked in fiction, streaming from that love of words, of senses, from that inexhaustible impropriety of languages which delights and disappoints us in turn, that coming-and-going which carries us or carries us away.

(It's as if one were to say: Aphrodite comes from Africa, from the aphorism, or the abominable [*affreuse*]. And it is clear that one would not be uttering a falsehood, for it all falls under the *etymon*.)

From elsewhere and everywhere, daughter of the islands and the coastlines, she puts the Greeks to sea and sees off Helen, who is pursued by all the kings. Hurt by the game she dared to play, she waves off her dear Trojans, Anchises to Aeneas, *Aeneadum genitrix*, mother of the race of Aeneas.

She displaces and mixes up principles, harmony, pleasure, and strength. She leads far from their origins peoples who came from afar, bearing traces of mysterious provenance, fleeting foundations, invented and grasped in an instant, gilded palaces and peacocks. Her true temple is the foamy city of innumerable temples and secret passageways. Yet to the rhythm of triremes heavy with slaves and spoils, and in the footsteps of the legionaries, comes the age of the imperial religion of Love.

Aphrodite tamed, subsumed by Christ. Cast into the depths and the infinite heights. Earth and sky—withdrawn from the sea on which, however, she has just walked.

Can one imagine this gentle step, brother of Atys, amidst the foam? No: all the gods went with him. Advent of a world of exile, peregrinations, great migrations, of cares and concerns. End of the coming-and-going: history goes on the road.

Aphrodite returns, reborn as the mother of God. Wise as an image, ready for the painting of love and flesh, the already ancient, withered troubles of a young culture. Rebirth through mourning, in God's widowhood. But Aphrodite was never a widow, any more than she was ever a virgin. Haven't we understood? How should we put it?

It's an ancient business, and our most cherished tradition: the Greeks were *superficial in their profundity*; they conducted their mourning with a serene smile. They did not expose themselves. Or, rather, to expose themselves was, at the same time, a way of concealing themselves, hidden in gracious nudity. Aphrodite is the Queen of the Graces: the Charities weave her dress. Veil, skin, grain, the reflections of the wine-colored sea, breasts, thighs, hair, and smile.

Aphrodite, the most Greek of the Greeks, and the least recognizable. Arche-Hellene, and somewhat Semitic. Trojan, Babylonian, Syrian, Ethiopian, Jewess, Arab. Helen raised in Greece, taken back to the Orient, lost in Egypt, given back to the Occident. Hybrid Aphrodite. There is no "race" in her, not even the race of the Gods.

The foam of peoples with the foam of their words, with that of the waves on their shores and beneath their oars. The foam of their days: imagine seven thousand years of speech and of rite, of navigation and fatigue, from the idols of andesite, of indeterminate sex, to us, tracing the foamy wake of their names on the brightly lit screen of a computer.

(In Strabo there are twenty-six cities and ritual sites bearing the name

"Aphrodite," including Aphrodite Polis, where the sacred cow of Egypt was raised, not far from Crocodilopolis and what is called, in Latin, Veneris Portus, Port Sell.)

The foam of their nights: the goddess guiding their members, their fondlings, putting them to sleep on soapy stones, holding in her hands her breasts, exposed above her dress—Aphrodite, with her marvelous neck, *perikallea deire*, and magnificent breasts, *stethea imereuota*, "Milky Way, o luminous sister / Of the white streams of Canaan," the color of melded liquids, mixing tongue, blood, and tale. Imagine the unimaginable night of time, depths without thickness looming in front of us, *hominum divumque voluptas.*

(We are tired of this imagination. To which communion do you proudly lay claim?

—You understand nothing. I speak merely of a certain doggedness.

—And that isn't derisory?

—Allow me a smile.)

Myths today are interrupted. They have not disappeared: for millennia now, we have been frolicking in their foamy wake. But myths no longer say what they were supposed to say (or what we say they were supposed to say): this discourse uttered from the things themselves, from the simple or fundamental (the atom), this utterance of a nature, a world, of an origin redeployed in language and signs. Myth no longer utters this foundational discourse; indeed, it must speak it no longer. An epoch is upon us in which it is no longer possible for the origin to announce itself without fury, in anything but the language of the charnel house. Myth has become will-to-race.

And that is also why there is mourning without serenity, and exposure without a smile and without poetry. A congealed froth, aphrodisiac pornophilia, and the obscenities of torture and hunger. And nothing and no one to render reasons or grace.

Myth no longer speaks the discourse of generation, in which sense is engendered and in which the world unfolds. It no longer speaks the language of its own sense. That myth has been interrupted means that this mode of sense is interrupted. The interruption of sense: here, very simply, is the epoch named "the West."

Interrupted myth no longer speaks as it did, mythically (as we think it spoke: for the Cypriot idols in fact told us nothing of what they pronounced, if they pronounced anything at all).

It's not that there is no longer anything to say, or that the silence of the Apocalypse has descended. From the very site at which myth was interrupted, a certain voice is heard. This place is nothing other than the surface of myth, where the depth of its sense ends, Aphrodite's foam.

Sense is no longer given, if it ever was. But the foam of words implies sense. Something wet, slithering everywhere, disappearing, insinuating, evaporating. One sense always mixed up with another, with something other than sense and the sense of something else, a hybrid sense. But the miscegenation of sense is not another myth. It is what we all are, an ordinary, unrepresentable mélange, something so common yet as distant as a formless idol, seven thousand years old. There is nothing substantial about crossbreeding; miscegenation is not another deep resource. Rather, it is just the very slow movement of men mixing together, and of men mixing with gods, men with women. The saliva of confused words uttered lip against lip, faithfully.

Sing me the foamy sense.

Sing to me of the island fringed with foam, your land in the middle of the water. Goddess of Cyprus, where three towns bear your name. The island is not dry ground, nor is it isolated. Its soil is bathed, drenched. Foam collects there, and forms a surface and a skin: *chros. Amphi deleukos aphros ap'athanatou chros.* Immortal skin from the young girl: *toi d'epi koureethrephthe.* Skin and color, *chroma.*

Aphrodite is an island. All the islands are Aphrodite, but hers has the name Cyprus. Chromatic Aphrodite has the tint of copper, *Chyprios chalcos, cyprium aes, cuprum.* Only metal from Cyprus contains cadmium, calamine, vitriol, and ash. So Posidonius attested, and Strabo after him. The whole of the Orient comes seeking copper; Crete and Egypt also. The Myceneans come, the Phoenicians, the Assyrians, and the Persians. They come and dig, filling their vessels, occupying the towns, constructing forts and warehouses. The Greeks come, the Romans, Paul of Tarsus. The Byzantines, Arabs, Richard the Lionheart, the Order of Templars—they all come. As do the Venetians, Eudes de Montreuil, the Turks, and the English. They come, they go, and come back again.

Coppery Aphrodite, bronzed, the color of the two-edged sword and the shield. Cyprus-at-war, sea of Orient and Occident, bearing the rape, the hatred, and the wounds of all continents. We no longer see the smile of the foam, no more here than on the other sea, the Gulf beyond the sands. A soldier says: "When you're a kid, you think it's funny. It isn't."

(There are no more victory hymns. The epoch has silenced all song. War without legend.)

(What remains, the veiled voice.)

The deep that rises up is birth. The foam is always emerging, only emerging. Aphrodite is not born: she *is* birth, emergence into the world, existence.

Birth requires foam. Mixing and moistening are necessary if the thing itself is to be born—in its inimitable form. "The humid is the cause of the shape taken by the dry," says Aristotle.

Empedocles calls the birthplace "Aphrodite's slashed turf." Goddess of gardens, *Aphroditeen kepois.* Sea of grasses, seagrass, seaweed, sargasso, kelp, lettuce, glossy hair, soaking fleece, crack opening. What comes to the surface, and froths, is a crack. The crack is not a cut but a fork in the seaweed, a fruit, a fig half-open on warm foam. These are lips, licked by the swell. Birth: the name of being. To be delivered, to come into the open.

The rough sea piles laugh upon laugh: Aeschylus calls it *kumaton anarithmon gelasma,* the multifarious laughter of the waves.

A crack, but without abyss, gulf, or depth. *Hystera,* that which is behind, at bottom, coming forward. *Hysteron proteron,* a rhetorical figure also known as hysterology. The speech of the goddess is a mild hysteria of foam without anguish or power. A divinity without strength, *analkis theos,* from which *ichor* escapes, when bleeding, the immortal blood whose shiny flow does not bring about death.

Nothing less than an elevation on the water, birth of the crack that shows on the surface of the water.

*Mastos,* too, the breast: the birth of breasts. Once again, the *etymon* belongs to the moist or the humid. To be wet, running, overflowing. Drunk. Senseless, *aphrosune.* Cypris's drunkenness: exuberant existence. *Uber,* teat, generosity. Once more a smile on the wine-colored sea. And man envies in the woman's breast the modest swelling, peaceful elevation and abandon.

Breast, wave, fold. Wave, particle, light. It is the subject of the verb "propagate-at-the-speed-of-light." The breast is born like light, like the dawn at the fold of sky and sea. Aphrodite with the eyes of light, *ommata marmainonta*, gifted Aphrodite, *chruse Aphrodite*.

The fold multiplies the occurrences of existence. The fold is not the fold of being: the fold is being itself.

At the tip of the breast, everything submits. At all points, at all ground-less elevations, everything submits, curls up, unfolds. The folds of the cloth supporting the breasts of the goddess, *poikilon*, embroidered with drawings of many colors, in which everything is retraced with tenderness, out of love. "Love": that in which there is nothing mythical.

Aphrodite thinks [*pense*]; she weighs up [*pèse le poids de*] the foam. This vague weight that does not bear down on the depths. *Argynnis aphrodite* is a brilliant butterfly found in North America. The weight of a gossamer flight that does not stake out territory. That cleaves the seaweed, the waves, but leaves them melded in a foamy fleece, *aphrokomos*.

Not "superficial through profundity." The dialectic breaks down, as well as myth, liquefied by the foam. Driftwood, nipples, and buds, shells washed by the waves.

Marine extension, deferred in all senses and all directions, in contact with the clear sky.

This clarity does not blind, yet there is nothing to guide oneself by in this naked birth of the senses. Neither a grammar nor a logic, neither faith nor politics.

This frantic flight of sense that must be the origin comes back to us, just the same and entirely changed: the panic of beginnings, the memory of our murky depths, bleached with foam, put on the water, weighed, licked by the crests of the waves.

*Translated by Jonathan Derbyshire*

# § 7  Les Iris

*For Irizarry, Manhattan*

(Don't sound the first "s"; don't make the grammatical link, either: don't make the liaison as the French language here requires, and don't make the link between subjects, as thought—French or not—everywhere requires. But don't mistake this dual prohibition for an introduction, either. Don't go looking for a key in either this direction or the other, even if it is obvious that "les iris" [irises] is the plural of "l'iris" [iris], with the apostrophe *eliding* the "e" to avoid the hiatus, without which what we would have here would be "le iris" [the iris], needing only the capital letter that goes with proper names for it to become, at last, the author on the roster today: "Leiris.")

Say to yourself instead that things are now under way: there we are, we had to begin somewhere, and this is how it began. We cannot say why this was; in any case it would be boring to find out. All that has been said so far is already a yawn, anyway. The reason is of course that a *hiatus* is already the same as a "yawn" [*"bâillement"*]: when the mouth gapes wide open while vocalizing its accumulation of vowels. The tongue [*la langue*: tongue or language] does not want to yawn. A tongue is constantly busy, with plenty to do, plenty to worry about and enjoy, and never lets go of the person it has in its grip. Leiris is gripped by his tongue, day after day and step by step: infinitesimally, intimately, minutely, and preciously gripped.

To a grip like this there is no easy access. Nobody touches another's tongue. Idioms never meet. They are like parallel lines, paratactic structures, dense particles. Each and every one, in its idiosyncrasy, is the result of slight, irredeemable pressure on the tongue by diction. Each and every one arises from an impression produced on the tongue and by the tongue, an inimitable impression amidst the vast labor of imitation that is language itself, that is both fleeting and durable, both vague and precise. Things start up, start getting said, with that impression, up until the age of manhood, and beyond.[1] Things are already under way, and as for what happens next, we shall see.

"We shall see": the pupil is at the center of the iris. That's how we can see, we are told. We can see by means of the hole through which a small *pupilla* or doll-like figure (oneself, yourself if you look into an eye) may be seen, and this hole, or *operculum*, is surrounded by an iridescent halo, shimmering or glistening like a rainbow, in a word by a goddess, the goddess of the various distinct shades of color even in their proximity with each other. By a rainbow arch tinged with peace, an inaccessible peace surrounding the scurrying movement of all these doll-like figures. By a goddess clasping that doll, like so many shimmering reflections encircling the image.

(Iris is the messenger of the gods. But what is crucial here is what comes to pass when the gods no longer have messages to pass on. Nothing violent or spectacular, though, no "death of the gods." Less seriously, but perhaps more insidiously too, just the simple everyday comings and goings of signs, ground into insignificant dust—and yet all rather like an endless discussion with an obstinate little sphinx. He does not make a fuss, mind you, but, when it comes to it, insists on haggling. There is no question of playing at being Oedipus, or putting out your eyes. But, ultimately, "man" remains a riddle, up until the age of manhood, and beyond. It is like an old habit that is impossible to give up. Irises flutter about everywhere, bearing nonmessages, but on the ground there is still this obstinate little sphinx.)

We shall see—which is to say it is possible that we shall see nothing, or that there will be nothing to see (but how to tell the difference?).

But this is how things got started, and how they keep on getting started. Like when two pairs of eyes meet, or when a glistening surface shimmers momentarily. The moment is always too brief to be grasped. Or rather: it is there only for the time it takes to make you aware of what cannot be grasped, is not there to be grasped: as an impression. To invoke the moment—which is why one calls upon it: "O time, suspend your flight!"—is to be relieved of it.

To be relieved of the moment [*le dessaisissement*] may be shown here to be perfectly identical with grasping the moment [*le saisissement*]. What grasped me relieved me of myself. What grasped me relieved itself of me, leaving me more alone than I can know. Alone in knowing nothing of my "self" except for the solar stirring of a shimmering that did not even illuminate itself or even cast any light upon itself. An iris caught empty-handed, caught in the act of wrapping itself around a pupil gaping wide open (hiatus) at nothing, the solitude of its "subject." An iris never sees itself, as is well known, and never sees its seeing. The eyes of the sphinx are full of sand, splinters of mica, old powdery bones.

The pupil is wrapped in an iris: like a tiny Egyptian mummy at the heart of the eye. So many iridescent strips of bandage tightly bound around this nothing secret: seeing.

We have to go and see for ourselves. The name for this is an "autopsy," from *opsis* and *auto*, to see for oneself, to see with one's own eyes. That's proper seeing. The continuous autopsy of fragile life, like an anatomy of tiny details. All those things that grasp us, relieve themselves of us, all these impressions.

To see is for the subject to be captured, ravished, nowhere to be seen.

Nowhere to be seen, I'm confusing you. Grasped: caught, captivated. Relieved: freed, delivered. The two in one, but no "one" to say or image this "two-in-one" or "one-in-two." (Somebody's two eyes, and Leiris's irises.)

∼

It cannot be said there is anything exceptional here (but where is this?). On the contrary, it is the unaffected measure of banality itself. This is how things start up: we cannot tell how, and yet this unknowing [*non-savoir*] is what you have to put up with, and are stuck with, in an unshakable fashion. That's how it all starts up: with a definite, confused adventure, and a vague desire already made perfect by its getting going, finely sharpened like a blade, like the soul of the mummy, the soul itself swaddled, wrapped, bandaged, completely out of touch with everything, with the world, thought, feeling only the pressure of a hand, of the desert or the eye holding it ...

All we know is that there was an impression, for a moment, in the moment. (But "there was" is wrong: the impression is always there, or else you are still waiting for it; all we have is a premonition of it; time here goes in every direction at once, or doesn't go at all, time being merely spatial, spacious, spasmodic. Time here is not the trickle of sand through the hourglass but the operculum of the hourglass that bulges at either end.) Impression: something pressing against you, pressing down, imprinting a pressure or a movement. But not an image, or an idea. We are a long way from Proust: no "madeleine," no "uneven paving stones" here, no reconstitution or appropriation of the fleeting thing. (And as a result, no work of art?) But everything is turned upside down: typography without type, printing without characters, a pure state of Fleetingness, or rather an impure state since it is not posited in stability, nor has it escaped in flight. This is an impression that is barely recognizable as an impression. Which already runs and flows into this other thing, almost nothing, the flow of what does not even flow and has neither history nor memory. An evasive murmur through innumerable interstices. No date, no landmark, and even less of a monument. But the thing, here, grasped *insofar as* it is relieved of itself.

A mummy without a pyramid, simply dry in the sand and the spacious sun. Eyes and irises beneath the bandages, beneath arch-like rainbow strips, just like the neck beneath the ribbon of Olympia.[2]

Olympus: no more messages are forthcoming. We do not miss them. Things are simply within our reach. We quietly go about our business collecting together remnants of the gods, our eyes awash with transparent tears crystallizing our gaze for fraternal and conjugal autopsy. This is what Isis would do with the limbs of Osiris, and in the end so too the daring iris [*l'iris osé*] landing on the last remaining bandaged member.

The thing, here, grasped insofar as it is relieved of itself—that is, insofar as we are relieved of it.

What does "insofar as" mean here? It is a question from which no philosophy can be released. (Philosophy can be released from nothing: this is its great poverty, and its unique resource.)

Impression occurs, and things have started up. Impression prints nothing (no type, no monogram, no imprint, no character), but impression presses something up against this iridescent surface, this sheet of paper or this screen that is vaguely ready to set to work.

But so *vaguely* ready ... Already all that remains is froth—and even that is to say too much; there is no froth, or foam either. "Trail" [*"sillage"*], likewise, says too much (as does "trace" [*"trace"*]). All that there is is a grasping that is immediately relieved of itself, of all possibility of seizing itself. An incestuous wedding, fondling from a distance.

A rainbow arch spanning an almost finite cloud of fine tears.

This is how you grasp sand, how you are both grasped by it and relieved of it. The pupil, the little bandaged doll-like figure, the mummy, has nothing in it except for sand and more sand, the grains of mica of the iris. The hole in the eye is the hole in an hourglass, which time turns over, from time to time, to make the subject trickle back into the object, or the world into consciousness, then thoughts into things, and so on, without it even being remarked.

Banality: the impression that catches your attention, for a moment, this infinitely small fraction of attention *has no interest.* There is nothing to add, nothing to subtract. It could easily be put under the incalculable and uneventful column of "everyday expenditure." But the word says far too much: it implies measurement and assessment, and puts all the best and greatest exceptions to one side. But this is what is happening here: *everything* is so much part of the everyday that the category of the "everyday" is a pointless one. The everyday is beyond all measure, beyond the logic of the everyday and the exceptional. The everyday holds, and jealously holds back the relieving of the grasping [*le dessaisissement de la saisie*], that is all it is made of, inverting the hourglass.

Yet we are touched; something has touched a sensitive spot.

(Shall we play, shan't we play: this is the rule of the game.[3] All that is unbelievably, inestimably serious. We take pleasure in what is serious [*sérieux*]. Which is when you screw up [*où l'on serre*] your eyes. Dark irises, flowers and vulvas, so many vulnerable virtues, so many vulnerary touches.

This, then, is the everyday: there is worrying news in the air. Politics is perhaps on the edge of the abyss; our nearest and dearest are suffering from incurable complaints; we are totally alone. But one minute follows the other, and if we do not commit suicide, it is because there is something infinitely small to which we remain obstinately, not "attached," as the expression goes, but exposed. There are no words for this, yet it is constantly murmured, and it is this murmur that constitutes idiom.

A murmur like sand. If you were not careful, the sand would gradually engulf all the Sphinxes and all the Pyramids. Here, nobody is entrusted with the job of looking after them, so the riddles, tombs, and secrets are like so many documents that are now effaced.

Effaced. With faces sagging. Ruined. Decomposed. Collapsed. Shredded. Bit by bit. Pulverized. Particle by particle. *Partes extra partes.* Dispersed. Spilt. Deconstructed. Fragmented. Disseminated. Scattered. Emulsified. Blunted. Unfolded. Folded up. Incomplete. Becalmed. Calmly. Carefully. Continuously. Obstinately.

~

Obstinately. Obstinacy. *Ostinato rigore.* You stay with it; it goes past, exceeds exceptions. It proves the rule, reinforces and upholds it. Obstinately, the infinitely small undermines booming magnitudes. What does that prove, one may ask? But who said anything about proving anything, proving what? Proofs, when they succeed, show only that what was proven was already in evidence, outside the proof, and there was no need of any proof in order to touch it. Iris here could be thought to mean: this hardly perceptible glistening of the not-needing-to-be-proven.

A self-evidence that scours the eyes. The self-evidence of sand.

Things that cannot be explained are perhaps no more interesting than those that allow themselves to be proven. But what interest is there in the fact that there might be some "interest" in it? The selfsame iris, no further than on the surface of the eye, insignificant and superb, dreams quite superficially of the undreaming mummy.

(A mummy does not dream but disguises itself in dreams. The mummy as mummer, its childishness and carnival quality.)

Whoever looks and retells his dreams (*he* likes to do this, is quite attached to it and attached by it), and does so merely for the sake of the impression, without meaningful intent and without trying to fill in the meaning, knows he is letting the dust of the improbable and unprovable run through his fingers. In which case, his pupil is the internal operculum of an hourglass that can be turned over for the desert to escape into intimacy, or intimacy into the desert, measuring out the everyday.

~

What is really impressive, and has no interest: what if it were possible to identify here a cardinal rule for "literature"? If so, indeed, literature would give up on all forms of Celebration or Representation, all Academies of this or that and all Pyramids- and Sphinxes-of-the-Text. It would itself turn to sand. In reality, it never stops doing this. But it is hard to see; it can barely be discerned.

"Les Iris" [The Irises] could be the name for a seaside villa. It would be a rather vulgar form of ordinariness. You could imagine a burglary, a crime, a death taking place, a whole detective novel. You can imagine the next-door neighbor, friendly enough, but who is perhaps just joining in the fun and names his own villa "Osiris." Another detective novel. The neighbor has some further inquiry. But that itself is vulgar. You can carry on, and use "Les Iris" as the name for a small condominium. Alongside the names of other flowers, like tulips or periwinkles. A whole floral neighborhood, both nature and culture, a policing of the novel.

As soon as "culture" is peeled away like a thin layer of skin and displayed for itself, glistening beneath the spotlights, at some advertiser's candlelit dining table, its vulgarity is unbearable. The same is true of literature, when it tries to make itself "interesting," and so too of philosophy, when it draws attention to the importance, profundity, or anguish of its thinking. And of art as well when it guarantees that it is art, and not just anything.

But the "everyday" is not cultured, not even the "everyday" of the cultured neighbor who has heard of the Egyptian gods and, who knows, has even read Plutarch. The "everyday" is therefore not vulgar. But no doubt, as I have said, it is already vulgar even to refer to the "everyday" at all. It is no doubt vulgar to want to categorize what happens, and the fact that it does happen. Just as much by proffering "History" as by referring to "the everyday." But for instance, you say "les iris" without giving it much thought, because you always have to provide a title, and because, no doubt, an impression has been made—a fleeting and futile one: a flurry of syllables ending in "-ris." I could have come up with *Ris-Orangis*, the name of a Paris suburb. The suburb is the place of the banal; and the banal is a place of abandonment. You abandon yourself to your impressions, the hourglass of impressions.

It is always singular, every time so singular that every time is an exception, and the exception is the rule, and the rule is indeed very regular: it is that existence is exceptional.

Existence is exceptional, but this is not something that can be seen. This is what is exceptional. For everything can be seen, everything is *phainomenon*, except for *that*. That may be written, but even written, it cannot be seen, and this is not the reason why it is written.

A detective fiction: For whom was it written? Who profits from the crime of writing?

If I write that existence—this existence here, or that one there—is exceptional, and exceptional in a banal way, I do not do so in order to theorize it, consider it, or contemplate it.

It is written for the time wasted in writing, a few grams of existence, a few instants of insistence.

It is written for the impressions that leave no trace, except for the fact that we have abandoned ourselves to our impressions. It is written for the hourglass, its minuscule fall and the fact that it can be turned upside down on its own axis.

The axis of irises and an axiological anthology: Augustine, Dante, Montaigne, Blake, Rousseau, Et Cetera.

Augustine: "What we are currently seeking is how you love wisdom. You want to see it, possess it unveiled and naked, so to speak, with your eyes, in a perfectly chaste embrace."

Dante: "Like him that sees in a dream, and after the dream the passion wrought by it remains and the rest returns not to his mind, such am I; for my vision almost wholly fades, and still there drops within my heart the sweetness that was born of it."

Montaigne: "I uncover things more than I discover them."

Blake: "The daughters of Mne Seraphim led round their sunny flocks / All but the youngest. She in paleness sought the secret air / To fade away like morning beauty from her mortal day."

Rousseau: "Being dominated by my senses, whatever I may do, I have never been able to resist the impression they have had upon me and, so long as the object continues to act upon my senses, I never cease being affected by it."

Et Cetera.

But basically, nobody, basically, nobody in particular. An insatiable and unquenchable desire for anonymity in the guise of literature whose origins are immense, infinitely small, infirm, and infinitesimal. Et cetera, and the pulverized limbs of the gods slipping between Isis's fingers.

Which is to say, just as much: nothing, no literature. On the contrary, an endless pursuit, an unremitting hunting down of all kinds of literature: of all the ways to believe that, by hanging up a sign saying "Les Iris," your tawdry villa will thereby be transfigured. And there are thousands of such ways. Thousands of ways of representing or figuring how, while setting sail from a humble fishing village, you will reach the spice road, the gold and silk road, and the path to the Indies. But there are not many ways to turn the hourglass upside down.

There is no road leading to the Indies, even from the quaysides of the

most powerful empires. There is the slow glistening of the boundless, iridescent sea, with salt in your eyes, and sickness, and you end up somewhere else, or do not arrive at all. There is no gold road, no silk road, or
self road, or any road leading to the self, but there is this long impression-
able gaze touched every day by millions of golden birds, or by a few fine
rods of rain.

*Translated by Leslie Hill*

# § 8   On Writing: Which Reveals Nothing

This is an awkward situation. I promised a paper on Flaubert's *Temptation of Saint Antony*. For a long time I had the book in mind, even had a certain fascination for it. I was convinced it represented a kind of limit experience, and had a magnificent abundance—of both structure and chaos—bordering on the sublime, with a grandiose quality, writing about which, even in a rough and ready manner, struck me as an intimidating but nonetheless thrilling task. But having been forced by my promise to read and reread the text (together with Flaubert's letters, which clearly show his obsessiveness and seemingly hysterical identification—*psoriasis*—with Saint Antony, as well as Foucault's piece on the book),[1] I find myself with nothing left to say, except to draw the conclusion, bluntly, that *The Temptation of Saint Antony* is an exemplary case of literary disaster. Foucault saw this with admirable clarity: *The Temptation* is a companion piece to *Bouvard and Pécuchet*. But it is also an entirely distressing one (Foucault does not say this, of course, and as a result perhaps fails to take his reading to its logical conclusion), whose author is quite unwilling to acknowledge that he himself is Bouvard, and Pécuchet too. The book is an act of stupidity. No doubt Flaubert realized this, but that does nothing to alter the text such as it is.

Admittedly, the text may be read ironically, as an entirely critical account of the *temptation* that is literature in the absolute, literature when it aims to (re)present totality and embody a vision penetrating to the core of being and the origin of all things. But if so, what is the point of such a long-winded, creaking caricature? What is the point, except to attest to the fact that Flaubert himself, despite all else, did have this dream of being—that is, writing, being by writing—life and matter themselves, as his Saint Antony ends up proclaiming? And to the fact that, having had this dream and knowing it to be a dream, he nevertheless applied all his energy to flaunting it. And even to the fact that he enjoyed the bitter pleasure of parading this idiotic dream before the world—that he enjoyed it, or ended up not even enjoying it, or indeed enjoying the very fact that he did not enjoy it. As Flaubert famously put it in one of his letters: "Literature, as far as I'm concerned, is a dreadful pain, like a dildo stuck up my arse without me even being able to get off on it." Writing this, Flaubert finds enjoyment in not finding enjoyment and suffers from enjoying himself. Indulging and rejecting his own suffering, he finds every possible way of getting writing to penetrate life, and does so obsessively and obscenely, but ultimately in a way that is ludicrously metaphorical.

So what is the point of this long, ponderous enterprise that is *The Temptation of Saint Antony*, if the result is to tie us in knots such as these? What is the point of putting together a text that ends up being a dreadful pain, designed solely to demonstrate that it gets nowhere? Flaubert's *Saint Antony* is a strange text in that everything in it hinges on the ending, whereas the main body of the text is stuffed with images and information, with clichés of hieratic or esoteric language, with nothing that actually affects its writing. It is a text that does not call for any further commentary, interpretation, or "reading," and that does not inspire any other writing either on the basis of the text or between the lines of the text (except for scholarly glosses, which are of no interest to anyone, or psychobiographical ones that are similarly irrelevant). All it is good for is to make the reader feel the stupidity of a typically Romantic phantasm, which is none other than that of the joint engendering of reality and its diction/fiction (*Dichtung*), in other words, the phantasm of *myth* as we take it to be, precisely, since Romanticism. Or to put it even more precisely: "Romanticism" *is* the obsession with a *poetic making / making poetic of the world*. We, on the other hand, have to contend with something quite different, which is: being in the world. Which is why we want nothing more to do with Romanticism.

The fact remains, and in a sense this is the most important thing of all, that Flaubert (indeed like most of his friends and contemporaries) was himself convinced that *The Temptation* was a failure. This failure, though, was the success of the temptation to which he fell victim in writing it. At any event, the ending of the text is perfectly ambivalent: either Antony finally delivers himself from temptation, or he ultimately succumbs to it. Unless, according to a third possibility, he delivers himself by succumbing to it, thereby acceding to vision *in itself* once he emerges from all the visions that have so far befallen him from the outside, and once he himself enters infinitely into the *vibration* of the thing itself ("vibration," appearing as it does toward both the end and the beginning of the text, is the word that best describes what is ultimately at stake in "vision," which is a palpitating material togetherness with the heart of things, their origin and fundamental principle). Vision, then, is sublimated into an ecstasy of the eye, a visionary seeing that generates its own luminosity, and an imagination that is creative of the synthesis of imagination itself . . .

This whole business is Christian or post-Christian, and it is not by chance that it finds its laughable and bungled *acme* in Flaubert's *Temptation*. The whole point of Christianity was to put to work the equation Man = God's image = Creator. (Which of course immediately backfires, turning into the realization that since man is merely a creator of images—and this is the hopelessness and misunderstanding in which the "West" as we know it was indeed born—he must manufacture a God for himself, an absolute Idol, whose own creative masterpiece is his own image. The circle of imagining subjectivity is itself an imaginary one, and an unleashing of passion in relation to images. *The Temptation* is full to the brim with this motif, to the point of nausea.)

There is one great model in literature (but can we use that word here? we should perhaps call it "pre-literature") for this postulate, which is Dante's *Divine Comedy*. I was struck to find at the end of the *Paradiso* (Saint Antony himself is cited shortly before) an exact prefiguring of the ending of *The Temptation*: "I saw that it contained . . . that which is scattered in leaves through the universe. . . . I think I saw the universal form of this complex, because in telling of it I feel my joy expand," and earlier: "Look now on the face that most resembles Christ, for only its brightness can fit thee to see Christ."[2]

From the very moment when I was struck by this correspondence, which is evidently not due to chance (even if it was, i.e., if Flaubert had not read Dante, it would be all the more convincing, all the more profoundly necessary), I realized that there was nothing to be said about *The Temptation of Saint Antony*, because its true model was quite alien to the world in which it was conceived. It is like a brothel or fairground stall designed with the idea of it being a cathedral. It is quite possible—it is indeed necessary—to assume that Flaubert was perfectly aware of what he was doing. But this hardly matters. Despite Flaubert's transformation of one thing into its opposite—"assumption" into "temptation," "Beatrice" into the "demon"—and despite the withering irony he displays toward literature, it serves merely to confirm that the relationship he had with his model was a grandiose and morbid one. Flaubert dreamed of a profane form of holy script, but this was a contradiction in terms, if not indeed the last jolt by which literature finally detached itself from what was not literature. And it was this monumental failure that made modernity (which we are still in the process of coming to) both possible and necessary.

By the same token, what Flaubert did was to measure up to the fact that literature excludes holy script. It reveals no transcendent world; it is neither traced nor dictated by a god. It is not *inspired*. On every page, *The Temptation of Saint Antony* bears the mark of a grandiose predisposition to inspiration—as if the thing in itself were about to leave its true imprint upon the surface of the page, a page not unlike the space described in the very first scene of the book, in which "there hangs such fine gold dust that it is as one with the shimmering light [*la vibration de la lumière*]." At every point, the writing testifies to the fact that what it is after is *vision*, that it considers itself to be a vision, a vision *fused* with the universal vibration of light and matter, outlines and shades. Not to see but *to be*, such is Saint Antony's cry at the end: not even *to feel* in general, but rather *to be felt*, to be the point of convergence of all the sensible qualities in the world, thereby offered up to a kind of absolute sensibility that is both absolutely diffuse—and absolutely identical with the very being of whoever thereby gives himself up to feeling.

*The Temptation of Saint Antony* is entirely structured in order to end in this way. The book does not lead to that conclusion gradually by moving one by one through a series of figures and categories of temptation; any such progression is only an artifice of historical reconstruction of which the reader quickly tires. It leads there by rehearsing endlessly—this too is exhausting—all the possible variations on the single theme of light, the penetrating into light and by light, in every sense and from every perspective: as illumination, revelation, brightness, shimmering, form, vision, spectacle, images of every kind, wonders of the world, circles of light, reflections, mirages, suns, stars and torches, apocalypses, scenes, heavens, piercing eyes, rainbows, things glowing, things transparent, even including the pure idea and the face of Christ "in the sun's very disk." Christ himself, *lux in tenebris*, is the solitary *subject* in this whole book, which lies strewn on the ground like a fallen asteroid, a damning witness, itself already burnt to a cinder, to the effects of thousands of millions of years of light.

With *The Temptation of Saint Antony*, literature takes its leave, whether it likes it or not, of "creation" or mythologizing, poeticizing re-creation. And it leaves behind a testimonial to its departure that is damning, affected, even passably ridiculous in its unrelenting desire to paint a huge fresco depicting a revelation that reveals only a frantic desire for revelation.

But was there ever any *other* subject of revelation than the desire for revelation? And was there ever any other *temptation* than the temptation of revelation itself? It is not hard to see how a whole exegetical program could be devised here to look into this business of "original" temptation and "original" sin. Moreover, the possibility that the temptation of Christ may be based on a transposition of initiation rites arguably practiced by the Essenians is now well established. To be tempted is not simply to desire, which presupposes a gulf between the subject and object of desire; it is also to touch the object itself, and thus already to try out—to make an attempt at—one's enjoyment. It is to be on a par with being itself, to reveal its power and reveal oneself capable of such power or be invested with it. It is to reveal oneself dangerously in possession of the very power of being or of life. And thus to be a sinner. To commit sin is to be in contact with the violence of original emergence. But this whole logic hangs upon the possibility of revelation: the possibility that there is something like an origin to be revealed.

There is nothing more to be revealed, but everything to be written. This is the threshold upon which Flaubert leaves us standing, and the threshold where he leaves himself standing in the sense of both positioning himself and giving himself nowhere else to go. Writing may be likened to revelation, but only insofar as what is revealed *precedes* revelation whereas what is written ... demands still to be written. Nothing precedes, nothing is given—and in the end nothing will ever be given. It is a case of staying, quite exactly, on that thin line along which sense both proposes and dissolves itself, where it dissolves itself in the act of proposing. That is the only way to describe a line of writing, and the only way to describe a drawing or a painting that is not a *vision*. In such circumstances, writing never *vibrates*. It traces its line, the end of a pencil sliding along the edge of a ruler.

Admittedly, things are not that easy. There is something in *The Temptation of Saint Antony* that resists and obstinately insists. It is not the text doing this, however, but its consciousness. Or rather, the text itself is merely the text of its own consciousness, consisting entirely in a kind of implacable self-consciousness, simultaneously radiant and numb, which the text constantly projects upon itself. (Truth to tell, this is a repeat of Descartes, an *ego sum* entirely taken up with engendering itself while measuring itself against all manner of evil spirits. That too is overwhelming, this redundancy of Self, always more *interior intimo meo*.) Perhaps Flaubert's book is merely the frantic external demonstration of its own consciousness of the fact that it cannot write, that it is doing its best to appeal to an unmediated exteriority just like one of those sumptuous entertainments it describes in its own colossal, overloaded stage directions, *and*, simultaneously, of the fact that this is how it most surely fails to allow this exteriority to penetrate between its lines. This, then, is an absolutely, irremediably unhappy consciousness; it embodies, in its most acute state, something that has so often been revived throughout the whole of modern literary and philosophical history: the bitter knowledge that the book is not the thing, that the thing is somewhere else, and that the book still needs to be burned if we are to have the thing. *Ego sum, ergo res nulla est.*

For example, Bataille had one dread, that *drinking* alcohol was without common measure with speaking or writing about being drunk. This might be called the dread of the "on": not to write "on" something, but to write that thing itself, to write on a par with the thing, to be the thing in its inscription or exscription. As if there indeed was *the* thing *in itself* somewhere. Or rather, as if the *in-itself* could indeed be *revealed*.

This unhappy dread may be said to be the incandescent extremity of creative consciousness: a creator grasps himself outside of his creation, plunges it into the emptiness that precedes it and from which he alone emerges, alone with the void as the truth of self.

*The Temptation of Saint Antony* is therefore the simultaneous product of a somnambulist submission to the model of holy script and literature as revelation, *and* of a resolute defiance toward that literature—which is exactly the same—that reveals only its own effects and sanctifies itself when it can no longer be sanctified by anything else. It plays the one against the other, submission against defiance, defiance against submission, and exists as the terrified, frightened consciousness of being perpetually caught between the two.

That also—this consciousness that borders on its own eclipse and yet resists—it persists in entrusting to an exercise in writing. Everything is beyond writing—the recopying of treatises and sacred books, the manufacture of Hollywood-style sets, religious incantation and chanting—everything, that is, except for the slender trace of obstinate consciousness underlying everything, which is present without ever appearing, yet remains without mystery. On every page the text, like no other, forces one to ask: who is writing all this? What compiler of texts, what rhapsodist, what *son et lumiere* enthusiast, what fanatic, what schoolboy dazzled by his own knowledge is responsible for all this? Might it be a writer? But, then, why did he give up being one?

What is a writer who, in the process of writing, gives up writing? What is an abandonment of literature that comes to write itself as such in the text?

The answer to these questions lies not in the text but in the fact that the text exists, that there should be this pointless and exhausting enterprise, these years in the wilderness of visions, of which all that remains in the end is the trace of their passage, like a gap between all these lines and scenes, these cries and hymns, a gap consisting of nothing—except for the strange necessity to tempt and attempt the ordeal to the limit.

In a sense, all modern writers are descended from Flaubert's Saint Antony. One of these writers, Roger Laporte, gave the name "biography" to the frantic enterprise, in book after book, of writing about the attempt or temptation—which defies itself, undoes itself, while all the time declaring that this is what it is doing—to identify life with writing and writing with life.[3] The enterprise is an exemplary one in its nakedness, for no writer eludes this fate, if one thinks about it. (I first meant to write: "no writer worthy of the name," but this is excessive. There is no "dignity" to be claimed here, at least none that can be measured. The loyalty or probity of the enterprise cannot be evaluated on the basis of any accent or code of "loyalty," "probity," or "dignity.")

The truth of the matter lies in what the ending of *The Temptation of Saint Antony* indicates: in the writing that becomes life and matter, but which, even in that very movement, withdraws or excludes itself from the process. The question is whether the relationship between these two sides of truth leads to irony, or despair, or madness, or something else: something else that might have the appearance of a strange kind of serenity—on the verge of irony, despair, and madness, and, despite everything, a serenity that would accept the fact that life is indeed writing, and that it has to be written, but because writing and life do not attain their sense, therefore do not attain one another. They cannot touch it, meaning of course that they tempt it, and are tempted by it, but their sense is not to attain to it.

This sense is not a sense; and in the fact that it is not a sense lies its sense. In the minute interval between these two formulations, which has no room for any revelation, it is necessary to learn to live, or pass through (which is the same thing). Which also means that the interval must be forgotten. Not in order for it to be filled in, but because its truth is to be forgotten.

*Translated by Leslie Hill*

# § 9 Roger Laporte: The Page

I am writing this during the summer, a long way from my library and my collection of books by Roger Laporte. I have no desire to reread them in order to analyze them, or comment on them, which in any case would be an activity without proper meaning or import, as all those who know these books will readily grant.

(How, though, are these books read? I should say that they frustrate all those things that, as far as ordinary reading is concerned, have to do with appropriating the text, or incorporating yourself within the text, all those things that have you "enter into" the text or make it "penetrate" within you. With Roger Laporte, you can only "follow" the text, slide along it, on a par with the page itself: in a certain sense, there is nothing else to appropriate except this movement.)

It may be deemed more consistent with the singular nature of these books—or this single book in several sections (it goes without saying that I am referring here to the series constituted by *Fugue* and what follows, up to and including *Moriendo*)—to look only for the trace that reading them has left upon me today.[1]

There are many books of which, without rereading them, it would be quite impossible for me to convey much more than a general impression, immediately engulfed by an overwhelming sense of remoteness and of the uncertainty of remembering (I also have a poor memory). But the situation is different with Roger Laporte. It is not subject to the vagaries of memory, which forms its traces selectively, by distortion or loss. Laporte's book is already in itself a trace, a simple, solitary trace. As such, it tends to efface itself. But this self-effacement is still constitutive; its tension is quite precisely its own, its intention, so to speak—that by which and toward which his text abandons itself, projects itself, or throws itself. It was written that this should happen—but what? Only writing. Or if you will, it does not write but describes "writing," yet without in any sense constituting a "theory" of "writing." It could be said to be a singular kind of *ekphrasis* (that Greek literary genre that describes objects, especially scenes)—the *ekphrasis* of the thing called writing—and therefore a kind of infinite reflexivity, an abyss, an annulment.

According to its fundamental tendency, inscription, then, is null and void and as such indelible. Contrary to at least one well-established version of modernity, according to which all books are to be considered as palimpsests indefinitely reworking, overlaying, recovering, and interweaving other writings, Laporte's work presents itself, in its fundamental tendency, as a scored parchment returned to something like its original state for fresh writing or another inscription (which is perhaps not necessarily destined to come).

"Something *like* its original state," not its original state: not untouched by any pen, but, on the contrary, worn away by so many pens, ancient as well as recent, and in addition worn away by the scraper that has erased all trace. The trace of Roger Laporte is itself a wearing away that would tend to offer itself as a new chance. It is an exhaustion of literature that places literature—one cannot say face to face with itself, but face to face with all that might befall it, for better and for worse: face to face with the possibility of still occurring or ceasing entirely, with the necessity of risking itself entirely by dint of its own exhaustion.

Some might say, as some, no doubt, have certainly said—"nihilism." I would sooner call it an annihilation or annulment of that literary exaltation that, from Romanticism to surrealism (and some later avatars as well), wanted to transfigure life in poetry.

Here, then, an end to transfiguration. No defiguration, either. Unless, perhaps, it is a case of the one and the other, taken to the limit, and of the one in the other: life transfigured by total defiguration into a pure movement of writing (the strange usage, the strange twist that Laporte imprints upon the word "biography"). But this movement itself, as inscription, tracing, and scoring out, like graffiti fading, touching truth, is the page become blank again, like the success of a carefully calculated failure—gravely calculated, or never evaluated at all, precipitated rather by blind will ...

And yet the page. The page, like the vastness of the sea when you reach the ends of the earth, like a glimpse of the limits of the universe at the furthermost extremity of the most powerful telescopes. The page, not as a support of inscription, but as a surface of expansion. The page, not matter, but in itself already form. Itself a trace, and more (or less) than a trace—an indelible demand.

It is as if Roger Laporte had arrived at a double result, both intimate contrast and violent discord: both completion, the end of Romanticism ("infinite poetry"), *and* the infinite task of writing. An end to the revelation of the poetic secret of life *and* the sense of existence as indefinitely to be inscribed. An end to the belief that life could be written (as narrative or effusiveness): in a word, an end to religion, once again, in order once again to take the risk of being alone and naked.

Today, there is a kind of literary suspense (but is not everything today in suspense? Is our whole consciousness not one of suspense, hanging between aporia and expectation, between what is all too familiar and what is unprecedented?). Literature has repudiated itself, and only cites or evokes itself, whether as *remembrance* or as *comedy* (let us treat these words as titles and proper names, as heraldic devices held aloft in the course of the adventure of literature), as *trial* or as *wake*. All it has left are the niceties of taste, and the role of "cultural" adjunct to the "human sciences." None of this will last, as all of us are only too aware.

What is to come will be known only when it has come. In the meantime, what remains, hanging in suspense, is a large-format page, scored and naked, its surface uneven, scratched, and relatively smooth or rough, across which the pen struggles to make headway. Or perhaps this is just a screen, an expanse of word-processed text flashing past at the speed of its own software. Excessively slow or excessively fast, sense wends its way along unsuspected paths. Let us not be impatient; we will see. The page is free, spacious, a page of writing and a page to be turned, also the page or city square: an open space, with room to pass by, with room for a gesture or simply somewhere to stand.

The enterprise of Roger Laporte at times has fascinated me but also at times irritated me. It seemed to me in the past to have the courage of the impossible, and the naive demand of the whole of the possible. Today, I feel differently when thinking about it: rather a solitary solidarity with all those who *really* put an end to the fondness for prettifying sense, the naked truth of sense—as well as the possibility of doing so—and therefore all those for whom the history of sense is beginning anew before our eyes, unreservedly, without intent or expectation: unreservedly, in both senses of the word, without limitation and without available resource. Neither possible nor impossible; a self-evidence that is neither literature nor silence, neither life nor death, but the insistent holding onto an utterance, which is what from this point on we are for one another.

*Translated by Leslie Hill*

# § 10  In Blanchot's Company

This twentieth century of ours began in a spate of feverish literary (and artistic) activity and with a profound upheaval that is also often seen in terms of revolt, subversion, or revolution, and viewed as a reaching toward the dimly perceived—or at any event yearned-for—possibility of over-stepping the limits of the sayable in order to write the impossible and to produce thereby the secret formula of a mode of signification capable of grasping the insignificant and unsignifiable, the immemorial and uncon-scious, the unspeakable and unknown. Beyond the exhaustion of all pre-vious mythologies, the idea, once and for all, was to reassert the whole power of myth and harness it anew to a fresh set of rules.

But amidst this feverish turmoil, disaster was lurking, and the whole of "culture" soon revealed itself to be merely a hateful pretext for barbarism. Thus began what, for us, soon turned into an "age bereft of naïveté"—the age of the impossibility of believing in any literature at all.[1]

But emerging as it were from within the interval between the one and the other, between the fever and the shame, came the voice of Maurice Blanchot, tortuously weaving its way, still persisting, slowly and dimly, in the attempt to measure up to the difficulty of a situation in which every move knows itself to be a trap (as it is), still persisting, with heightened, painstaking vigilance, always alert—to the point of unstinting repeti-tion—to the signal failings of a civilization and its many games of sense or truth. And Blanchot's was a voice that undertook to hunt down the ne-cessity of writing, as a movement not of self-apprehension but of self-abandonment.

The murmur of Blanchot's voice is unceasing, even when it is as close as possible to what should cause it to falter: it speaks of the certainty of the moment that will neutralize it forever (and moves forward on that basis); but equally, as a result, it remains as close as possible to the risk that the movement of abandonment itself will become just another object to be grasped, another literary enterprise—whereas in fact what is really at stake in Blanchot is the need to "free us from the usual literary world."[2]

In this way, Blanchot's voice understands—or declares—itself to be the voice of someone alive yet already reported missing or believed dead: dead, that is, while still living on in his own words, according to the sameness [*mêmeté*] of those words that still persist (even though history itself may have been rent in two), and yet who can speak only with that break in his throat. And what sustains such a voice is the "absolute responsibility" of having to be responsible for what is always without guarantee and without response.[3]

With this perpetual risk and extreme fragility accompanying us both, and affirmed as such, Blanchot and I will have been fellow travelers and partners in conversation, necessarily so. Just as I was slowly discovering, while still at school, literature's vast riches (as the phrase goes), his was the voice that became interwoven with them, blurring the image and disrupting my attention. Though disorientated at first, I was later to find in Blanchot the most familiar and strangest company of all, while also the most secret and hidden, because of the light cast by the singular obscurity that is his.

This company was familiar to me in that, already from Flaubert onward, literature had been worried about itself, as though it had no alternative but to be alone, and alone in turning aside from itself in disgust (it is worth recalling Flaubert's fearsome confession, "literature, as far as I'm concerned, is a dreadful pain, like a dildo stuck up my arse without me even being able to get off on it"), and yet strange in that, appropriately enough, the voice of absolute worry, alone just like any voice, had no alternative but to isolate itself even more, to turn aside and lose itself in its own infinite turmoil. And no one has the task of finding it again any more than they have the task of challenging it. But it restores to each one of us, strangely, the chance and duty of risking ourselves in our turn ...

Amidst a world that is made up no longer (at least not immediately) of the violent contrast between fever and shame, but of a care [*souci*] that is itself uncertain of what it means and hesitates as to whether "literature" still has any sense, even the sense of casting suspicion upon itself, or whether sense does not now run somewhere else (but certainly not through religion, science, or philosophy), given that it always runs somewhere, even if it is against the flow, in its own absence, or furtively.

*Translated by Leslie Hill*

# § 11   On Blanchot

There appears to be no end to attacks on Blanchot (at least, as far as those who even got started are concerned ... ). So how long do we have to wait before we move beyond this flimsy and unnecessary episode? The question, in any case, relates to a more general one: how long do we have to wait before we move beyond smug, knee-jerk reactions flailing around making hasty judgments about the past without properly measuring up to the questions the past poses or the tasks it bequeaths to us? Which is a way of saying, loudly and clearly, that denouncing all forms of "totalitarianism" and all forms of "ideology" (in aesthetic terms, all forms of "Romanticism") is not a conclusion to anything but simply repeats the same old consensual refrain that is hardly even a prerequisite for tackling the real issues.

Staying for the moment with the attacks on Blanchot: these are moral and political on the one hand (the charge of anti-Semitism), and literary and theoretical on the other (the charge of mysticism and/or nihilism). Sometimes the two are treated separately; sometimes they go together (i.e., right-wing Romanticism, and/or overcompensation for anti-Semitism by mysticism).

These attacks are morally (politically) derisory, and literarily (philosophically) pointless. This much needs to be said, at least as a simple statement of principle, in order to say not that Blanchot is beyond question but that the question cannot be asked in these terms.

They are politically derisory: the few anti-Semitic expressions used by Blanchot in the 1930s (and used alongside other expressions that are quite categorical in their opposition to Nazism and to the persecution of the

Jews) are a concession—which should of course be condemned—to a vulgarity that belongs to that period and speaks volumes about anti-Semitism itself, but says no more about Blanchot than *their* anti-Semitic statements say about Flaubert, Baudelaire, or Kant.

That sociological anti-Semitism and doctrinal anti-Semitism (as perfected by Nazism) are perhaps closely related—that is one thing. But that the distinction between them, both *de facto* and *de jure*, is necessary (at any rate in the period before 1940)—that is another. Not only was anti-Semitism, in Blanchot, never a thought, but his thought was never complicit with it, even when his position was politically on the right.[1]

As far as right-wing thinking in the 1930s is concerned, it is essential to be able to distinguish clearly (which admittedly is not always straightforward) between various classical reactionary motifs and those that belong to another, more deep-seated reaction to the disarray of the modern world—indeed, sixty years later (even in the light of the events of May 1968, which Blanchot understood), it is still apparent that ritualistically trotting out democratic humanism and its "values" is no adequate response in the face of it (and often quite simply, and cynically, serves as an ideological façade for continuing domination and exploitation).

To sum up quickly, democracy, freedom, the rule of law, and the secular state have not always been equal to a challenge that is nothing short of a mutation in history and civilization, perhaps in capitalism as such. To be more precise: this does not mean we should do away with the political opposition between left and right, far from it, but demands that we think it afresh (and not on the basis of a past that has been simplified for the needs of the cause), in the absence of established certainties and without blinding ourselves, whether willingly or not, to the real state of "humanism" and humanity.

"In the absence of established certainties," here, means at least: having no confidence as far as community is concerned (and no availability as far as the "people" or "polis" is concerned). On the other hand, it also means the certainty that each and every imaginary representation of community denatures it, but that at the same time there is no sense except in common—and not in communion. These twin propositions define what lies behind fascism and behind the death camps, which is harshly, nakedly, brought into focus by the camps, and also define a task for thinking, in which without hesitation Blanchot assumed his share.

The attacks on Blanchot are literarily pointless: there is no doubt that

Blanchot's work is not free of Romanticism, if by that one means the religion of art and especially literature (of and in community). Blanchot's work will always have its source in Romanticism; but if one leaves to one side the laborious routines of the skeptics and positivists, what work of this century, in one way or another, does *not* find its source there?

However, if one carefully considers Blanchot's movement, it is apparent that it is also made up—uneasily, with difficulty, perhaps sometimes even reluctance? but also tenaciously and scrupulously—of a constant process of resistance to the religion of literature. There is no nihilistic mysticism of literature in Blanchot, if only because, increasingly, literature's object is not "literature," but on the contrary the withdrawal from literary fascination (or distraction). Everything, it could be said, has always turned, and continues to turn (to hang in the balance, too, and be decided) on all the different possible ways of understanding and elaborating the following sentence from an article first published by Blanchot in 1932: "The fine epithet of human or humane [*humaine*] conferred upon our [French] literature would be unimaginably unwarranted, if it dealt with man merely in order to abandon him to himself and turn him into a useful object of study."[2] Blanchot's entire writing speaks of this and by way of this.

Blanchot, finally, under the names of "writing" and "worklessness" [*"désœuvrement"*], deals with the condition of sense, its production and circulation, once all forms of fascination and distraction, all plethoric figures of signification and communication, in a word, all forms of myth are suspended. The break with every "new mythology" (which was admittedly not given to Blanchot from the outset) defines a turning aside from both Romanticism and "literature" as such.

It is of course this question of myth that underlies the question of fascism, just as, today, it runs through the issue of thinking community and history otherwise. More precisely: what makes all the difference here between these different ways of thinking is the relationship to myth, and to the mythic or mythological idea (this can be verified on a daily basis, and could be verified too by a reading of Blanchot's texts in historical sequence). This also means: the question of how to tolerate and uphold the absence of myth, in other terms, the question of how, in the future, the imaginary can take account of the symbolic (i.e., of bonding, or sense). Alternatively, to put it in entirely different terms: how, in the future, will what some call "subjectivization"—meaning the appropriation of an identity (and) of its being-in-common—how in the future will this work?

There is no "literature" in all of this, no "literary theory," no mysticism either, but an arduous questioning, demanding that thought "allow itself to be unbound, by writing, to the point of the fragmentary," words in which what may be heard, at the very least, is the decided refusal of all forms of imaginary totalization.[3] Of literature, if it is necessary to do so, it is possible to begin talking again only from the other side, and the same goes for politics, too. (Of course, all this can be put quite differently; it could be claimed that what is at issue here is only literature; but in that case the very name of literature, in the enigma it has maintained since taking on its modern meaning, is only a coded allusion to the effacement of myth.)

This, it seems to me, is the elementary clarity we are entitled to demand before entering into any debate around Blanchot, that is, around ourselves and our way of being exposed to the fragility of the present time, which itself is heir to a fractured history.

*Translated by Leslie Hill*

# § 12  Deguy l'An Neuf!

"Deguy l'an neuf!" came to me *just like that.*[1] I mean, the title came to me immediately, as soon as I was asked for one, immediately, without delay, without thinking about what I could or might want to say in relation to that title. It was all very quick; it was of course all too quick; but that is Deguy for you, already. We are both of us like people in a hurry, always rushing in. I did wonder afterward where, *just like that,* the title had come from, knowing full well that with Deguy it would all be a matter of "as" or "like," "as-ing" or "like-ing" [*"commer"*], as he might put it, in every possible way, but without knowing how [*comment*].

(All I know is that on New Year's Day this year, having already submitted my title, I had my bag stolen, together with a first draft of today's paper. I was forced to change course, and set off in a different direction.)

But I don't really know why I like mistletoe [*le gui*], and the tradition of mistletoe at New Year. I quite enjoy cutting down mistletoe for New Year's Eve when we spend it in the country, and I rather like the strange, star-shaped plant, which is hard and brittle, with a quite definite outline and little white globes like glutinous pearls. What is mistletoe like? On trees where it is found growing, like the parasite it is, it seems completely at home, and it is like a foretaste of spring in the depths of winter, with its name, *gui*, snapping or cracking like a shrill cry [at least in French]. There is also the druid connection—Norma or Getafix—a whole legend that never quite became a proper *epos,* that had its development arrested at the *as if* stage of an *epos,* in a word, a Latin *satura*: a miscellany or mixed bag, something like a hot-pot, or hodgepodge.

So, Deguy, then, as all these things. Deguy as always brand new in the midst of winter, Deguy as poetry that itself lives on *as* poetry, as if there were something called poetry, as if it were still possible for there to be something called poetry, living on and renewing itself in that way, as before, as such, yet quite unlike anything else, displaced, diverted, today more so than before, today as both threnody and prose, yesterday a rhymester, always an occasional poet but never a poet of state (his words, not mine): finished the state of poetry and the state of poet, finished and—as it were—put off for a fresh occasion.

∼

I said "Deguy l'an neuf!" with the same enjoyment and enthusiasm, the same sense of entertainment and curiosity, as fills me with each of Deguy's books, which are always fresh and unpredictable, which is not to say that they are totally different from the previous ones, since just like every one else he returns repeatedly to a small number of propositions (the word "propositions" is his: he "puts forward propositions," he says, and says that poetry puts forward propositions), and therefore repeats what he has to repeat, just like every one else, and very simply, for basically he is a very simple poet, but he does so afresh each time, as for the first time. Others plough lengthy furrows, speak in a tone that is tense, *recto tono*. Deguy plants his sprigs of mistletoe all over, rather indiscriminately, a parasite in every respect and every genre, dotting about here and there, in unruly fashion, changing styles, changing turns of phrase from one page to the next or within the same sentence. Changing manner and mode, turning, without moving, at every turning, because, he says, "there is no proposition that is not turned or troped in some way,"[2] and, as he also says, precisely measuring his words:

> Every three hours a poem
> Becomes new then fades
> With reading grows again in the silence.[3]

∼

(But, as happens, as often happens in my case, having joyfully dispatched my title, I was overcome with anxiety. Which became all the more intense later because of having to speak after so many learned discourses, in every sense of the word, of course, on Michel Deguy. Every-

thing will have already been said, and I shall therefore no doubt be repeating bits of everything.)

~

To talk about poetry and about a poet (even an absent one, since a poet
is not what Deguy is but merely what he "seeks to be"),[4] even to talk
therefore about a sought-after poet—nothing is more risky, and there is
perhaps nothing less possible than this. For ultimately—and this should
be said from the outset, even if it is a cliché, indeed precisely because it is
a cliché—it is the poet's job to discover the poet. No discourse will be adequate to that task, and philosophical thought [*la réflexion*] knows in advance that it lags behind. Deguy says this:

> *Philosophical thought lags behind;* there is something irreducible in the presen-
> tation or staging of the thinkable that forces it into a kind of endlessly sup-
> plementary metaphoricity, always seeking for a new sort of figuration or alle-
> gory, better equipped to bring speech, as it grapples with what lies beyond its
> bounds [*aux prises avec ce qui n'est pas elle*], back within the language of words
> [*en langage de langue*].[5]

Philosophical thought lags behind. Philosophy lags behind, lags behind
poetry and lags behind *in* poetry. It is the philosopher, in Deguy, who
seeks to be a poet—in Deguy, as in every one else, for it is a predicament
shared by all. But the poet is the one who says this is not what he is, that
he is a "poet without state," which is perhaps also, once again, a predicament shared by all. Philosophy and poetry lag behind one another—lag
behind, just as they supplement, metaphoricize, allegorize, heterologize,
heteronomize, cut across, and cut out different shares for one another, the
one *as* the other. This is not the result of any constitutive inadequacy on
the part either of the one or of the other. It comes from the fact that, together and separately, the one like the other, precisely as a result of the *like*
that holds the one in relation to the other while disjoining it from the
other, they are the mode of existence—the necessarily double mode of existence—of the lagging-behind as such of speech [*l'être-en-reste de la parole*]. Speech lags behind because "it grapples with what lies beyond it."
But this is not the result of any constitutive inadequacy—as regularly pro-
fessed by those philosophers who dream of "ordinary" language or those
poets who spend their time thinking about silence. Nor is it the result of

language's supposedly being in a state of infirmity and forced to measure up to an absoluteness of sense that would have the effect of simply abolishing it or ultimately disposing of it. It is a result of speech as the mode of existence of being-in-the-process-of-grappling-with-what-lies-beyond-it [*l'être-aux-prises-avec-ce-qui-n'est-pas-soi*]. It is not that there is speech *and* something else, like being, world, sense, or truth. There is being that lags behind itself—being in deficit and in excess of its own identity and singleness as being. Speaking being [*l'être parlant*], then, which is quite different from the concept of man, is rather being itself and as such, being that is always more and less than being, being that happens to be, or not to be, to be beyond its being, being existing life and death.

As he says, "nonbeing is a euphemism,"[6] a mild way of speaking that assuages, refuses to accept the crashing violence, the dazed sense of loss, and the bitter realization that says, "I know that I cannot bring her back alive."[7] What he describes here as a "scrap of Orphic allusiveness," which opens this lament for the dead, or threnody, should of course be taken to refer to both Monique and poetry too. Or rather, not to Monique *and* poetry but to the one *as* the other. Not the one absorbing the other, in order to prettify it or make it more touching. Not intimacy exploited but intimacy exposed, precisely because it *has* to be laid bare, and this has to happen to avoid its being poeticized. Philippe would call this, I think—and for once he would say it in the manner of Michel—the intimation of intimacy. Not a poetical trafficking with death, or a morbid trafficking with poetry. But the one as the other because the same nonliving bringing back of the past that is past, the infinite past, which is infinitely over and with which the bringing back of the past must grapple. The word "euphemism," he reminds us elsewhere, "was invented by the Greeks to mean: to *pass over death* in silence."[8] To restore death to its silence by speaking it, which also means to allow death to speak amidst our human, all-too-human silence, and to speak with its ever-fresh, ancient voice. To pass over death: not to pass beyond it, nor to endure and maintain oneself in it, but to pass with it, within it, on a par with its eloquent silence, if that is possible.

~

Deguy writes: "in our experience of the impersonal *it* that, so ordinarily, does the raining or is sunny, and of the *doing* that is none of our doing and is closely related to the expression 'there is' [*il y a*]—there is nothing

I can do about this—the day dawns and the world comes into being."[9] Being is always fresh, and speech grapples with this freshness. Always fresh: that is to say, it always was fresh, and its freshness is more ancient than anything. Always fresh, returning always, always the new year—the beginning again of what is most ancient and goes on for ever. A reminder of the unforgettable: that the "there is" [*"l'il y a"*] starts up and goes, and passes on. A *threnody*, therefore, with every new year. One by one, then, he counts out all Monique's birthdays, enumerating, simply, and as a finite sum, the infinite passing, giving to understand nothing other than the verb: to *pass*, in the infinitive, calculating incalculable passing [*passer*].

Enumerating each one, as in an implicit metrical pattern, as in the schematic prosodic structure underlying the poem, on a par with the positioning of speech on the edge of what lies beyond it, grappling with what lies beyond it. Speech: the mode of existence of what thereby grapples with the absolute passing of absolute freshness—meaning, ultimately: the mode of *existence* as such, the very modality of existing (of ex-isting), this absolute mode—mode or measure—being itself the conformity of being with that which is even more remote than nonbeing, which withdraws from this euphemism, and which might only be called blasphemy (a curse upon existence), so long as—

—so long as speech is not indeed a grappling. Speech grappling with what lies beyond its bounds is before all else speech grappling with what within its bounds lies beyond its bounds, with a blasphemy that is always close at hand, always imminent, always insistent, speech that would curse being and itself into the bargain.

Speech grappling with its own blasphemy: there lies the common source of philosophy and poetry, the one lagging behind the other, but not so as to substitute a blessing for the curse, nor to sublimate the cry or lament. To do without blasphemy is also to do without its opposite: it is to lose one's grip—or the will to get a grip—on "what lies beyond it," that is, the passing, the infinitive: to pass. To grapple with something is not to get a proper grip on it. Deguy writes: "There is no such thing as deathbed pornography. Horror is not sublime either, for the sublime is still bound to the beautiful."[10] There is no such thing as pornography at all: no writing that embellishes nudity, if nudity, being-denuded [*l'être-à-nu*], is that with which existing or existence [*exister*] grapples, and grapples as with *nothing*, with nothing on which to get a grip, because it is nothing—passing, in the infinitive, what is freshest and most ancient alike.

Consequently, if the poem "calls up the extreme elsewhere [*le très ailleurs*],"[11] this does not mean it brings it back from that remotest of places. The reminder of the unforgettable is also a reminder of the immemorial: that of which no memory exists. Death reminds us of that of which no memory exists. So too does speech. The poem calls up the extreme elsewhere *as* an elsewhere, and does so by keeping it elsewhere. This is also what is meant by "I cannot bring her back alive." I come back with the extreme elsewhere, but cannot get over it, cannot retrieve it, cannot bring it to book. But to pronounce either a benediction or a malediction is the same: it is to try to bring to book the extreme elsewhere. Deguy wants to hold speech at a distance from both the one and the other, and thereby hold it, not by malediction or by benediction, but by *diction* alone.

~

This, too, is how Deguy is a poet "after Auschwitz." He writes that the camps show how a specifically modern twist has been applied to the euphemism of the Greeks. Extermination could be spoken only by passing over itself in silence, by passing over itself in the language of the "final solution," and by calling the ovens an "international *information* center," as he puts it, emphasizing the euthanasia-like euphemism involved here (which is quite incapable of leaving death to itself, and to its elsewhere, and confiscates it by edulcorating [*en bien-disant*] the relentless curse [*maudire*] of piled-up bodies).

After Auschwitz, we can no more speak badly [*maudire*] than speak well [*bien-dire*]. This is perhaps the sense of the double injunction imposed by Adorno on poetry after Auschwitz. And this is the sense of any poetry "after" Auschwitz that writes itself as such, knows it, and says so. It has the sense of resolutely leaving to one side both benediction and malediction, the one as obscene and the other as derisory. It has the sense of leaving behind all declamation and all poetical poses in general. Adorno's verdict makes no pronouncement on Auschwitz, perhaps, that may not be found elsewhere. But it does make a statement about poetry "before," and about the nature of blessed or imprecatory poeticization. (It therefore makes a statement about what it was that "poeticized" poetry, well before Auschwitz, and about what simultaneously exalted it, put it beyond itself, and put it into crisis ... ).

Expressly replying to Adorno, a contemporary German poet writes as follows:

> We believe that poems
> have only now once more
> become possible, that is, insofar
> as only in a poem may that be said
> which otherwise
> would make all description laughable.[12]

Something has retreated from saying, from euphemy and blasphemy alike, from both incantation and imprecation. Something has retreated that formerly guaranteed saying, whenever it sought to go beyond itself, and did not leave it denuded when it came to grappling with what lay beyond it. Something that made it possible for Orpheus to bring back Eurydice—or at least believe he could. What has retreated is poetry itself, insofar as it was once a foretelling of the words of the gods, a voice plunged deep into death, birth, creation, love, and destiny: a speaking that could tame and put a spell on what lay beyond its bounds.

Or at least this is what was believed, or what people wanted to believe, and this is how poetry has been represented, how the thought of poetry, surrealistic and overblown, has been overdetermined and overessentialized: as the thought of a transcending of speech by speech itself. This was when the hatred of poetry began,[13] and when Zarathustra could claim that the net cast among poets only ever hauled in "the heads of former gods." When it then became a case of insulting beauty.[14]

What then began had something to do with prose, that is, with speech that could not be transcended. The prose of Hegel—that is, the prosaic quality of a graying world, deprived of living color, regretful of poetry and hopeful for it, for poetry, or pure thought—gave way to prose as a refusal of poetry, to the prose of a world that was no longer gray, indeed was neither gray nor in color, that was not the point—but a world in which speech openly grapples with what lies beyond it. Where poetry no longer has the need to curse—or bless itself, either. It deposes itself, lays down its tropes, advances straight ahead, *prorsa,* straight ahead toward nowhere, like every other mortal being. Straight ahead from the extreme elsewhere to the extreme elsewhere.

Or else, it is poetry itself that comes back once more from the remotest of places, the most ancient of times, *as* the most ancient and the extreme elsewhere, *elsewhere here in this very spot.* Prose: or the new year of poetry renounced, not brought back alive.

Deguy slowly explores this history of poetry "to be put back into prose [*à remettre en prose*]," as the title of one poem has it.[15] (He ruminates ceaselessly on the history of poetry; there is no shortage of evidence of this.) He goes about it slowly, gently, feeling his way, without violence, without overdoing it, playfully rather, with syncopated prolixity. Rhythm stirs in the shadows. He says: "Everything is dark and yet densely it dances, dances and cadences."[16] He wishes for "an art of poetry that disconcerts poems."[17] Not a ruin, not refusal, not an anemic sublimation of poetry. But the poem losing its composure and self-assurance, its pose and transcendent authority. Deguy cuts across and unsettles the poem—both work and substance, the very thing of the poem, the hymn or *epos,* the poetic song ready-formed, already confirmed. He prefers to choose the poet. The poet is not the subject of the poem. The poet is not substance but displacement; he is not a subject but is still to come, is the to-come [*l'à venir*] of the "it" that there is [*il y a*]. "Long time a poet and not yet, not ever"[18]—a poet, the growing back of the most ancient, which does not return but comes afresh, bringing back the old *as* the fresh, the freshly ancient. He can then say: "What you seek is at hand, is here—and is something else."[19]

His poem is not organized according to the organicity of a work. But it passes; it is the passage and passing of the poet, his being-in-passing scattering a calculated trail of little white pebbles behind it as it goes. "Everything resumes on each page; everything ends on each page."[20] Going elsewhere, always having something to do elsewhere, and restless, because it has things to do: not in order to produce poetry, but in order to help others out. It must be "a poem that does not talk too loud, as useful as Martha, translatable, reducible, and exportable, which goes into battle with other emergency help."[21]

This is his response to the great question, the question that will have preceded and prepared the possibility that poetry might disappear: wherefore poets in times of distress? From now on, the question becomes: wherefore poets in times of distress for poetry? He replies simply by the patient, discreet, and fleeting usefulness of what "does not talk too loud."

(At least, he makes every effort to believe this. Finding it hard to do. He still has to curse the modern world: still, as though it were the reflex action of poetry threatened in its sacred livelihood, whereas we have moved on, and he is already seeking something else: seeking to restrain speech from talking too much and to control its excesses.)

This reserved, restrained way of speaking, always restrained by the remote place back from which it comes, to which it returns—this is what grapples with what lies beyond its bounds, and grapples with it in order to summon up what is lacking in distress, or to meet it halfway. What is lacking is the "extreme elsewhere." The "extreme elsewhere" is presence, and the silence that goes with it. He says: "presence is something that can be established"; "silence must be imposed."[22] That is the task; that is what poetic making does; that is the emergency service that should be provided. To come to the assistance of presence in passing. Not to subtract it from passing but to pass with it, discreetly, almost furtively. Furtive eternity is what we lack, and what is within our reach. To pass over in speaking silence, to speak in the passing of silence. Elsewhere, extreme elsewhere, this very spot: undying places all.

~

The presence that must be established, the silence that goes with it—this does not mean the immutable presence of the gods. It is the fleetingness of being: its timelessness. Poetic "making" is therefore not a "producing" but a proposition. What the poet proposes is nothing other than "how it is like it is [*ce comme quoi c'est*]."[23] How it is like it is—is what, here or there, in the moment, passes. The thing itself. He refers to what he calls a "proposition of acknowledgment."[24] To acknowledge the thing itself in passing. In passing, to acknowledge the thing itself. In this selfsame passing, to acknowledge the thing. This could be called "circumstance." He says, "each poem is an occasional poem, a poem of circumstance"[25] (all in all, the poem is situationist). The presence and silence of circumstance must be established and proposed. They must be *pro*posed, because neither presence nor silence are ever posed. Neither supposed, nor deposed either. Proposed only in passing. Take them or leave them, without delay, traveling at the speed of poetic light, which is speed at the limit, speed that calculation approximates and decides on arbitrarily so as merely to fix the limit and say when the limit is reached.

What has to be acknowledged in passing is the presence and silence of "how it is like it is." What has to be proposed is the acknowledgment in the circumstance, given the circumstance, of *the* "how it is like it is"—or *of* "how it is like it is"—that is, of the presence and silence of the thing or of being. They have to be proposed as what they are, and consequently, be proposed without being withdrawn from their reserve, their distance, their passing. The thing or being: what basically happens [*se passe*], basically passes [*passe*], the basic event. He says: "What you seek is at hand, is here—and is something else. The treasure is buried in the field; that is how prose turns the soil, how language holds things at a distance while acceding to them."[26]

But to leave the thing, the being, to its presence and silence, in order to propose it, is nonetheless to imply—to give or take—the turning of a particular, circumstantial proposition. For there is no thing *in itself.* In itself the thing is *something*, and being is some taking place. He says, "there is no proposition that is not turned or troped in some way." Every time, "how it is like it is" requires a singular turn. Deguy is a poet, a writer of prose, a proposer of turns of phrase and turnings, of tropes that turn aside from presence, as do the turns on a turner's wheel or the hand that turns itself to design or drawing.

Such is the craft or handicraft of poetry, the poet's work and his daily grind, of which he says, "it is a makeshift sort of working life, putting things together without properly knowing how, living in poems."[27] Without properly knowing how, but with considerable know-how, all the tricks of the trade, and the *Handgriff* that philosophers despair of ever picking up, just like the trick or sleight of hand of schematism, the tracing of the arch-design of things, their sensible identity, and the trait of their presence.[28]

Naturally enough, *ut pictura*, as he is fond of repeating, the turning of the proposition, the turning capable of offering how it is along with how it is like it is—this is the drawing or design of presence. Circumstance—that-which-stands-around—is the exact contour of the turning of being, each time in its turn. Such is the imperious necessity of his work: "I must," he says, "draw her life exactly, and say what its courage, devotion, endurance, and discouragement were like, and the resoluteness, the limitations, the unchanging fear and laughter, the defeat and horror of it, too."[29] Already there is no need to go into detail: each one of these words, which in itself says only something vague and general, resonates differently because it is placed under the injunction of being exact. It gives off the muffled, almost silent sound of a single circumstance, the contour of someone, of some *one*, whose face does not appear. ("If I focus my memory on her petrifying face in my head, tears fill my eyes, as though my soul had a head cold; my soul floods out between my body and my memory.")[30] Exactitude is not precision, has nothing to do with precision. Precision approaches, aims to get as "close as possible" to presence, which it thus assumes to be approachable and therefore in some way fixed. But exactitude is not found in proximity, which always leaves the "closest"—even the "closest possible"—prey to the indeterminacy of "more or less." Exactitude is exigency—that is its *etymon*—exigency "exacted," accomplished, carried to term, without remainder: the strict observance of the thing, its presence, without the slightest approximation. The thing is not approached, nor is it approximated to anything else: it remains in its elsewhere, the distance of its being, its passing. It is solely, strictly, exactly retraced upon itself: just as (he says) in drawings by Rubens and Watteau,

> the perfect line happens to repeat itself so exactly
> that several drawings of the same thing
> draw the thing as though it were superimposed upon itself.[31]

Superimposition, or else—to use another word to say the same thing about sameness [*mêmeté*]—coincidence. He asks, "What is it that favors things that silently expect nothing in the grayness?," and answers the question, "coincidence."[32]

The thing *itself* [*la chose* même], then, *falling* by itself *with* itself and as though upon itself. The thing itself, which is itself the philosopher's "thing itself" or "thing in itself": the matter itself of the being-in-itself of something in general, something-and-not-nothing, but the thing itself grasped in passing in its self-sameness [*sa mêmeté même*], according to its presence and silence, according to its presence elsewhere and the resonant silence of its being-itself [*son être même*], being the same as itself. As he writes:

> The same [*Le même*]
> on a par with [*à même*]
> in addition [*en plus*].[33]

The thing, then, or the some one, the no one of whom it has to be said: She took her words with her, and was buried in herself.[34]

And she is the one who cannot be brought back alive: she herself. Not only does he not bring her back, but he himself does not come back either. Not bringing her back alive is something he cannot get over either. He stays with her, alongside her, this thing, this person who is no more. He remains alongside her, fallen upon her with her.

But this is how, with her, he too takes his words with him; he takes back all his words, and brings them back to the coincidence with the thing. All these words in this language, of which he repeats at every opportunity how much he loves it and is indebted to it,[35] this language that he cannot get over, that remains on a par with the thing into which it retreats.

Long before, he had already written: "Turning toward the word 'fountain,' it is the thing fountain in whose presence he finds himself, and which he succors: he does not drink from its water, which flows, grief and sense, in his memory."[36]

The thing itself as the coincident retreat of the word into the exactitude of its design ... When another poet might say "wherever the word defaults, let no thing be," he says instead: the thing is where the word defaults, but this default is the very exactitude of the word. The unheard-of character of the thing is heard here, with its distinctive timbre [son timbre même]. Just "as a phrase makes language vibrate, or a brass instrument makes musicality resound, so each time language is like the invention of the viola for the ear, the triangle, or oboe too."[37]

~

From the unheard-of to the audible, from the elsewhere to the here, the hiatus remains:

> Unfailing hiatus,
> only the storm of the poem
> little by little repairs its perpetual worsening
> every now and then makes worse its perpetual repair.[38]

A hiatus—the opening of coincidence, the retracing of exactitude, the yawning of the same. To repair it and make it worse, both together, one by way of the other, one like the other, this is what is called being exact, professing exactitude. (In Horace, hiatus sometimes comes to mean "speech.")

The audible exactitude of the unheard-of is called timbre [le timbre]. Poetry is like an emancipation of the timbre of speech, within speech itself. "Just as Valéry, whenever he was about to enter into a state of musicality, preferred the sound of the orchestra tuning up, running through all its timbres, so too do we, readers and writers alike."[39]

Timbre for itself, released from the attunement of the chord and from the vocal composition of song—the song behind the song, the song within the song—timbre opened up within itself to its own background noise, the thing itself at bottom struck or stroked against itself, vibrating with nothing other than its own tension on a par with itself, with the stridency and cadency of coincidence.

(It might also be said that prose is the poetry of timbre, the inverse relationship of an autonomized, almost unmodulated timbre, or rather: a timbre whose modulation, mode, measure, and turning could be described as the sounding, beating, or immanent echo of timbre as such, the resonance of the *same*. As if one were to say of a poem: a piece for solo rustling of paper, or unaccompanied throat clearing.)

This is how, for him, music could be thought to belong "elsewhere," "in an *unheard-of* space, by which I mean one that is nonallegorical, nonreflexive, nonrecognizable, in other words, not even *enigmatic*, rather: without any answer, if the enigma and its answer belong together."[40] What is not allegorical is *tautegorical* (according to Schelling): which says the same on a par with the same [*le même à même lui-même*], and by the same itself [*et par lui-même*]. Deguy wants the same to resonate of itself, as such and without resemblance, without *returning to the same*. This is what he wants to hear, he who cannot get over it.

But he also says, and underlines it, that "it would *seem* there is some non-semblance . . . , basically something strange and novel."

The nonsimilar [*le non-semblable*] cannot itself but seem to be such. The thing itself displays its self-evidence and certainty by virtue of the exactitude of its "as itself" [*son "comme elle-même"*], its perfect "superimposition upon itself" or coincidence—and this "as such" cannot present itself only *as* (as if it were) identical with itself. There is a vertiginous collision in the coincidence of "*as* as" [*"comme comme"*]. This is not to say that the thing itself and as such is not; certainly, it is—and is *as* such [*en tant que telle*]. But being as such, it is immediately similar [*semblable*] to itself. It reverts, without any interval and yet not without hiatus, from the same to the similar [*va du même au pareil*]. From the depths of its withdrawal it is already in a state of acknowledgment. At the height of its exception it is in a state of resemblance. In apposition with itself, it is in a state of "apposition controlled by the word 'like,' or 'as' [*comme*],"[41] and this is how it may become an object of proposition.

If a proposition is always a proposition of acknowledgment, this is because it is always achieved by the use of an "as" or "like." And if there is no proposition that is not turned or troped in some way, the way common to all these turnings is this "as" or "like." Deguy's poetics is a poetics of the "as" or "like": it is the common assumption [*assomption*] of a rhetoric, a logic, and a dialectic of "as" or "like," just as his philosophy has "as" as a transcendental. It is like he is mad about "like" [*il est comme fou du comme*]. For hardly is the "as" or "like" inserted, or slid, more like, into the intimate hiatus of sameness, than it sets off a whole series of crashing waves of resemblance, collisions of proximity, family likenesses: "There is something like in being / A family likeness an unassuming air."[42] The resemblance between self and self, the *as* of *as such* [*le* comme *du* en tant que tel], the joining of the same to the same—which is also to say: the barely perceptible disjoining of one from the other—opens up all manner of resemblance. If the one is like itself, as the one that it is, so it is also already like the other—like the other of the one as its very own other. Deguy is fond of these dizzying possibilities. No sooner is the series of resemblances declared open than these gradually prove more different from one another in their very resemblance with one another, and the *as* or *like* extends to the resemblance, general difference, liberty-equality-fraternity, of the *as-one*, the "as-one-ism" [*comme-unisme*, i.e., communism] that he applies as a rule to "us," an "us" of which he declares, "we are neither German nor Jews, yet we are just the same [*pareils à eux*], 'trait for trait,' sharing a communal trait [*un trait comme-unaire*] that is not visible in the visible,"[43]— and to the same disparity and disproportion, the same deployment and multiplication, that populates presence with incalculable semblance and resemblance.

He addresses the thing as follows:

> That to which I compare you celebrates, multiplies you,
> Adorns you beyond compare. For what
> Would you exchange yourself, shall I decide upon the barter
> And the transformation I seek to measure
> All things against you.[44]

All things can be the measure of all things. All things can be the common measure of the incommensurable commensurability of everything, and of the indifferent difference of everything, its proportionate disproportion. *As* or *like* provides the measure: the common measure of being is what makes one presence be like another presence, and being *as such* nothing other than its own analogy (Aristotle refurbished in the guise of a poet), whence, too, his singular ontological frivolity, genial gravity, and childlike application to playing as though not playing.

~

The "how it is" (yes, Beckett's too, which he re-cites and treats as his own),[45] the "how it is" of being communicates necessarily with the as or like of "that's like it is." In which case it is the poet who finds words to propose the multiplied turning of the *as* or *like* of being.

To be proposed, it must be transposed: "Blind, they used to say of poets, in times gone past, because they would transpose things in order to find them."[46]

The poet transposes, transports, assembles things, assembles (he says) "the character of a *thing*, a qualification that transfers a certain number of 'things' in advance . . . or: the world emerging in a commonsense perspective (common: as-one). . . . A character that may be said to be ontic and transcendental."[47] Deguy thinks like an empiricist, or like an analysand: he makes associations. He takes it upon himself as a poet (which is how, in an absolute sense, *he takes it upon himself to be a poet*, albeit only as the one he seeks to be) to carry out all manner of "metaphorical transactions," starting with the transaction between resemblance and assemblage, and trafficking—turn and turn about—in trope-like transportations in every possible way, from puns to metaphors, malapropisms to prosopopoeia, and with all the prolixity and insolent laxism that comes with anxiety. "That which cannot be spoken," he says, "must therefore be written."[48]

To write is to allow oneself all the tricks and turnings of proposition; it is to write one thing *like* another, despite and in accordance with *disproportionality* (despite and in accordance with the "sad fact of Disproportionality itself,"[49] the "sad fact revealed" in the death of the woman who "tucked in, and held together both sides of things over which we have no control"),[50] to write, for instance, "the ill-starred poem of the ill-spoken word"[51]—and like this poem, consequently, like this single poem common [*comme-un*, as-one] to all the poetry of this poet seeking himself as a poet, like this poem whose very title satirizes every sacred institution of poetry, to write all these "metaphorical transactions between this thing and that (he says) which will be found, in reading, to be 'mutually compared,' similar to one another,"[52] to write, then, for the sake of the reading that in effect will bring about the similitude of what writing will have put to one side, the reading that thereby creates a second nature, a new space of proximity, the very proximity of what is distant, words like their things and things themselves like something else, and always, first and last, *Worte wie Blumen*, those words of Hölderlin he recites,[53] words, that is, like flowers—

—but he immediately adds: "the like of poetry is not metaphor, but something else"; the like of poetry is not like the like of simile (the question is one of passage: what like is like the other kinds of like, and which is different? and why is it that in French there are so many kinds of like [*comme*], homonyms and synonyms alike, or synonyms by virtue of their homonymy, as Deguy wishes, unless of course it is the other way round, or both at the same time); the like of poetry is not the like of a simile that metaphor condenses (in one poem in the collection *Ouï dire* [*Hearsay*], he denies the right of simile to serve as a name for the language of tropes in general).[54] The like [*comme*] of poetry is the like of *as* [en tant que], not the like of likeness [*pareil*].

(In this way, and in more than exemplary manner, the point should be that poetry *as* [comme] prose—as argued by Lacoue-Labarthe, who is a very different philosopher, in order to emphasize the *like* [comme][55]—is indeed nevertheless the *as such* [en tant que telle] of poetry, the essence, the Idea of poetic demand itself: the demanding essence of poetry is there as prose, *in prose*. Prose is not the same [*pareille*]; it is far less and far more; it is the insistence and resistance of poetry itself. In this respect, prose is still, absolutely, a poetic proposition, a proposition of poetry in general, a *way* of saying, or rather of making poetry as such. One way *contra* [contre] another, but *like* [comme] another, also, similarly. *Contra*, against, up against: together with (*con-, comm-, cum*), in the mode of (*comme, quomodo*, like).

The *like* [comme] as Deguy wants it is the similar [*pareil*] as *as* [en tant que en tant que], or the similar similar to the as. It is as if Hölderlin had written (as he should have done) *Worte als Blumen, Worte wie Blumen als Blumen, Worte wie als Blumen* ["Words as flowers, words like flowers as flowers, words like as flowers"].

It is the similar to the extent that it makes visible the as [*en tant que*] of what it resembles. *Worte wie Blumen* makes words visible as [*en tant que*] flowers, that is, to the extent that [*en tant que*] as [*comme*] words they are, in their being, flowers. But how are flowers? For Hölderlin, they open and bloom. For Mallarmé, the flower arises, absent. For Angelus Silesius, it grows without reason. For Novalis, it speaks, and the poet becomes a bloom. For Derrida, a friend of Deguy, there is always a dried flower fading abysmally in a book.

The flower is the ill-starred spoken word [*le mot-dit*] par excellence, poetry to the extent that it is clinging (Bataille) or unacceptable (Denis Roche), but this is because it gives rise to the incomparable like [*comme*] that compares nothing—the how it is of being that resembles nothing— what can also be expressed by referring, as he does, to the "sense of a life that is without sense any more—in other words, . . . sense."[56] In Derridean terms, one might say "there is no such thing as difference *as such*," and that is what the dried flower in every book—and the inappropriability of any single or *proper sense* as such—is all about. Deguy's retort, however, is that there is an as such of the as such [*un comme tel du comme tel*], and that is the as-similarly [*comme-pareil*], the pareil of the nonpareil (as the age of Louis XV put it): the nonpareil radiance of the pareil, giving rise to another bloom, that of desire.

What resembles nothing, starting with itself, what differs endlessly from itself and transports itself from word to word, gathers desire for an image without resemblance nor illusion. The object of desire is always what resembles desire, like the blooming of a flower. He says: "What I call an image is what makes a naked woman appear as a woman; nudity gathers together beauty and desire; what resembles is desirable."[57] To make a naked woman appear as a woman is to superimpose her upon herself, to acknowledge or present her as such, or to be exposed to her as such; it is to make being (the woman) coincide with appearance (the naked woman): it is to make being be, nothing less. The image is being *as* such; this is what this definition says (and it is not by chance that, at the same time, it consists of a snapshot-like allusion to a whole vast swathe in the history of painting, photography, and film).

The image—and consequently, one can imagine, the whole of poetry— is the *as such* of being; it is this "as such" itself emerging from its concept and discourse, the "as" *as* [*"en tant que"* en tant que] gesture, showing, *deixis*, the presentation *of* being. And this presentation itself as desire. The showing of being is desire for being, desire for the *as such* of being, for what is desirable is never (naked) being on its own, but the showing in which it comes to be offered up *as such*. Here is how Deguy puts it:

> Palms rolling out the pastry of buttocks
> Or the left hand supporting the right breast
> And the thumb softly excising you . . .
> The horizon of thighs displays purple nymphs
> Without an image the sex appears
> And then like a face it is . . . [58]

Coincidence as coitus superimposed upon its own image like an ocular—not oracular—bloom. For nothing of the uninscribable is revealed; nothing is revealed, and all is written, written like the "natural comparison" of the uninscribable, disproportionality "itself," and its own image. The image is the desirable exactitude of being, and desire is what conforms to this exactitude.

~

But the image or figure made in this way by the "as or like" as an order to appear [*comparution*] and collision, as a summons requiring the extreme elsewhere to put in an appearance while remaining elsewhere, this is no trompe l'oeil figure nor, as he puts it, any "trompe-l'âme" one either.[59]

The flower, or woman, is also the one he cannot bring back alive. Some time ago he wrote about the orange blossom Nicolas wore to the wedding. He wrote, "hydrangeas prefer indoors / (I describe life to her with exactitude)."[60] And now he writes, "Here is the stonemason's garden."[61] The tombstone is the flower, the tombstone as a flower, like a woman naked. The word says like a flower like a tombstone, and it is on the tombstone, he says, that nothing should be inscribed to deceive the soul [*en trompe-l'âme*]. And this is why "I shall leave the tombstone with only the name engraved upon it."[62] The flower that blooms once more in this new year is not a flower but a mistletoe berry, dry and brittle like the plant that bears it, and parasitic, too, on its own "as" or "like." That very thing, however—he at one point said that it was like a resurrection: he always acted as if they could commune [*comme-unier*] with one another in the religion that was Monique's and went with her to the grave. Indeed he wrote:

> I believe that something like an air of resurrection
> is at work with death and that it is the task of the poem . . .
> to say of poetry that what you bind
> in its name will be bound to this earth.[63]

The poem (re)suscitates the world as world, including death as death (the incommensurable commotion of as or like), and no afterworld, no other world.

Resurrection is all in the tombstone, as the name is in marble: the poem stands there *like* the name, and as though it was thereby fulfilling the very being of the poem and its desire. He brings back alive not her but instead her name.

He also says, a little later: "Return toward the actress of gathering night Vega / Like Yvette Guilbert or the eyelashes of a Degas."[64] He also says elsewhere: "Ut musica Ut pictura Ut poesis":[65] all alike, their triple "like" in common, which is to bring back night into night, but each time alone and with no other relation to the others than the distance of this *ut* (meaning: in the same way as, just as). Among the arts, there is no assumptive unity; all there is is this *ut*, like the tonic of their chord, and therefore like their spacing, their difference. There is no such thing as art as such; there is always art as the plurality of the arts. And poetry is never like painting or like music except insofar as it is neither one nor the other: but poetry *as* poetry.

Similarly, the name, the elementary prose of the name is neither the face nor the voice. It is the distance inscribed between the one and the other alike, and the putting at a distance of the one and the other. It is there, as alone and fresh as ever. The new year takes place in the midst of winter, like the winter solstice. The extreme elsewhere is much further away than any sky or any other world. "But," he adds, "since we cannot live except as if there were no death, the thoughts that wear the veil of incurable sadness add nothing to the truth."[66]

Immortality as though there were no death: all the *as*es or *like*s refer back to this *as if*, this *als ob* with its Kantian regulatory function. But this regulatory function does not consist in simulating what does not exist and fomenting the poetical lie of immortality. It consists in regulating itself absolutely, exactly, upon what has no object. There is nothing objectifiable about our immortality, and in that way it is *nothing*, absolutely, but it is absolute as such, as *ours* and nothing else. Immortality *as* death. This is where we already are, and "resurrection" is no heavenly phantasmagoria: it is the asyndeton death/eternity.

In other words, what is at work with death, what the poem binds to this earth—this is nothing that passes beyond it: truth has nothing to add, no supplementary negativity to join to sense. The truth of sense is solely in sense *as such*: the sense that speaks itself, and insofar as it speaks itself, by all the *ases* or *likes* of all the tricks and turns of writing, by all those *ases* or *likes* that return to the same only by never ceasing from differing indefinitely from each other, in the absolute dispersion of all resemblance and of approximation.

Of the right to disproportionality, among all the tropes and turnings that make something like sense, there is nothing to write, nothing except for a proper name, the properness of which is that it has no sense. Poetry is "the one withdrawn"[67] (he recites Hölderlin); it too is in the tombstone. Not underneath, as though nobody remained, whether some thing or some one, but inside, compacted, pacified, in peace.

He writes: "reading myself, like a foreigner"—and he reminds us that we will have always remained foreign to the whole of sense to which he will have appeared to summon us—" . . . do you not hear the euphemy of this prose—that searches for itself in truths, which differentiates between the diverse ways in which sense is caught within it."[68] This prose is the euphemy of poetry abysmally ruined and withdrawn, of poetry that remains extremely elsewhere and is not brought back alive. Among all the different propositions with their many turnings, there are differences, but there is no supplementary turn for difference. What is sought, and makes all the difference, is the poet. The poet seeks himself, though he cannot be found, cannot even be sought. He seeks himself as a poet and finds himself *as though* he were a poet: facing further forward than himself, without subject or object, following a trail already effaced, grappling with what lies beyond his bounds, and those of speech. He writes straight ahead, and goes nowhere other than the elsewhere common to all common sense, engraving on the tombstone the asyndeton of name and dates, like a poem named yet unspoken.

*Translated by Leslie Hill*

# § 13  The Necessity of Sense

On the topic of the poetry and poetics of Yves Bonnefoy I shall not speak directly or thematically; that is beyond my competence. This is not to say that I have not read Bonnefoy, far from it. As for so many others in my generation, *Du mouvement et de l'immobilité de Douve* (*On the Motion and Immobility of Douve*) and *Hier régnant désert* (*Yesterday's Desert Dominion*), while I was still at university, were for me more than just books. They were the voice of the present moment of poetry. I remember saying to myself: "this has just been written, now."

But I did not become a poetician. And if I have taken on the task of saying something here today, it is with the idea of accompanying Bonnefoy's work from a distance (a distance necessarily my own), as though from another shore, perhaps, and in the expectation that providing a counterpoint of this kind is the most appropriate way in which I can pay homage.

For Bonnefoy's work does not appeal to what goes under the name—to use an ugly word—"consensus." It appeals to sense, and appeals against sense, but only insofar as sense is thereby shared out and divided up, if needs be, to the point of its absence. Bonnefoy writes:

> I can hear the piercing cry
> Echoing in the music, I know in myself
> The poverty of sense.[1]

I shall take this as my theme.

Another word for poverty is "neediness" or "necessity." I have not sought to establish whether "neediness" or "necessity" belongs to Bonnefoy's vocabulary. But at least the sense of need as constraint or imposition may be found in a line of his like this:

Speech itself is in need of matter.[2]

Between these two quotations lies everything I should like to say, in my own fashion, about sense and necessity. By virtue of what, and in what way, does what can and must be represented as the "poverty" of sense require "matter"? How must the sense of speaking, the incorporeal *lekton* of the Stoics, be embodied, and what effect does this have upon sense? What are the implications for its poverty?

Let me say straight away that, in following the trail of sense, I am following a trail blazed by Michèle Finck.[3] I am indebted to his powerful study of Bonnefoy, which is both patient and demanding, and I want to try here merely to prolong it, as best I can, by adopting a slightly different perspective on the question of sense.

Returning to this question of sense, then, and the question of its necessity—both in the sense that it is unavoidable and in the sense that it is irreducibly needy—we should begin by noting to what extent it seems not to be possible, today, to speak about poetry without taking into account the celebrated question (whose impact on Bonnefoy Michèle Finck explores): *Wozu Dichter in dürftiger Zeit? Wherefore poets in times of distress?*

Admittedly, to our ears, this question may appear to be a hackneyed one, whose point has been worn down or blunted as a result of its near-obsessive or near-incantatory repetition. However, if this is the case, it is only insofar as Hölderlin's words have always been interpreted as though the "poet" were being contrasted purely and simply with "necessity" (in the sense of wretchedness, distress, or need), in other words, only to the extent that the question makes one expect the answer to explain ultimately how poetry belongs to necessity, and pacifies or remedies it. The abundance of grace is meant to replace or, in the end, to overcome the constraint of need by dialectical means. Some form of "salvation" is involved. This is Heidegger's interpretation, as well as that of many others, and no doubt it features in a major way in every philosophical and poetical—or, more precisely, "poeticizing"—interpretation of the question. Ultimately, perhaps, it is the only possible interpretation, one that is already implicit in Hölderlin's original formulation.

But one could (and perhaps should) try suggesting something else, more along these lines: that the poet is in a state of necessity, or neediness, which he espouses and obeys. To take it a step further: of necessity as lack, the poet speaks the necessity as constraint. The poet does not replace it with salvation, and yet does not plunge into distress, any more than the poet falls victim to autism.

To give some sense to what is being proposed here, to give the argument the exact sense it demands, based neither on compromise nor on dialectics, we need to begin once more as follows: today, more than ever before, with a kind of self-evidence that is itself a sign of the age, the necessity is for sense. "We need sense"—such is the cry, in both senses: sense is lacking [*fait défaut*]; and sense is what we need.

And what if what we call "poetry" (irrespective of whether or not it is between the covers of books of poetry), what if what we call "poetry" were the taking into account and the taking on board of an imperious failure, constitutive of sense? (I use the word "poetry," but perhaps in the final analysis we need a different one.)

If there were time, the whole history of poetry from Romanticism down to the present would need to be retraced here. It could be shown how that history was punctuated by what might be termed an overinvestment in sense, in the postulate of Sense (with a capital letter) and, in correlation with this, by a series of disinvestments in Sense. (I cannot deal here with the reasons for this double movement, which are too immense.) It could then also be shown how the end result, in the age in which Bonnefoy, and others, receive this legacy, is a kind of standoff between this "prophetic-oracular" postulate and what declares its "hatred of poetry" (to use the words of Georges Bataille). Bonnefoy, for his part, puts the demand as follows: "One has to be suspicious," he writes, "of any poetry that, in respect of the need for closure or form, is not expressly negative."[4]

In truth, it is not solely this or that more or less "closed" or "formal" determination of poetry that is put in doubt here (even in Bonnefoy's own eyes, unless I am very much mistaken); it is rather that all poetry is placed under suspicion, with the result that no non-"poeticizing" use of the word "poetry" seems possible any more. What I mean by the "poeticizing" use of the word is the sense of a metaphysical or mystical revelation of Sense, or the sense of an "alchemy of the Word" as found in Rimbaud, which Rimbaud ultimately rejected. In which case (and this is another aspect of the same history), it is impossible to avoid the obstinate insistence of the idea or imperative demand for a kind of *prose* as what lies beyond an assumption of Sense—which is to say, in truth, that it in fact remains on this side of it.

(I do not have the time to go into this here, but one would have to consider carefully the reasons why it was *poetry* that became, so to speak, the key or symptom of the West in both its desires and its failings. Let me just recall this, emblematically, by citing the words of a character in a Pirandello play who tells us he has become a Turk "owing to the bankruptcy of the poetry of Christendom." Relations between our history and poetry are necessary ones in the sense of being both imperious and needy. Far from poetry's floating free beyond the bounds of history, it could be even shown that the question of history will have been for the West a question of poetry—that is to say, of the necessity of sense.)

For the moment I shall simply say that the poetic (or poetico-metaphysical) sense of "poetry" has become, in a coordinated history that is itself the history of our philosophy of History, the sense of an infinite assumption of Sense or, alternatively, of an oversignification, even if it surrenders at times to silent exaltation, or the sense of infinite accomplishment, sense gathered, promised, and projected into what Rimbaud in an early poem calls "future Vigor."

And it is this that has become impossible, untenable, intolerable (and began by becoming so for Rimbaud). (And this is the other history of our history, the present state of our time.)

Indeed, the "necessity of sense," in our case, no longer points toward the febrile injunction to provide ourselves with ecstatic states of signification. It points instead to the fact that sense—sense itself, taken absolutely, both with and without the capital letter—cannot be appropriated or signified. Sense consists in nothing else. But there's more. The very fact that sense cannot be appropriated as the truth of sense is not to be understood within the terms of a reassuring dialectic, by which the death of sense may also be said to be its resurrection. There can be no dialecticization or aestheticization of what touches us within the semblance of a generalized and progressive loss of sense. No dialecticization, no aestheticization either, because the two are indeed the same; both belong to the logic of sacrifice, the sacrifice of available signification in exchange for the advent of a higher sense. The point is to consume (whether bodies, things, or words) in order to subsume and to assume a sense that may be summed up in its pure ineffable presentation, its pure unnameability.

Such, we may say, is the metaphysical state of things, which is also to say: the last gasp of metaphysical poetics.

In these circumstances, how do things still stand with poetry? What can be said about poetry that does not poeticize it? And what can one say to acknowledge the need or necessity of the exhaustion of sense, of sense itself when it is exhausted? These questions, I believe, are the same ones Bonnefoy encounters, too.

Let us return to some simple remarks on the subject of the different senses of the word "sense" (here, too, I refer to the work of Michèle Finck). Two ambiguities, two collisions or instances of oxymoron may be noted here.

The first is the one picked out by Hegel: "sense" refers both to an element of signification and to a means of perception. The second is present in the history of several European languages in which sense [*sens*] as signification is mixed with sense [*sens*] meaning "direction" or "path."

In the sense of "sense," "signification" (*meaning, vouloir-dire, Bedeutung*) is inextricably linked with one or the other of these other semantic values, if perhaps not both at the same time.

Signification today (whether understood in terms of a final signified or a signifying intention, or in terms of truth or communication) is suspended in a state of essential suspense that, without doubt, is the event of our history. The significant sense of sense is in a state of suspension of sense.

(The question immediately arises: is this not what has always been at issue in "poetry"? But let us not get ahead of ourselves.)

If so, what do these two other senses tell us about sense?

Sensibility speaks to us of a way of being two in one, both feeling and felt, two subjects in a single act, as Aristotle more or less puts it. What is sensible is not an immediacy in which one partakes immediately; it is the being-outside-of-self of a passive activity. The sensible is an erotics, not a semantics. An erotics represents not primarily a pathos of desire but a syntax of feeling.

The other sense of "sense" provides perhaps a first way of articulating such a syntax: sense [*sens*] as "direction" is sense as a being-*to* [*être*-à], a mode of being that is neither in itself nor for itself but *to*—"to" itself just as it is "to" all the rest. It is another way of being outside of oneself, of being to oneself as though sent, thrown, or dispatched, not having arrived, still coming. It may be said to be a kind of ontology of the Latin *ad* in all its different meanings. *Ad* is what is transcribed in the accent on the French word *à*. But accent, the word "accent," is from *ad-canere*, meaning the reinforcing of the voice for purposes of singing, that is, in-tonation as an intensification of sound, the tonicity and tension of articulation. The Latin word *accentus* was used to translate the Greek *prosôdia*. Poetic cadence may be said to have something to do with this articulation of sense.

In a way perhaps not too far removed from all this, Yves Bonnefoy has it that "sense becomes music."[5] The idea of music itself should be examined in its turn, not poeticized (or turned into an assumption or sublimation of sense). This is why, for the moment, I simply want to say: whether as "accent" or as "prosody," sense is articulated as for song, but it is not song itself, nor a form of harmonic resolution, nor is it any form of resolution at all, but articulation, the one into two—both an erotics and a tonics, if I can use such terms.

In the first instance at least, this may be reduced to that most elementary of differences between poetry and prose already formulated by Plato: "if melody, rhythm, or meter were to be removed from any piece of poetry, what would remain is discourse."[6] Prose for Plato is defined negatively, as "discourse without meter,"[7] therefore without measure, in all senses of the word: without cadence, without limit, without caesura, without suspense. In Latin it is termed *oratio prorsa* (*pro-versa*): discourse turned to the fore and always going forward, discourse in a straight line, without inflection or turning, without *versus* except for the indefinite straight line itself.

In this sense, at the end of the straight line, at its indefinite or infinite extremity, there is Sense both as terminus and as destination, Sense as padding or revelation, but equally, by that token (since an infinite straight line comes back to itself as a circle), Sense as principle or origin, Sense as intention, vector, and finality, all at the same time. Whether rejected or projected into a regulatory or mystical infinite—and perhaps *even more so* in those conditions—Sense is the necessity or neediness of prose, or at least of prose understood in this way. Let us say it is the necessity or neediness of discourse. It imposes itself on discourse absolutely, orders it through and through—and, by that token, discourse misses it, but misses it as an object of desire, as its own intimacy projected infinitely outward.

On the other hand, there is the caesura [*coupe*]. To quote the words of a young poet of today, Pierre Alféri, "The accent falls somewhere else: in the impetus of delivery as it leaps over the gaps in the text or agglutinates them, in the suspense of irregular breaks in the line and of the caesura, and in enjambment."[8]

"The accent falls somewhere else": I would also say that somewhere else is where the accent is produced. Somewhere else, that is, other than the straight line: the *versus* the line suddenly has to contend with, interruption, the act of starting the next line (in Latin, *versus* first meant a line). To start on the next line when nothing material (like the edge of the page) or discursive (like the order of exposition) makes this necessary. Yet this does not occur arbitrarily. The act of moving to the next line is prompted by (or is on the lookout for) a quite different necessity: the necessity of undoing sense.

Then, sense stops being produced or occurring. But it is accented. It is tense: not in the sense of tending toward completion, but in the sense of tense to the point of breaking—indeed it does break. Caesura is the dismissal of sense.

It is remarkable, for instance, that when Bonnefoy uses the word "sense" [*sens*], he often breaks off straight after. This can be seen, in particular, in several caesuras or enjambments in *Dans le leurre du seuil* (*In the Lure of the Threshold*).[9] It is rather like a caesura echoing or voicelessly rhyming with these breaks in sense, saying: "See the true fruit grow, you who consent [*toi qui consens*]."[10] "You who consent": this is both a rhyme and a caesura in (muted) sense, suspended, breaking on its own closing hiss: consenting to the caesura of sense, consenting to no longer sensing the sense in any sense.

The caesura breaks off sense like a fruit plucked from the tree: this is how Hegel wanted to view works of art, detached at last from their religious function. A detached fruit is a true fruit: neither destined to rot so as to be reborn, nor offered up for consumption in order to be incorporated, but a fruit that is merely fruit, endlessly, without ending. This is the perfection of a fruit that is not a completion of the fruit, the truth of sense that is no sense, but not any "nonsense" either, the truth of sense as its body, matter—and its matter as caesura.

This truth may be said to carry the necessity of sense: its need and the neediness of this need, its incurable indigence. Sense itself, in a word, breaks into sense, detaches it, retrenches it.

Retrenches it even to the point where it is necessary, above all else, to guard against making the caesura make sense, guard against investing the caesura, enjambment, or syncope, or start of a new line with any oversignificance—that is, guard against poeticizing what, in poetry, is necessity itself. We must not make what suspends sense make sense.

The whole of erotics is there, with its tonics: in the caesura in the symbolic.

But there still has to be a caesura, which is perhaps never simply visible at the level of the "jumping between lines" on the page. Thus, in this simple but abrupt caesura—"The roundness of their breasts / Beneath their tunics"[11]—sense itself may appear to be suspended just as much as it is maintained, both sensual sense alongside meaningful sense, and the one within the other.

It can no doubt be said that the poem is striking an ancient-style pose, which in its turn is both sensual and significant, one by virtue of the other.

(I say *pose*, and not *pause*. So long as there is suspense, there is no immobilization, nor any relaxation of tension. There is tension, intensity, that may be part of a pose, in the sense in which one refers to a "flattering pose," or else it may belong to a caesura. An accent may belong to a pose or to a caesura, to the one alongside the other, to the one against the other.)

But it might also be said that the pose here is being cited, or recited, merely in order to be interrupted in its turn.

Poetry is always threatened by poses, whether plastic, rhetorical, harmonic, or mystical ones. The danger of the pose comes very close to the caesura. Therefore the caesura must interrupt the pose just as much as it does the content of discourse.

In this way, on the one hand, it is not enough to introduce a caesura: it has to come at the right moment, in the right place, according to the right measure. But, on the other hand, there is no measure for that measure, no yardstick or model for it. It is rather as if the caesura had to be its own measure every time, a single measure, measured against nothing, therefore without measure, measureless—and yet, as both measure and cadence, regular rhythm and syncopation of what is thereby joined together but in order to be joined, gives itself the free play and entire interval of the *versus*: the reverse and obverse of sense.

No doubt, the caesura [*coupe*] is itself necessarily, needily double. It both separates and brings or gathers together at the same time, in the same way that a caesura is an incision, a section, as well as a vase.[12] This, too, seems to be in evidence in Bonnefoy when he writes, "In my hands held out / For a cup [*coupe*]."[13] Comparison remains within the realm of proximity, that is to say, within a distance that is infinitely reduced and thus endlessly open. The caesura will be the slot that does not open by accident in the vase, but presides over its very ordering. The break [*coupe*] between the hands divides the cup [*coupe*] formed by the hands. There is no collection.

Sense, in order to be Sense, demands in exemplary manner to be a collection, a gathering, and a sheltering. Sense demands a temple, a metaphysical horizon, a God, an ancient-style pose. But the necessity or neediness of sense—which perhaps constitutes the whole of our "modernity"—demands the caesura, the transport elsewhere, the disparity between places and situations, the interruption of truth.

One might say poetry is still a metaphysical, onto-theological category. Whereas verse [*le vers*] is simply atheistic, or rather, atheological—as such, it remains calm and composed; it displays, that is, no single pose; it is without a pose, but in the manner and the time of the caesura.

*Translated by Leslie Hill*

# § 14  Ja, Bès

"Our names might be thought to be no more than the reflection of an absence of name," Jabès once said, and never stopped repeating it. How many texts—perhaps every one he wrote—he devised to reflect this absence! He said, "*our* names," thereby including among everybody else's, with everybody else's, his own name—which, being his, must therefore be supposed to be clearly indicated by his own texts, in accordance with the maxim "Being what one writes. Writing what one is."[1] As a maxim, this is mad and unacceptable, but it is the only one admissible—supposing maxims are there to be given or followed, which is a question I shall not go into here.

Jabès, then, may be thought to have written his name everywhere, and nothing other than his name. That is my hypothesis, consistent with all the different uses to which Jabès put names. Supposing, of course, that that indeed *was* his name, and that he indeed *wrote* it. But both these suppositions are pointless, since he was a name, or wrote his name, no more than anyone else; at most he signed it, at most he signed with his name just as Christians "sign," or cross themselves, in the *name* of their three nameless gods. But such suppositions are necessary since our names are, for each one of us, the more-than-frail, solitary clue as to the being of our being; all the rest is existence in the world without clues or proof or consequences.

Supposing, then, what all his books suppose, like a lengthy exordium on the name itself, and supposing that he was his name and that he wrote this name interminably, from beginning to end; in that case, *ja*: one can say he wrote first in German, in unheard-of manner [*inouï*], in order to say "yes" [*"oui"*], combining this with *bès*:

> [French] prefix [says Littré] that, when used pejoratively, has the same meaning as *bis*, as found in words such as *besaigre* [sour] . . . ; *bis*: prefix with pejorative meaning, as for example in *bistourner*, to turn out badly or go wrong, and an alternative form of *ber*, *bre*, *bar*. What is the derivation of this particle? One proposal is that it is related to German *mis*, which has the right sense, as in *mes-estimer* [to underrate], but it is hard to see how *m* could have become *b*. . . . Diez takes the view that it is Latin *bis*, meaning twice over, given that in various compounds the word shifts from meaning *double* to meaning *oblique* or *askew*, as for example in the Spanish *bis-ojo*, meaning cross-eyed or shifty. Of these various conjectures, the last seems the most plausible.

*Yes, twice over: a double yes, oblique and cross-eyed.* Cross-eyed because belonging to more than one language. Cross-eyed because both German and Latin. Cross-eyed because nothing other than *ja, ja—ein reines Jawort, das Jawort als Name, was heisst das, oder wie heisst das? mag das Ja heissen?*[2] Cross-eyed because no more a Jew or an Egyptian than that. And yet one just as much as the other, yes, yes.

In any case as much of a Jew as a lost tribe, or one gone astray:

> And they said, What one is there of the tribes of Israel that came not up to Mizpeh to the Lord? And, behold, there came none to the camp from Jabesh-gilead to the assembly. For the people were numbered, and, behold, there were none of the inhabitants of Jabesh-gilead there. And the congregation sent thither twelve thousand men of the valiantest, and commanded them, saying, Go and smite the inhabitants of Jabesh-gilead with the edge of the sword, with the women and the children. (Judges 21:8–10)

~

"What if the letter were only the secret of the name?" That is, the letter taken literally as a letter, as a phonic or graphic inscription, not signifying as a sign, only signing a vacant space, the letter insofar as it is nothing other than what possesses the whole index-like power of being. And vice versa: the whole being of being [*tout l'être de l'être*], its whole is-ness [*estance*] or presentness [*prestance*], is entrusted to the letter [*la lettre*], the frail body of a mark, its frail sound [*son frêle bruit*].[3] So, the first letter in Jabès: the letter *J*, pronounced [in French] as *gît* ["lies," as in the phrase

"here lies ——," as found on gravestones] or *j'y* [as in "I ——
here/there"]: I am here [*j'y suis*], I am going [*j'y vais*], I am lying here [*j'y gis*], here I lie [*j'y suis gisant*]. In German, the letter *J* is called "jott," *und das heisst so viel wie* jota, *aus* yod, *das der semitische Name des Buchstabens ist, der in der Bibel als Symbol der Kleinheit gilt.* Jott *der Kleinste der Kleinen, die letzte Kleinigkeit des Namens. Der Buchstabe: so viel wie nichts. Geheimnis als Nichtigkeit.*[4]

But there is no such thing as a single letter: the letter in the singular is already multiple. Which also means, among many other things, that it is vocalized: not *j*, but *ja*.

*Ja*: "The Lord [*Jah*] is my strength and song . . . : he is my God" (Exodus 15:2). *Jah* as the letter and secret of Yahweh, not the sacred tetragrammaton but the grammaton, no heavier than an exclamation, no more weighed down by godliness than that. *Hallelujah*: "praise Jah" is almost exactly the same as saying "praise the exclamation of praise." *Jott, Gott,* God.

*Jabès* = *Yahweh*. God twice over: oblique and cross-eyed. A god who exclaims himself as his own exclamation, his own name only and his entire secret as a god weighed out for a grammaton, or a gram. A god neither absent nor hidden, who has neither turned away nor been lost, simply divided by an exclamation, open like a human mouth even before it invokes any deity at all. *Ja, jab, jott, Job. Je-*mand. *Any-*one.

Yes, Jabès, yes the tribe that has no respect, that says "yes" but to nothing that may be approved, that says *ja* only as the letter itself, has nothing else to affirm or keep except literally the letter, perhaps the Greek *diphtera*, which is hide or parchment. *Oder das Buch—Buche, Baum, Holz—durch den Stab gestrichen: der Stab, der senkrechte Strich der Runen. Jabès schreibt in semitischen Runen.*[5] Yes (to) the trace, the mark, the incision, made upon the surface scraped clean in preparation for the stroke or trait. Yes to the scratching of the surface.

*Gedankenstrich des buchstäblichen Namens: A–B.*[6]

∼

*Edmond* = the protector of property (to take Mallarmé's word for it, who was an English teacher). Edmond is the keeper of the mark [*le trait*], or rather he himself is the mark that does the keeping and is the property of property, since how could property be marked as such—whether eminently or properly—if it did not bear some distinguishing mark of quality or belonging? Any mark allocates property or properties: to the area on either side of the mark, or to the mark itself as it endlessly divides within itself. *Edmond* names and protects the double mark of the *Ja*, at either end of Jabès's books. The mark is always endlessly double: *ja, ja, A–B.*

This is all Jabès writes. Everybody knows this; everybody has read it and commented on it: or has commented on nothing else, whether knowing it or not, whether showing it or not.

Edmond Jabès wrote only the keeping of the mark—that is impossible to keep since it inaugurates all keeping. The single infinitely multiple mark of the acclamation of the proper: praise him who praises himself in his absolute distinction. The pure pleasure of impatiently scratching the impassive face of being. The childish pleasure of simply being *there.*

The most serious and the most childish: just to be there. Just imagine Edmond Jabès as a tiny Egyptian baby, just a name, with humble beginnings like all names, which could be any name, and yet suddenly is already irreplaceable—and at the other end of life a whole history that nobody will ever be able to recapitulate, a line dotted with shimmering pebbles, all marked with the same name leading nowhere except to the echo of the name, now dispersed among several different memories, several different libraries. What does it mean to be an Egyptian? For a whole swathe of the world, it is to be the absolute child, the baby who starts with nothing and will go far. In a sense, the Egyptian has already achieved everything; he is born unable to move, and his first cry is immediately as silent as stone. In another sense—is it not the same sense?—the Egyptian is pure derivation or drift, who can turn into a Jew or into a Greek, into an Arab or into a Christian, turn into every possible name. *Egypt* means the name, the suffering and joy of the name, its wealth and poverty.

⁓

Let us suppose that Edmond Jabès wrote nothing, except—everywhere—his own name. He could be said to have written only his own name—everywhere. Like someone carving out his own and someone else's initials within a rudimentary heart, mingling, interweaving, or inverting the two in a kind of reversible pattern: *E.J.* = *J.E.* Not "I," not "ego," not a substance, subject, or suppositum [*suppôt*]—but the mark of an utterance, the mark of an open mouth, the mark of a pen tracing a mark. *Je—la*: I am but my own exclamation (without proclamation or clamor). Not ego, but echo: *ja, ia, ya.*

Nothing, except for the imprescriptible saying-I [*dire je*], which is not just one saying among others, but saying itself: saying it about saying in all the modes of saying [*le disant du dire en tous ses dires*].

In German: *E.J., J.E., je, jemals, von jeher, immer unendlich ja sagend.*[7]

~

In Arab countries, *Jabès* begins and ends with the letters of Sura XXXVI, which is recited at burials: "I.S.—We shall restore life to the dead. Their actions and achievements will be written in the book of evidence."

Let us suppose Edmond Jabès wrote nothing except the book of evidence.

Wrote nothing, then. Except what can be clearly seen upon any letter chosen at random, presented and combined with nothing other than free or scribbled space: a vestige of writing, as exists in the world, without any key to its combination. *Vestigium litterae video.* A kind of Linear B, or primitive rune, or dubious trace resulting perhaps from an animal claw or tumbling stone.

Nothing to read, then, nothing to be deciphered. Which explains his dread of being read absolutely: to the limit of this "leaping of words toward words," to the limit and in all possible directions, dispersed across endless wastes of sand, snow, or stars. Your name is dust, and you will return to the dust of the name. From the outset, everything disperses the patient, beaming, tenacious labor that consists in writing endlessly the same single imperturbable writing of the general immobile permutation of all signs under whose aegis is housed what resides in no sign or system of signification, that is to say: *the book that is nothing other than the unreadable deciphering itself literally and like an open book.*

~

Let us suppose that god decided to write illegibly, thereby illimiting the readability of all words, and that Jabès is his name saying "yes" to his abandonment, to the abandonment of the name of Jabès itself insofar as it will have ever constituted a name and thus constituted a god and thus failed to respect the reserve of the name itself that is incapable of naming and knows this and leaves no room for anything or anyone who might have a name beyond all names or an incommensurable name or no name at all, for that would still and forever be a name if indeed to name means to call to being.

All "nominalism" is inescapably confronted with this: the thing named may well be only its name, yet by that very fact, it already exists. Not that the name consists in itself in any way (that is what is generally called the "imaginary"), but nothing comes to being except being itself, and the name is the absolute share of that turning aside from self by which being comes to be and therefore separates from itself, from being *itself* [*l'être même*].

The name names nothing or no one: trace the difference between one "yes" and another "yes" of existence, and this difference is existing [*exister*] itself. Me Tarzan, you Jane. And so all names are Ja-bès. Yes, all names are equal; they are equal insofar as they name one another; and *Edmond* keeps this equal, indefinitely exchangeable, always unique value, which means that, with E.J. dead, that voice will no longer be heard that said the same identical thing, the same self-evidence as each and every other voice.

∿

*Ja!* Don't make any comment. For E.J. is already its own commentary.[8] *Its own infinite commentary on its own secret.*

This is the desacralized, perfectly concrete secret of names at every moment being reborn in a different sense: a sense different each and every time yet exchangeable with any other, as with the rows and rows of identical plaques or steles in a vast military cemetery, or one marking a natural disaster, where it was not possible to personalize the graves and where as a result the singularity of each name stands out all the more nakedly, self-evidently. But in the camps or a charnel house the exact opposite happens: there is no room for the substitutability of the dead; they are forced into something other than bodies, and something worse than any death. To expose a dead body to vultures or other birds of prey upon a stretcher or on a windswept, sun-drenched terrace, or to lay it beneath a gravestone or put it in an urn, is to expose that body, not negate it by changing it into mush. Decay should not be the work of man.

Burial should be—always has been—space open for another birth—not a rebirth into some phantasmagorical second life or afterlife, but a putting back into circulation of birth as a single putting aside of a place in the world—and nothing more. This may not seem like much, but it's a lot, indeed everything—that a place be made in this way and another chance taken for the sake of the sense of everything and everyone. This place is the place of a name: a name each time proper and each time anonymous: *yes, yes, that one, this person here.*

*Bès,* the grotesque midget gods of Egypt that were present at the bedside of women in labor, labile creatures with shimmering attributes mingling with everchanging animals. *Bès* with still almost formless bodies and yet already delivered from formlessness, deities of undivided individuation, who were both diverse and rambling: "body without number . . . , animal, vegetable, or mineral body; the body of a perfume, a sound, a presence or absence."[9]

Like all those giving birth astride an open grave already made ready, their limbs apart in the shape of an *A*: *A, A, Bès,* and immediately expelled firstborn, panting *A, A, Bès, Abba, Babel, Babylon, Beginn, Bethel, Biblia, Byblos,* reciting the endless alphabet of all languages, with names and places thereby coming into the world.

∿

The letter that is the secret of the name is the body, on which the letter is effaced as the extension of its transformations and deformations, its displacements and grafts and mutilations—this integrity being maintained on the basis of a general restlessness contained by nothing other than a space spinning in itself on its axis, by which, from one extremity to the other, one birth to another, it could be said to *resemble* itself: this body of which not a single grain of skin will have ever remained the same, yet which despite everything is the same skin everywhere, *ja,* as though naked and unveiled. Him, the selfsame self, like his name.

∿

We can now go to the secret of the cipher of the letter, according to the gematria of the Pythagoreans, as handed down and multiplied into the nine psephic methods of the Cabala. In this way, in the gnosis of Marcos, the cipher *la,* the first of the seven archontes, is 10 + 1, and that belonging to *Jabès* is 10 + 1 + 2 + 5 + 200 = 218 = 2 + 1 + 8 = 11. Jabès, the first archon and twice 1, the double unit, the runic Jew and Latin Arab, saying in all languages his secret name of *ja* twice over.

*Ja: Jabès musste doch deutsch sprechen. Musste, die für ihn unsprachbare Sprache sprechen. Aussprechen.* *Musste, von allen unbemerkt, das Wort und den Namen in diese Sprache so tief hineinlegen, so tief, dass der oder das verschwindet.* And never returns. *Mit jedem Buchstaben bejaht—jabès—die Schrift dieses Verschwindens, also bejaht sich das Schreiben selber. Was es je vermag.*[10]

~

*J'abaisse, I turn down* the name like the handle on a door, and open it: the great plains of prose are ready for the exodus.

*Translated by Leslie Hill*

# § 15   Robert Antelme's Two "Phrases"

For myself, and surely for many others, *Robert Antelme* is not the name of a "writer," nor does it point to a "body of work." This is not because he didn't publish or because he only left only a few books behind. It stems from his having what I will call, having no better way of putting it, a posture or a manner of enunciation quite different from that of the writer. Let me put it this way: Robert Antelme has uttered just two phrases.[1] (And this is why his is not the name of an "author" or a "signatory." The name Robert Antelme is hardly a name in this sense; it merges with a voice—without timbre—that expresses these two phrases. So when I say "Robert Antelme," I hear these two phrases. And nothing else.)

The first of these phrases is this: "man" (what makes up his *species*, what makes him *special*) is nothing other than an absolute, unshakable resistance to destruction. It says that man, who brings destruction into the world, is nothing other than the absolute affirmation of being—more precisely, he is being or existence as absolute affirmation. (And this affirmation suffices in itself; it is not affirmation of anything external. It is "self-sufficient" without having a "self.")

This phrase defines an ontology and an ethics: an ontology without substance or subject, an ethics without morals or rights. It defines the ethos of a being faced with the nothingness that we are. Our ethos: our bearing, our look, our comportment—even when it deserts us.

Robert Antelme's other phrase comes from a letter that he wrote to Dionys Mascolo (who published it) upon first returning from the camps: "To have been able to free words that were barely formed, and at any rate did not have any age . . . but were modeled only on my breath, this, you see, this happiness, wounded me definitively."[2]

This sentence bespeaks the coming of a new phrase, a new speaking, the entry into the vertigo of a sense that is breaking down. It defines a poetics devoid of poem or charm but not of song. It defines a poetics of being or of beings born into the sense that they are, born of meaning where meaning is absent, arising from and for nothing. It defines a poetics that engages the praxis of the same ethos.

These are the only two phrases uttered by Robert Antelme. His ethos and his pathos—his bearing and his suffering—have been uttered and them alone. For the moment, I have nothing to add. Not in order to keep silent, but in order to let these two phrases do their work, in order to allow them to make themselves understood (this is what *phrasis* means). We are now, once again, inexhaustibly at the beginning, and our words are barely formed. In any case, they are ageless.

*Translated by Sara Guyer*

# PART 11

*Art*

# § 16 Georges

Photography shows something, or someone, and shows, too, the reality of what it shows: it shows that this or that something, this or that someone, actually existed, at a particular time, at a particular place, sometime, somewhere.

Photography passionately shows the real, its fragility, its grace, its transience. Somewhere, at a particular moment in time, something or someone appeared. Photography shows us that this took place, and does so in a way that resists our doubts, our forgetting, our interpretations. It offers us an evidence.

For example, you drank this glass of wine. I saw you drink it. I saw that on this particular day you drank this glass. In the reflections on the glass, I can see the time of day unfolding, passing by, immobile. I see you drink: in a manner of speaking, I see the lived, the flow of time, the day. You, you don't see anything; you're drinking.

You were about to light a cigarette. As always, there are little wisps of tobacco around your lips. You're always smoking. You're about to use your lighter. The photograph was taken just before that. The impression is that you're a bit put out, that it's stopped you from smoking.

The photo shows me how direct you are. You look directly at the camera; you know exactly what all this is about: your picture—and that both tickles and flatters you.

It's as if the reality of you looking at your own future image—but also at me, busy taking the photograph—formed the very surface, flat, glossy, sharp, of the photograph.

You're sporting your eternal beret and a hair grip to keep your flowing locks in place. And you have a dress, pulled over the top of your sweater. You are badly shaven, as usual, and your hair is unkempt—apart from the hair grip. Once again, you look so squarely at the camera that one feels oneself not looked at but measured with utmost precision.

Photography doesn't show that you actually have difficulty seeing. On the contrary, it sharpens and intensifies your gaze, conveying its true reality: you see everything.

You're looking away, but you know that I'm taking your picture.

Might it be that some people are more real than others? No doubt. You are one of the most real people that I've ever known.

This photograph was taken in the spring: behind you, the wisteria buds can just be made out. In the sun, your old boozer's nose looks like another bud. There's a sense of joy here.

I wonder why you've pushed the sleeve of your other sweater up above the elbow.

Photography shows the reality of thinking.

When you're tired, you let your eyes fall closed, you let yourself fall forward, you slump onto the table to sleep. It's too much, always has been, too many sorrows, as they say, too much sadness and too much pain in your life. You sang, "The sad are mad, and those who listen even madder." You wouldn't listen to them; the photograph makes that abundantly clear.

You're eating, this evening—one evening, this particular evening. You look like something straight out of a prewar French film. You play your part perfectly, George, full of memory and knowing, full of mischief and ingenuity, as clear and unfathomable, as inexhaustible as a photograph. Clearly, you like photographs—and they, in turn, do you justice.

*Translated by Simon Sparks*

# § 17 Catalogue

The difficulty of writing on works of painting is well known. This difficulty is no doubt neglected or avoided more often than it is confronted, more often, even, than it is simply mentioned. Perhaps it's precisely because it *is* so well known that everything seems to strive to conceal it: the abundance of works on painting, the proliferation of critical texts and presentations of or adjuncts to exhibitions, an abundance that, it would seem, will continue to grow simply because such writings can be signed by anyone at all. In fact, from the moment technical study is cast to one side (be it historical, historico-symbolic, semiological, whatever), it seems that anyone who wishes to do so can write a text about painting. The idea of "writer" needs to be taken in its widest possible sense: novelist, essayist, poet, or philosopher ... So long as his or her profession is, in one way or another, defined by writing, he or she can write about painting. Now, I do not want to oppose this apparent "ease" with some concealed "difficulty." Rather, I want to try to show the difficulty that lies within this ease, to show one through the other. Still, there will have to be some detours, not least of which is the fact that I will myself have to write about painting. As we say, therefore, I am trying quite simply to understand what I am doing here; after all, it doesn't go entirely without saying.

The proliferation of texts about painting has been exacerbated by what would appear to constitute the general or generative rule of the specific type of work that we call a *catalogue*. Traditionally, the catalogue comprised a list of works exhibited (or an exhaustive index to a painter's production), preceded by a *preface* (itself usually signed by a curator, an art

143

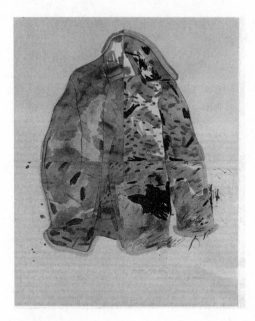

*Flight Jacket 5* (1978), by François Martin.

historian—in a word, an *expert*, moreover an expert doubly competent: in the matter of painting and in the matter of the catalogue or the inventory, the dating and placing of works). The preface to a catalogue might thus be reduced to the most restrictive understanding of a preface: an opening or informative discourse promptly effaced by the catalogue proper. But this latter, too, is doomed, by its very nature, to be effaced. It is not a text (or at least not on first sight, and, for the moment, I want to leave it there; we might ponder later what sort of *text* it is that could form or be a catalogue in the strictest sense); rather, it is purely an instrument of identification. To introduce a case in point:

> François Martin
> *(Air Show) Flight Jacket 5*
> *98x120 cm*
> *Collage, ink, pastel, acrylic on paper*
> *19/20 December 1978*

These indicators, these references are in turn effaced by the works them-selves, which, it would seem, can do perfectly without them. We close the catalogue (a finger held between the pages, to find the next such reference), and look.

Nowadays, however, a catalogue has become a different thing altogether, an entirely different type of work. It has even moved from being the simple instrument that it was and itself become a work. In such a work, moreover, the balance is reversed: the list of works is effaced, practically relegated to an annex (the traditional position of the preface), almost written off.

In the catalogue for François Martin's exhibition *The Air Show*, for example, shown in Amsterdam from June 21 to July 31, 1979, the only particulars given are those of the drawings reproduced in the catalogue—ten out of the thirty-six pieces being exhibited. These particulars, moreover, are much briefer than those in the example that I have just given (and that I have taken accordingly not from the exhibition catalogue but from the personal catalogue of François Martin). In the "official" catalogue to *The Air Show*, the date is limited to the year, and the technical description, identical for each one of the ten drawings reproduced there, to the remark (in Dutch) "*mixed media op papier,*" followed by their dimensions.

While what is properly termed the "catalogue" is basically an accessory or appendix to the *catalogue* that we hold in our hands, the "preface" to that catalogue proliferates from it and invades it. A text by a writer or by several writers, at times a substantial text (but quantity is not one of the necessary criteria for what I am calling "proliferation"; it is the status or the context of the text that decides that), the former preface has become the true object (which is to say the true subject) of the bound whole. In reality, what we are dealing with is a new type of *book*, in any case with something that actually calls to be read and not merely consulted. Indeed, the writer's name and the title of his or her text are often placed on the cover, rubbing shoulders with the painter's name and the title of the exhibition. This "book" is no longer either a catalogue or an "art book." The classic catalogue had no other role than to refer directly to the thing being exhibited; the art book, on the contrary, has tended to function as a study, often as a replacement for what was exhibited (or what could be exhibited), but never as an immediate index. Besides, the art book refers to museums and collections and not to the event of the exhibition. The reason why the new type of book is more akin to the catalogue is not simply that it is related solely to painting but, more importantly, that it is related to the event of hanging the pictures. It refers to the painting that is being shown, to when it is shown (and what painting is not shown?). What this new type of book shows, however, is not hung, nor can it be hung ...

As such, this new type of book—or this new type of catalogue—adopts a peculiar and double posture: along with the exhibition for which it is published, it has itself become an event. Its own commercial circuit is linked—in principle—to the time and place of the exhibition; at the same time, however, it is detached from the time and place of the exhibition. Indeed, it is often not even readable at that time and that place. It is to be read for itself, like any other book, and so at a remove from those things the sight of which it still presents, installs, and accompanies. This new type of catalogue is a monster: it shows painting by showing itself while effacing what it shows, sometimes the painting, sometimes itself.

This story does not unfold by chance, and that is why I was anxious to remind you of it (however crudely). It has often been read as the effect of a demand addressed by painting to writing. In this instance, "by painting" means by painters and by the painting or fine-art market. It is as if the operation known as "textual cataloguing" affords painting an increase in value. This can be explained, up to a certain point, as a function of "added value" or as a type of premium. Even this, however, explains nothing. For we would still need to know how a written supplement could afford an increase in pictorial value. And this requires that we understand whence, *within painting*, this written supplement. Equally, however, it requires that we understand whence, *within writing*, this supplement to writing (or to literature) that constitutes the genre of writing about painting. (And this further requires, moreover, that we understand in what way the writer profits from it in turn.) Both questions—or, rather, this singular and double question—would situate the contemporary genre of the catalogue's theoretical and historical dependence on the polymorphous genre of occasional writings about painting. We would need to go back, through August Schlegel and Baudelaire, to Diderot, and perhaps even further. I will not undertake this here; rather, I want merely to refer to that inquiry according to which specific connections would undoubtedly be established between the socioeconomic history of painting, its pictorial history, and the history of literature.

The question that interests me here, however, the question of the double supplement of painting and of writing—a question that I would want to call *the question of the catalogue*—will need to be approached from the side of the catalogue itself, albeit slightly dislodged. The catalogue for *The Air Show* offers another figure of the phenomenon (a figure that we can find in other painters as well; so far as François Martin is concerned, however, *The Air Show* is, to my knowledge, the first attempt at the genre). This catalogue—which, as I have said, contains not a true list of works but ten separate reproductions—begins with a text by François Martin. In this instance, the written supplement is the painter's fiat. And it is perhaps through this text—which provides, in short, both a limit and the strictest, most narrow form of generalized writing, both displaying and exceeding its principle—that we can best raise the question of the catalogue.

(Sending me this text before the publication of the catalogue, François Martin wrote on the manuscript: "Introduction to the exhibition (*Air Show*)." Note: *Introduction to the exhibition* and *not* to *the exhibition catalogue* ... ).

This text is not long; it has a quality that throws out of balance the classic relation between text and list. Allow me to cite it here (in a translation from the French original; the catalogue was published in Dutch):

36 life-size drawings.

For some years, my painting practice has been elaborated within the sphere of representation. By way of an object—which becomes thus the object of painting—this work is also a function of time insofar as, repeatedly starting anew from the same object, it carries on until the subject has been exhausted. These manufactured objects, taken up a dozen or a hundred times, are reproduced in their actual size [*leur taille réelle*].

The choice of the object is never neutral, even if I sometimes "forget" the reasons for this choice. This forgetting comes into play as the pictorial reproduction progresses.

My relations with the chosen object have to be quite consistent in order for this pretext for painting to be able to incite a lengthy sequence of works. The nature of these relations is varied: affective, cultural, everyday, narrative relations, etc., etc. . . .

*Flight Jacket* and *Leather Hat* would mostly come under this last category.

1974
During the Vietnam War, away from combat, the B-52 pilots kill the time between bombardments in the bars of Bangkok. Green and yellow satin-finished

jacket. The morning's napalm and the evening's beer. I squint and am unable to superimpose the images.

1977
The opening images of Chris Marker's film *The Base of the Air Is Red* (*Le Find de l'air est rouge*): a fighter pilot in action comments on his hysterical and murderous hunting down of Vietcong fighters.
Hat, headphones, and satin jacket.

1978–1979
36 life-size drawings of a flight jacket and a hat.

And me in there.
The attraction of aerial meetings, the complicated figures.
Childhood memories.
The tree that hides the forest.
The tree; (*Air Show*)
The forest; *Flight Jacket* and *Leather Hat.*
 —François Martin, April 13, 1979

That's it. That's all there is. That's all there is to *The Air Show* catalogue. And we should note that it has a title: the title of the exhibition, of the catalogue, of the text, of all three, whether at once or separately . . . In a sense, I have done no more than provide you with the catalogue itself (missing only its last page, the list—the catalogue—of François Martin's various exhibitions).

So what am I doing here, outside the catalogue (and what is the catalogue doing outside the catalogue and outside the exhibition)? I do not want to expand the catalogue. I do not want to add a discursive supplement, whether to the paintings or to François Martin's text. What I would like to do, however, is broach the question of the catalogue. And in much the same way, I would like to be able to see *The Air Show*, to arrive at a synoptic, albeit squinting, view of the exhibition (and) of the catalogue, of the painting (and) of its text. I would like, then, to see and to read with the same gesture. At the same time, perhaps something might come to be said as regards the difficulty of writing *about painting*.

Let us begin, however, with the catalogue itself. It is hardly by chance that the reciprocal supplementarity of painting and writing has proliferated in this type of catalogue or in this type of book (*The Air Show* in itself also makes a small, easy-to-handle book), guaranteed as it is under the pretext (if it is one) of providing an index to an exhibition. The particularity of the catalogue-book lies in its being in principle inseparable from the space and time of the exhibition. It is connected to them; it even forms part of them. The text that it puts forward is designed (whatever I might have said about it a moment ago) to be read in that space and at that time; ultimately (but everything here happens at the limit, at that strange shared limit between writing and painting), this text even provides the a priori conditions of a space and a time for visiting (as one says) the exhibition.

If you read Martin's text in the Kunstahndel Brinkman in Amsterdam, you would not see *The Air Show* with the same eyes. And yet, it is very much *with the same eyes* that you would read the text and see the painting. The text, be it that of a writer or, as here, that of the painter himself or herself (the painter-as-writer), would act, to stay with the Kantian vocabulary, as the a priori form of the intuition of the painting. Either that or it would constitute the transcendental of the painting. At the very least, it is what remains *to be seen*.

If François Martin offers this text at they very start of his(?) catalogue, this is because it can provide, in one way or another, the conditions for visiting *The Air Show*. That is, it can provide the conditions for *seeing*. The catalogue would produce the *conditions of visibility*, doing so through what is written, through legibility. Legibility, then, would be the condition of possibility for a visibility. Hasn't that always been the role of a catalogue, at least in its minimal form of a list of *titles*? Indeed, at times the painting itself, hanging on the wall, is accompanied by no more than a number whose reference to the catalogue allows a painting's title to be read. Including, on occasion, the exhausted form: *Untitled*. *Untitled* constitutes no less a readable syntagm than anything else, one that makes it possible to see the painting: its title is untitled and its visibility has thus, in some way, to be organized around this (il)legibility.

The question of the catalogue thus leads us back to the question of the title in painting. We can hardly imagine a painting that would not even have the title *Untitled*. How could there be a painting of which we could not *even* say that it is untitled? And what would be its relation to these equally exhausted forms of title: *Gouache, Aquarelle, Acrylic*? What is immediately apparent, however, is that this latter form, even when it does not constitute the title, still appears in the catalogue. Another example from *The Air Show*.

*(Air Show) Flight Jacket 14*
*Oil, graphite, pastel, colored pencil on paper.*

(And remember that all these citations in *The Air Show* are preceded and topped by a collective nomination that also constitutes, or so it would seem, the title of the painter's text: "36 life-size drawings.")

Various things follow from this. For a start, it follows that the title is inevitable. It does not approach painting from the outside; rather, painting in some way produces it from out of itself. From which it follows that one of the title's most minimal forms may well be the title of *painting* itself, in the sense of the material or the substance put to work in (or on? or as? or by?) this sort of exhibited work (something that cannot avoid opening peculiar perspectives from which, for example, painting can take the title "36 drawings"). From which it also follows that, if there is a title, a minimal condition for a title, if there are conditions for entitling painting, there has to be a catalogue. Whether the brochure or the book materially exist or not, there is a catalogue. Somewhere, in your head, if you like, in the ideality subtracted from the space-time of the exhibition, there is, at the bare minimum, a list of minimal titles. From which it finally follows that there has to be a centering, a partition, a distribution of works or individual pieces, even when the exhibition undertakes to present a single piece (it does happen) and its catalogue a single number, or even when it presents, as in the case of *The Air Show*, one or two repeated titles, distinguishable by their numbers alone.

The reason why there has to be this sort of partition and distribution is that there is an articulation. Painting is not founded on the space supporting it—it no longer adheres to it, partitioning itself off; it also slices into this space, articulating it. The catalogue enumerates the incisions that are primarily an enumeration of the space that they divide. Vision is itself dependent on this act of division. Although the existence of the catalogue may diminish ad infinitum, it will never be reduced to nothing.

Now, it seems to me that when a painter provides his or her own catalogue—as is the case here—it is because he or she notes the situation that I have just outlined and decides to take it into account. He or she decides to take into account what brings us back to the division that articulates vision, namely, the fact that the conditions for a painting's *visibility* are provided by a *legibility*, one that can never be absolutely reduced. He or she avoids the ideologeme that dictates that the admirer of a painting need only look and stay silent. More than this, however, our painter avoids the ideology that dictates that the painter can work only when mute, only when immersed in the immediate presence of the substances that he or she manipulates and of the gestures of that manipulation.

In a general sense, the catalogue-book, the supplementary character of writing in the modern history of painting, meets head-on the demand for a legibility, a demand that is neither superimposed nor superposed on painting but inscribed in and by painting, in and by visibility, giving painting a surface that would not differ from that of painting itself. At issue, therefore, is something altogether different from what might have been termed a painter's "writing" or "reading." It is not a matter of applying a linguistic or semiotic grid to the pictorial. Rather, it is a matter of what, within the pictorial, is *not* pictorial and perhaps a matter, then, of the fact that the pictorial is never and nowhere purely and simply pictorial . . .

Furthermore, the two regimes are wholly incommensurable. I am not talking here of an operation that needs to be done *to* painting; rather, I am trying to indicate a certain operation *of* painting. If we write "about painting," and if we go so far as to evoke any writing whatsoever, it is because there is something legible in visibility of and for itself. More accurately, we would have to say that there is in painting, in the nonpictorial at the very heart of painting, a certain writability or scripturality. The point here is that painting itself writes about painting, thus making itself possible. (By the same token, however, this is also what makes it so difficult, even dangerous, to write about painting from anywhere other than from within painting. This is not to say that the *painter* is in the best position in which to write. François Martin is in no better position to write about *The Air Show* than anyone else; as writer, his position is doubtless different from that of François Martin the painter. What it does mean, however, is that writing about painting—and hence the catalogue—must always begin with a written stroke, a stroke of scripturality and legibility that painting *itself* conceals, or whose layout, whose trace, sketch, outline, etc., it produces.) The nature of this writing-in-painting will not be easy to determine—indeed, will perhaps even be impossible, since it has, of course, nothing to do with painted writing, with calligraphy, ideology, or hieroglyphics.

In this regard, *The Air Show* offers an extraordinary sequence of inscriptions. What is *The Air Show*? It is the title of a catalogue, of a cata-

logue-book (a pure catalogue only has the minimal title *Catalogue . . .* ); it
is also, perhaps, the title of François Martin's text (unless that title is simply what is written as a nominal first sentence: "36 life-size drawings," a
sentence that would provide, for the text in question, a minimal title for
the catalogue ... ); and it is the title of the exhibition. The exhibition,
then, has a title. (It has no theme, like collective shows do; nor, like most
personal shows, does it take the painter as its theme.) Its title is the generic
title of two series of titles: *Flight Jacket* and *Leather Hat.* That's all; there's
no additional move toward individual titles: each piece in *The Air Show* is
either a *Flight Jacket* or a *Leather Hat* with a number. This most minimal
articulation is perhaps also the maximum articulation; it displays the
repetitive division of the *same* object (or the same "subject"). Undoubtedly, this has to be the starting point in any reading of Martin's text and
of what he says there regarding the consistency of this repetitive procedure. Curiously enough, he calls this "representation," as if it were not
properly understood that painting is essentially representative. But this is
the case only if representation is itself understood in advance as being essentially pictorial (remember Descartes: "the ideas in me are like paintings"). With his use of the word "representation," Martin breaks the circle. By "representation" he means, on the one hand, the reproduction of
the object (this is idea of "life-size"; I will come back to this); on the other
hand, however, and in the context of the specifically temporal gesture of
pictorial *resumption,* he means the re-presentation of that object, the repetition of its (life-size) presentation, and so the division, articulation, and
di-vision of this *same* object.

In truth, however, so far as these two series are concerned, or so far as
the double series of *The Air Show* is concerned, can we speak of titles?
These titles are all-too-simply the names of the two represented objects.
As titles, they are re-presentative in turn. This is yet one more form of the
minimal title. It refers to the entire tradition of what used to be called
"still life," in which titles such as *Apples and Pears, Guitar, Newspaper, and
Pipe,* and so on, tend to be used. Such is, it could be said, the most minimal form of reference, the title extended into a referential index. In it,
painting is said to be nothing more than the reference to what linguistics
terms the referent, the thing, the real, the material or ideal object. *Flight
Jacket*: this refers to a flight jacket. It refers to the flight jacket worn by
American war pilots and as could be found in the catalogue of a company
that produces such jackets or among the lists of the U.S. Air Force Supply

Corps. The painting announces itself as nothing other than a catalogue; it is itself the numbered inventory of a series of references. Its catalogue (*The Air Show*), therefore, is the catalogue of a catalogue.

Here, however, we are not simply dealing with a game of Chinese boxes or with a *mise-en-abyme*; the catalogue constituted by the painting itself complicates this entire schema. The various *Flight Jackets* are both what announces their legibility—an (American) catalogue of flight jackets, the flight jacket itself remaining thus a referent of the painting—*and* what gives them their visibility—reproduced or produced "life-size," "real size," they are themselves the referent of the catalogue. In this instance, "life" or "real" refer to painting alone. This is hardly a revelation. To claim that painting or the pictorial object is its own referent is rather dull. In this case, though, something else is happening, namely the blocking and suspension of the system of reference. It is not that there are words referring to representations that, in turn, refer to things or to themselves as things. Quite the contrary, in fact. Things (the jackets and hats being painted, the painted jackets and hats) are referring to words (and not just to any words; not to *blouson*, as I would say in French, but to "jacket," the English harboring a whole frame of reference, brought out in Martin's text, both in what it says—the Vietnam War—and in what it only half-says—the weight, the grain of the English words: "meeting," "flight jacket" ... ). Equally, however, we have something else again: neither the words nor their referents nor the painted things constitute a singular and ultimate sense (even if that is all that there is: the *sense* of painting). Nor is there any plurality of sense. Rather, what we have here is the re-presentation, the presentation (exposition), repetitive and divided, written-painted, of the same thing: the phrase "flight jacket," the flight-jacket object, the history, the fantasy, the painting of the flight jacket. What we have is the indefinite (is thirty-six finite? a finished saeries? if so, up to what point?) partition of the same thing, the indefinite division of the *sameness* of the thing and of the sight of it. What we have, in the simultaneously open and closed, singular and divided interplay of three instances (the words, the painted things, individual and world history), is something that is not of the order of process (no one instance precedes or, still less, engenders the other) but of the order of oscillation, vibration, or undulatory interference. Interference—the interference of three things, three indicators, or three indices (what are they to be called?): world, words, painting—is substituted for reference. And this, curiously enough, acts like a sort of sub-

stitute for the great metaphysical trinity: world, I, God. You can work out
which one is which . . .

Now, something is produced in this interference—and this something
is undoubtedly what we call "painting," François Martin's painting, for example. What needs to be understood, therefore, is that painting is painting only within the context of such an interference. In other words, *painting* has no independent essence and existence; rather, "to paint" means to
be subjected to this interference of world, word, and painting. In this interference, each term constitutes a supplement, the reciprocal supplement
of writing and painting endlessly opening onto a supplement of world.

Whence the singular position and exemplary role of the catalogue: it is
at once party to the interference *and* the site of its disturbance, of its trembling. Equally, however, effacing itself, it gives free play to the interference.

But that's not all. What is at issue here in this interference, in this painting? Essentially, in the interminable terms of the re-presentative division,
it's a matter of what Martin's text says and of what the exhibition makes
us see; it's a matter of an "exhaustion of the subject." *Flight Jacket* and
*Leather Hat* are repeated, verbally and pictorially, until they are exhausted,
until this disturbingly ambiguous "subject" has been exhausted. In the
text, it is the *object* (the jacket, the hat) that is exhausted; at the same time,
however, everything points toward the exhaustion of the *subject* (a certain
François Martin) who decides as to the cessation—the final cut—of the
painting (and so, too, of the catalogue).

Exhaustion involves both saturation and wearing out. It is from the perspective of just such an exhaustion that I can begin to see *The Air Show*:
the object is exhausted through its altered, erased, blurred—in short,
*painted*—presentations, but exhausted in such a way that, far from being
undone, it reemerges each time as if *cleansed* [epuré], clearer, more distinct, and more schematic (and we can see this in the nearly constant relation that Martin maintains between color, material, and drawing; drawing is neither primary nor secondary but incessantly (re)emerges from its
own interference with the glues, the grains, the supports, the collages: "36
drawings" ... ). This exhaustion provokes the insistent and discreet appearance of a contour, albeit an unfinished one, of a trace, albeit suspended; ultimately it's as if this trace, in an infinitely exhausted unbind-
ing or delineation of painting, were once again to be traced out in words,
on the painting, at the bottom of each drawing: *Flight Jacket, Leather Hat.*

These words, these titles, these referents are still there. Equally, however, it is as if there is nothing legible, as if everything legible is there only in order to be unbound, delineated—colored, coated, daubed with color right up to the point of exhaustion, to the point of nausea in the visible of the drawing.

And this visible, too, is in turn exhausted. It is exhausted not only in its interference with a world and with its history (the exhaustion of war, the exhaustion of the thought of war, of the horror of war, of the horror and the grotesquery of war, the exhaustion—as the text says—of the look that is unable to accommodate images of war, that of its violence and of its insignificance; here, horror—our own horror—is not denounced but, in this exhaustion, is simply overwhelming; how can we see this?) but also in its own visibility. Here, as always in Martin, drawing, color, support, alterations are gently undone through one another, by one another, in the very beat of their assembly. This assembly is so light, so transient, carried by sustained though clear vibrations, vibrations that are linked to serenely clear places or traces—a rigorous abandonment, then, a geometrical carelessness on the part of the painter—so light, in fact, that it is carried, of its own accord, into the whiteness of the paper that it divides. An immense tenderness—either that, or a spasm—of whiteness resorbs everything, that is, makes everything appear, that is, suspends everything. The legible, the visible, the world, all of these are suspended by this white—absolute painting, absolutely suspended.

And what if it were here, in this exhaustive whiteness, saturated by colors and by materials, that the truth of the catalogue was played out? The truth of its title, for a start. A little earlier I asked: What is *The Air Show?* In purely humdrum terms, it is an aerial meeting. In terms of legibility, it is the cloudy and captivating gathering of the objects and meanings indicated in the text. In terms of the visible, however ... air spectacle, spectacle in the air, spectacle of the air. *The Air Show* is the vision of the medium itself, of the element of vision. That, too, is something we know: painting only paints what needs to be seen. Here, however, it also paints the fact that to see is always to see in the air, to see air with everything that we see—to see an impalpable yet sensible transparency, to see the *medium* ("*mixed media op papier*") of visibility, which is not only the same as *almost* seeing nothing (whence it becomes a matter of reading *The Air Show* or "36 drawings") but also the same as *almost* reading nothing (whence it becomes a matter of seeing the air show). Martin brings to light what we might call an ethereal or aerial essence of painting. Yet what is brought to light is not an essence but a detachment or a trembling, a way of keeping things suspended in the diaphanous element of their evidence. And this evidence—absolute vision as the evidencing of vision itself—belongs neither to raw presence (to the world) nor to the order of signification (to the text) nor to the visible. Rather, it is the medium without medium of a perpetual excess of each one of these over the others, a perpetual exhaustion of each one by the others. Ultimately, as Martin says, the painter forgets the reasons for his choices; he forgets what he was looking at, what he wanted to say, what he wanted to see or make seen. This exhaustion of the referentiality of a world, of the intelligibility of a discourse and of the subjectivity of an artist, opens onto the inexhaustible actuality of a painting.

All of which allows us to understand, for example, these remarks from Kant: "Among the pictorial arts, I would award the palm to painting, partly because, as the art of drawing, it is the basis of all the other pictorial arts, partly because it can penetrate so much further into the region of Ideas and also expand the field of intuition in accordance with those much further than is possible for the rest."[1] But also this, from Heidegger: "In the work it is truth that is at work, not merely something true."[2]

Now, it seems to me that the very idea of the catalogue, at least as I am trying to understand it, has much to tell us regarding the role here (in *The Air Show*, in François Martin, in painting) of the *Idea* or of *truth*.

*Katalego* means to arrange a series of things in order, to arrange them according to *logos*, according to saying, to discourse and to calculation. It is an enumeration; it implies discretion in the mathematical sense of the term, the successive isolation of each unity (it's the same flight jacket each time, even though you can only see one at a time; it's the same painting, but it's never possible to see more than one at a time; it's always cut up, divided. Indeed, I would cheerfully go against the prevailing tide and say that music is the art of the simultaneous and painting the art of the successive). Above all, however, *katalegos* denotes an exhaustive enumeration; that is, it denotes what completely exhausts the series of its object(s). *Kata-* denotes downward movement, a movement toward what grounds [*vers le fond*], a movement right back through. The cata-logue leads enumeration and division right through to that extreme point where it no longer takes place, where *logos* touches on what it is that grounds and withdraws or suspends itself through its interference with that ground.

The ground in question is not that of *logos*; rather, it is, as we say, of the air. It is impalpable, inascribable air (air, nonetheless, that is still in the world), the most elementary of elements in which painting finds its *solution*, in every sense of the term.

In what does painting consist? In the general catalogue alone, perhaps: the exhaustion of everything, of every signification, of every point of view. Yet this exhaustion cancels nothing; rather, it brings into existence, starts to bring into existence, a presence of things—an obstinately re-presented presence—a layout of words, a way of looking. More than any others, Martin's paintings take on thus the character of a birth, of a coming into the light of day, a coming into the day's air, into the clear mumbling of an initial presence that has already begun to present itself once again, into the accompanying withdrawal of the very transparency of this presence.

I understand why painting is coupled with the catalogue and why the catalogue proliferates and exhausts itself in the book or in the text-catalogue. Painting is a provocation—insolent and exorbitant—to discourse. In order to take up the challenge, in order to bring the truth or the idea of painting to light, discourse catalogues it; it describes it. In doing so, however, it also *catalogues* itself; the most powerful, most knowing, most painstaking discourse on painting falls in with and is ultimately reduced to its most impoverished, most exhausted form, that of an inextricable involvement with what it describes, which disturbs its discursive project and curtails its intention. Such rarefaction, however, encourages it to speak, perhaps even to sing, in a most peculiar language, one that's always nascent, never wholly endowed with sense, the melopoeia of the catalogue:

> 36 life-size drawings . . .
> *Mixed media op papier . . .*

Inexorably bound to painting, drawn into its mixture or its *medium*, the catalogue turns out by the same token to be essentially detachable. It's what you can take from the exhibition. It's what is left over, outside a particular time and place, before an eventual re-presentation. What do I do with a catalogue in my library? It's a book. I can read its text. Yet it's never really a book. Its text is suspended over an interference. I can't resolve this interference by returning it from my library to the exhibition. I can't fill the gap. I can't seize the articulation between the trace of painting and the trace of writing, any more than I can the gap and the articulation between this double outline of the Vietnam War or François Martin's childhood memories. Here, however, the gap and the articulation are the *same* thing. They fit together in the same place. But I will never find this place—I am in it; it's the air. In other words, it's painting.

*Translated by Simon Sparks*

# § 18 Interviews

## I

—What do you see when you think about François Martin's paintings?
   —Que voyez-vouz, lorque vous pensez à la peinture de François Martin?
   —Was sehen Sie, wenn Sie an die Malerei von François Martin denken?
   —Ladong am seoung thesim inja François Martin am palang dejim?

—There's no need for you to translate, I understand.

—I know. I was just wondering what language to use when talking to you about painting.

—That's something else you already know: no language whatsoever. Language is radically improper when faced with painting. Language touches on all the other arts, even if it only skims over them. Through modulation, through signification, or through inscription, it can deal with the calculations of music, dance, architecture ...

—But so far as painting is concerned, it would be no good?

—No, no good at all, definitely no good. Painting doesn't speak. There's a silence where painting's concerned, an absolute muteness.

—But to say that painting's mute doesn't mean it's ineffable. These are two different things.

—Of course. I didn't say that we can't speak about painting. We should. Still, language does remain essentially improper to it.

—Should I give up asking you questions?

—No, no, you must, as I said. But nothing that we say will count for anything. What we have to do is exchange ideas, views, ways of looking at things, rather than questions and answers. François Martin's painting should circulate from your eye to mine; it should touch our eyes together, carry one eye toward the other.

—Let's assume that that's possible. Do you think you can isolate his painting from all the others?

—I wouldn't want to. To my eyes, the sight of his painting is mixed with all sorts of other paintings, and to your eyes, with others, too. You could say that it functions as a disclosure—as a private viewing, even—of any painting you like, even of painting-in-itself! What we would have to do is to see all these paintings in his, and to see ourselves in them at the same time. I have to see you in his paintings, just as you have to see me in them. There has to be an interview rather than a dialogue, an interview in which painting itself can be made out.

—That was actually my point. I asked you what you see, not what you have to say.

—When I think of painting, I see ... painting. I mean, I see that it's there to be seen. There you go. There's not much more that we could say. Or maybe it's that before saying anything else we have at least to say that it's there to be seen. I'm not talking about perception. "Perception" is always overloaded with significations or manipulations. Here, it's simply a question of seeing. Painting is there in order to bring out, broadly, at length, endlessly, that thing, that type of pure material essence: seeing. I'm not talking about a discourse or an operation or a perception. No, I'm talking about seeing, maybe only about glimpsing. About glimpsing seeing, glimpsing that it's seen. I'd say: to paint is to be seen.

—Is it worth it?

—Yes! It's certainly worth turning away from perception and from conception. We have to turn completely to seeing, or maybe bring about a complete turn in seeing. Painting doesn't make itself seen in the same way as everything else that we can see. It makes itself seen as a reversal of seeing, as the ability to deceive all sight, in order to make us see precisely the opposite: not *what* we see, but the fact that it is seen.

—You're joking ...

—We'll see.

## II

—Que voyez-vouz, lorque vous pensez à la peinture de François Martin?

—Alors ... je vois ... blanc, always white. Of course, when I see his paintings I see all the different colors he's used, and white may well be one of them. Actually, white is there rather often. It's not actually a rule, and I'm not sure that I could even say he has a certain fondness for white. But there are often various shades of white in his paintings. But that's not the white I'm talking about.

—So what are you talking about?

—To be honest, I'm not sure if I *could* talk about it. I see it, yes, but that's all: the fact that I see it. You asked me what I see when I think about paintings by the particular painter François Martin ...

—And if I asked you the same question about another painter?

—Yes, I would see something else. Black for Goya, yellow for Vermeer (you know why), violet for Apelle, green for Picasso, green and white ... But with François Martin, it's white. No hesitation.

—You've already mentioned this, in another text on François Martin.

—I have? I'd forgotten about that. You see, though? This proves how insistent it is. I see white—or, rather, I see whiteness; I have a vision of white. My seeing is white, immersed in whiteness as if in its own substance. That's what François Martin suggests to me: that seeing equals whiteness.

—But if that's the case, what is there to see in whiteness?

—You're asking this because you're taking "whiteness" to be the disappearance of colors. Newton's white, as Goethe said ...

—Yes, I know. "Newton has taken all the other colors and made white . . . "

—" . . . and he has very much deluded you." The whiteness that I see, however, is also something very different from a color, something very different from the disappearance of colors. François Martin's white is what makes me see the thought—the weight—of his painting, what makes me see how seeing weighs on painting and how, in it, painting weighs on the eye. What is being thought there, in his painting, heavy and light, is seeing reversed in painting, turned around on itself, on its skin.

—Painting's skin?

—Yes. I own a little piece by François Martin entitled *Peau de peinture*, painting's skin. But let's come back to whiteness. The point here would be that seeing has left the eye, has been tattooed onto a skin, spread out in broad daylight.

—I don't understand. Surely the condition of vision is the clear division of shadow and light, of black and white ...

—That's not the point. This has nothing whatsoever to do with dialectics. The white that I see, the white that François Martin's painting makes me see, isn't the white of sight or the white of the visible. It's the white that constitutes seeing itself, its matter, if you like, its hard and precise texture. In a certain sense, there's nothing that can be seen.

—You mean that it's night?

—It's something altogether more blinding, more shattering than the night that kills our eyes. It's the "white deprived of form," as Hegel says, "pure identity." But Hegel wanted to drown this in "the emptiness of the absolute." To my way of thinking, however, what's at stake here is plenitude, identity replete with eye and canvas, in and through one another, an embrace and not a vision. This whiteness doesn't dissolve colors but, on the contrary, presents them, pushes them to the fore. It's the tender and joyful surge of the colored thing in something quite ... other, something more primitive ... How can I put this? It's not the colored thing, the tint or the pigment, but the thing-color, the mass of coloration, the truth of mass overflowing its surface. It's both the white crust *and* the translucent grace of every color whatsoever, of every surface; it's their seeing dazzled, ravished, whisked away to a sort of extremity that's its own place, the white of the canvas as much as the white of the eyes. Have you noticed the painter's look? François Martin's look? He looks at you with the whites of his eyes, verging on the very limit of absence.

## III

—What do you think when you see François Martin's paintings?

—But I don't think of anything, if, by "thinking," I'm to understand what's ordinarily and inevitably understood by the word. I'm actually no longer thinking. Thought crosses over into seeing. It makes itself seen.

—And where's the white in all that?

—Seeing painting or seeing-painting, if you like, is a white thought, the flashing of thought that has become thought itself. Let's say it again: *das formlose Weisse*, formless white or, in any case, white devoid of ideas, of forms in Plato's sense of the "idea," if you see what I mean.

—Yes, I do; the great essential forms, the intelligible models, as when he says "an idea of the beautiful in itself that is equal to itself."

—There's nothing like that in painting. There, there's no idea. There's this white, which shouldn't be thought of as abolishing the forms of drawing but seen as extending beyond them. Far from suppressing them, it makes them seen and so fills them, thickens them, marks them out. Have you seen the marks? The stains, the striations, the slides, the strokes that stride across the edges of forms and figures? When we're immersed in them, we don't have the faintest idea of what it is we're seeing; all we know is that we're there and that it's there to be seen. In a sense, it's ideal, it's the ideal of seeing, the beautiful in itself. There's a kind of jubilation that gives the eye to painting and painting to the eye, far beyond ideas, opening the eye of the mind to what it can neither see nor conceive.

## IV

—Can we conclude from our last conversation that the painting of ...

—But it wasn't a conversation! Merely an interview: a view, between you and me, of the painting of F.M., or of his view of us, this painting that looks back at us ...

—Would you say that there are paintings that look, and others that don't?

—Certainly. True painting looks. False painting doesn't. It lays colors, it proposes spectacles. But true painting ...

—Would you say: the painting of truth?

—Yes, yes, I would, if I had to. True painting, well, it looks. It looks at you. Its surface is a luminous look cast on itself and open wide onto you, absolutely lucid, and making you see in return. Listen: "What do I see? A whiteness for which snow is black / Eyes ravished in themselves, by themselves bedazzled."

—But that was a woman: doesn't painting lack the depth to be such a look?

—Precisely not. By reducing itself to the two dimensions of its surface, it achieves the "concentration of the soul on itself," as Hegel explained somewhere. "Painting must break the total extension": it renounces the totality of space and makes itself superficial through profundity. And that's all that whiteness is: burst extension, the soul. This whiteness that Martin assigns to all his surfaces, to all his colors and contours. The white of the eye of painting. It's not the dissolution of colors, but their thickness, their instant depth. This whiteness is always coming and offering itself to the surface.

—Does that mean that we have to understand it as truth?

—Yes, undoubtedly. In any case, it's as present and concealed, as un-predictable as truth itself. It's free, without pretension; it reveals nothing; it's not sublime, but everything's there: pleasure and pain, something that touches you right there, a divine simile that no longer holds any God. It's this, whiteness, a fire that burns without flame or ashes. It's beyond the blaze, this white burning of painting. It consumes colors, their patterns, and F.M. along with them. Look ...

—Yes, I see. Thank you.

*Translated by Simon Sparks*

# § 19 Res Extensa

One often thinks of sculpture as originating in a gesture which, from the outside as it were, hews a block of inert and formless matter into shape. Admittedly there is no lack of evidence to suggest that this gesture is invariably accompanied by a sort of motion, if not an *emotion*, coming from the matter itself, from the way the block is arranged, from the nature of the material, its lines of force or of weakness. Even here, however, the image of cutting and boring still dominates; it is still a matter of carving, trimming, and stripping away, of smoothing and shaving. Or else of crafting and molding, of a lump touched, impressed, or marked in some way.

(The first series of images here refers back to the etymology of the word "sculpture" and to hollowing or digging more generally: *skalpos*, "mole" in Greek. The second series, meanwhile, is closer already to painting.)

Ordinarily we speak of sculpture in terms of *impression*: a form is impressed on a lump of matter, twisting and bending it into shape. More rarely we refer to an *expression* of matter. Not "expression" in the sense of "signification," as when one says that someone "expresses" his or her feelings, since in this sense expression is just another impression: form given to some content. Rather, an expression that would be literally ex-pression: material pressed to the surface, pushing itself outward, making space for itself and thereby pushing some other material out of the way, in this instance the fluid element of air and the hands of the sculptor. An expression that would be, first and foremost, an extension or expansion, and perhaps, ultimately, an expulsion. In any event, an exposition; not a signifying process or a translation.

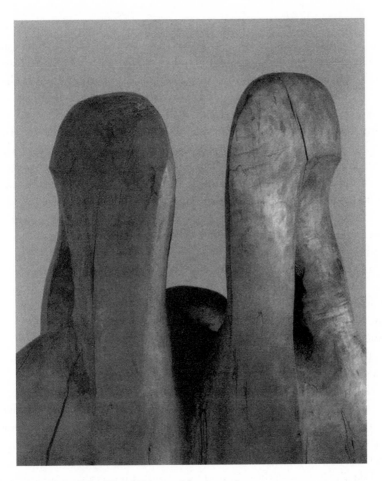

*Janus-Torso* (1969), by Henri Etienne-Martin.

It is this that one has to reckon with in Etienne-Martin's sculpture.

Here matter is not worked over and crafted from the outside; instead it responds to the pressure and expansion of its own massy thickness. The *Dwellings* (*Demeures*) themselves proceed less from the clearing or construction of a habitable site and more from the mute and heavy dilation of a honeycombed mass that arranges itself in volumes, places, and passages in which the "inhabiting" would be that of the material up against itself.

In these *Dwellings*, what *dwells* and *remains* [demeure] is mass,[1] the crust and grain of a substance, barely taken out of itself, but distended sufficiently for its "remaining" to be an act, a praxis, rather than a persisting sunk in itself. But this is also matter expressed, pressed, and raised right up against itself, coiling around itself, remaining the matter that it is.

And what is a piece of matter? *Materia* or *materies* is thick wood, the hard part of a tree, *mater* designating the trunk from which the offspring emerge (and there is another sculpture, from 1984, entitled *The Tree-Look*). *Materia* is the maternal trunk, the phallus employed as a stomach or stretched like a breast. It does not spurt sperm, nor does it fill with milk. It merely inflates its mass, enveloping itself as it spreads out.

Sculpture can also present itself as an art of extreme equilibrium, an arrow in the void. Or again, as an art of excavation, in which case it is something material and substantial.

*Sub-stance*: that which subtends, ground, foundation, support, receptacle. Extended substance stretches out. Thick substance thickens. Density shows itself without letting go of that internal adhesion by which it is bound together. Immanence puts itself on display, only so as to be touched straight away. Barely visible, in a flash, and already it is a finger that sees, a palm, skin that has already replaced the iris and the cornea. A look alighting on the sculpture and becoming opaque.

Little or no discourse. Titles, though. But what is a title? It is not so much a piece of writing as a notice. It is an inscription (*titulus*), engraved matter. For the most part the titles here are names. They signify, for sure, but they signify only so as to trace the signature of substance. Matter signs and identifies itself, but its does not hold forth.

Take the following title: *Janus-Torso* (1969). It is exemplary because it is often repeated in Etienne-Martin's work: *Janus II* (1970), *Janus or Life and Death* (1963), and also *Gemini* (1984). *The Two of Them* (1956). The list of double sculptures, structures or statues, goes on. *The Spiral* (1983), *Opening Night* (1945–55), *The Cry* (1963), *Tarot's 21st Blade* (1969), *The Son of Time* (1979), *The Tree-Look* (1984), and so on. With Etienne-Martin, one must pay attention to the motif of division and of doubling, of splitting and dehiscence.

A *torso*: here again we are dealing with wood. *Thyrsos*: the stem of a plant; the thrysus of Dionysus, a stick bound with vines and topped off by a pinecone or often a phallus, and waved by the participants in a bacchanalian revel. A cut stem or trunk: fragment. *Torso* in Italian is a cut stem, a section. And in German it is a sculpted fragment, or a fragmented sculpture. From the same root we get the Old French *trou*, as in the stalk of a cabbage. (Or there again, *tronchet*, the silversmith's block, or the cooper's. And *tronce* or *tronche*, the large wood stump for Christmas Eve, or "mug," a peculiar visage.)

The torso is the detaching and coming away of a substance that comes out and comes up. It is not the *body*: there is both more and less than a "body" here. There is emergence, bursting forth, *and* a truncated or abbreviated body. The thing remains suspended in its truncation. Held in the moment of dilation and the expression that frees substance and puts it there, with nothing more, no roots or foliage, with no organic activity. Bounding yet immobile, jumping on the spot. Plantlike, mineralized; a fossil of the origin.

Janus, god of gates and public byways. God of entrances and access, god of beginnings, first named in the liturgical litany, January.

Janus: the acephalic torso is bicephalic here. At least if the *frons* is a head. There are two *frons* in Latin: foliage and the brow, the face, what is open to view. Aspect. Matter faces up here and offers its aspect to view, as opposed to becoming head and thought.

Immanence is turned away from itself. A slow torsion disassembles it just enough for a vague evocation of the head, of the fringe on one face, the mouth of an other. So much so that the *frons* is quadrupled, two trunks, two necks or spines, and two faces or sides, a front and a back, femininity and virility, a hollowing out and a swelling up.

Matter turned away so as to burst forth face to face with itself. The interior facing the inner. Seeing itself without sight, speaking without voice or sign. Place of beginning, simultaneity broken in two, turned backward and forward, coming naked.

The material mass, amassed matter, is not freed for who-knows-what kind of spiritual assumption. Solid, face to face with its own dehiscence, with no membrane between it and its own substance; nothing but the air it displaces by its own volume, slowly like a heavy vessel whose anchor drags in the depths.

Indecent and secret, obscene yet discreet exhibition, it neither engenders nor absorbs. It neither projects nor digests. It does not operate. It springs forth, it is sprung forth, from the immobile, silent heart of things

and from there, without delay, surrendered to the rhythm of a pure outside.

The outside does not express the inside; it neither translates nor trans-
figures it. But a more ancient exterior of the origin, in the origin, expresses
the inside that it has filled since time immemorial: it pushes it and
stretches it outside, though what emerges in this way remains the inside,
and stays inside. A *res extensa* contemplated or inspected by no *res cogitans*.
The *cogito* here belongs to a substance, not to a subject: *cogito, ergo exten-
dor*.

What is sculpted is this, the subject. This is what gouges out the *skalpos*
of the outside, the evisceration of the ground of things. A subject sculpted
and hewn, a substance dense in expansion, naked, *exterior extero mec*.

*Translated by Jonathan Derbyshire*

# § 20  Lux Lumen Splendor

Light is not itself a luminous substance: it is the give and distance of the world, the absolute velocity of the appearing of bodies, the sculpture of their mass, the curvature and brilliance of their edges.

It is thus that it is *lux*, the light that used to be called "absolute" or "primary": the radiant source distinguished from *lumen*, the secondary or incidental light in the translucency of surfaces or bits of matter, their reflections and refractions. At the very edges of bodies, *lux* is folded, modulated, and diffused in *lumen*. The limbs that supply the title for this series, Lux Lumen Splendor, are a name for edges or frames, for what wraps around them, their hem, their nimbus.

"Photography" means "inscription of light," and the "light" here is *lux*. It was only the search for different qualities that led to this technique becoming that of the photo, understood as the recording or instantaneous ravishing of illuminated forms. Guerrero goes back to the primitive sense, the sense which undoubtedly will always be to come, and which makes all photographic art ambiguous: not settling for capturing that which is bathed in light, but instead tracking its momentum and range. Not referring it back to some luminous element, but penetrating it, bending, twisting, breaking, shining and erasing. Writing *lux as well as* lumen so as to get hold of *splendor*, the brilliance of the shine given off by illuminated bodies.

Undoubtedly it's a question here of a luminous desire for bodies (the opposite of an illuminated desire). The transparency of this desire has

Photograph by Guerrero.

nothing to do with the supplication of lack or absence: it desires in the
adoration and sharp intimacy of presence—of a presence set free from its
source, taut, elusive, ahead of itself—the precedence of *lux* over *lumen*, the
very ground of *splendor*. (A sort of fiat, except that nothing would be said;
a click would suffice.)

To this end, Guerrero arranges light in front of the lens, in a wavy,
transparent piece of material. This is not a luminous object; it is a piece of
*lumen* in something close to its purest state, almost the nascent state of
*lux*. This thing is solid, however. It is like an unveiled veil, a frosted screen
laid bare. This is matter that will never be plastic; rather, it is plasticity itself made material and elemental, the basic structure of the hollowing out

and sudden appearance of the body. Here, the body of a woman is reduplicated; that is to say a body, absolutely (perhaps men, perhaps even objects, only have feminine bodies). Reduplicated, hollowed out, bent, allowed or made to flee or to take hold. The tip of a breast, a nostril, or a shoulder more present than any exhibition, present for being denuded and cut from a visible transparency.

The torso, the breast, the shoulder, the neck, the becomings or births of the body: bent, folded, stretched, worn out, restive in abandon, surprised in the pose. The edges and surroundings [*les bords et les abords*] of the body: but is a body anything else? Occasionally something seems on the verge of being lost or ruptured in the extremity of an extension concentrated solely on its nullification, as if this skin were anxious to know that it would not be touched, that the transparency of its own nudity would withdraw it once more, so as to expose it anew.

What do I see if I see transparency? I see what allows me to see: *lux* behind *lumen*, or even my eye itself, a radiant eye, and the air of the emptiness in which *splendor* unwinds. The supplicating gesture of a woman, and with it everything that shapes my look: my consideration of its headlong flight.

The eye touches, and this touching twists and hollows it out at the same time, opening within it a clear abyss. Rest and an infinite calm are promised to the touch, just as an anxiety and sudden torsion lie in wait for them. The torso withdraws, as do the head and the stomach, yielding only lines of flight, of light spun in fiber optics, in hyperboles and fractal lines, an uncertain and sometimes painful gleam.

The transparent matter in which the body is bathed, sculpted (in no sense is it painted), offered, and withdrawn, all at once, this matter that bears the body as its desire to be and to be touched is like the diaphanous, detached membrane of things in the Epicurean theory of vision. Or else it is like the luminous doubles that, in the early days of photography, were thought to be stolen from the body by the *camera obscura* (people feared for the health and integrity of photographic subjects). At the same time, however, it's something entirely different: a coincidence or collision of the fluid and the solid, of the abstract and the concrete, of eye and film. It is light colliding with itself and vision in internal division, in this bit of raw transparency, with hints of unease, a slight twitching, fear and surprise.

Skin merges ceaselessly with light, the rays of its specter and their final resolution in the black of an eye, on a hair, or on the tip of a breast. *Splendor* coils around itself, *lumen* founders, and everything tends to a sort of dullness: *lux* is still further away, or else *it* is this dark, dull point.

*Translated by Jonathan Derbyshire*

# § 21  Held, Held Back

Two violences, one on the other.

Or else—who knows?—one and the same ambivalent violence twice over, one and the same fury turned against itself, taking itself in hand, flush against itself, amassed, massive, and agile, unbridled and restrained [*retenue*], in and through itself.

Two violences turned against one another and wreaked on one another: two buttressed pressures, two stereoscopic images for one and the same balance, one and the same relief, the same stance [*tenue*] on the ground. Before it does anything else, a sculpture holds and holds itself in place [*tient et se tient*]. Its entire coming lies in this stance or this holding in place [*sa venue est dans la tenue*]. With it, the two violences come and are held together.

The first of these: a blazon of suffering, bodies reduced to mere signs of bodies, the body itself absent, replaced by blows, by hunger, by infection, prison bodies, camp bodies, exiled bodies, bodies riddled with viruses: masses crazed with massacre; bodies buried before their time because there is no more that could be done; body-figures, bodies figured in such a way as to recall that there could have been—that there should have been— bodies there; bodies from where there is no longer anything but bodies or where there are no more bodies, it amounts to the same thing. Not the monumental or inanimate corpse, but the body, sculpted, hollowed open. The wounded, tortured body has long been a familiar sight. One of the great churches has one as its emblem. From this moment on, however, we have another coat of arms to bear: bodies hollowed out from within, undermined and gnawed away, bodies consumed by their hemorrhage or their diarrhea. And might we not see in this the image of all modern images? The faceless, the emaciated, the one who exists for no other reason than to confirm that he does not exist, the one who is nothing but the place that he ought to occupy, nothing but the event that does not befall him, the thought that he cannot think?

The other violence: a densely woven texture of open mesh, the body on the verge of what tears it apart, the infinite fragility of skin, utterly finished, utterly finite, hollowed out, released, an empty cage, a wire frame exposed to the touch. And might we not see in *this* the image of *all* images? The image of a body's originating in its singular extension or measure, the pure structure and sculpture of a small shard of a world *in statu nascendi*, of its originating in an uncertain separation, the whole of the inside suddenly outside, the absolute loss and gain of the other, of all others, and first of all of the entire self, of this body that I am by crossing through it, always behind and always before the body itself. The rhythmic configuration of a presence (without organs: no respiration, no digestion, no heartbeat; merely a tension, a fold, a step). Alongside one another, similar and disparate, similarly dissimilar, each given over to its original presence. The world in millions of open origins in every possible sense of the term, man without species or genre, violently singular.

~

The first violence refuses the second, and rains violence down on it. It does not look to tear the two of them apart or to tear them from one another. It is fear in the face of what cuts itself off in a self-absence that all share and no one wishes to acknowledge: fear before the vast strangeness of innumerable men.

It is not difference that constitutes the second violence; rather, it is the semblance of this absence, of this shared absence from one another, of this absence that means one can never see or touch the very thing that one might have expected to see or to touch: love, thought, the secret of being, and even something beyond all of these. But if one were to see or to touch these things, there would be neither seeing nor touching. The second violence is thus the separation of a birth, the severance of yet another. The first is the rage of refusing the fact that love, thought, the secret are, from the beginning, violently dispersed.

~

What we call a world is nothing more than this dispersal of origins, their dissipation, and their prodigality. Neither an absence of origin (what we call a universe) nor an origin compacted in on itself (what we call an earth), but the violent irruption of multiple origins and of the equally multiple sense of sense. Sense: nothing but sculpted shards of sense.

This is also why the world can destroy itself: this originary violence, however peaceable and devoid of violence its birth may be, carries with it a ferment of fury, regardless of how little it is able to bear itself, how little it denies itself. (Nuclear warheads, famines, the destruction of the ozone layer, overpopulation and depopulation, powers, productions, religions, millions of bodies promised to what?)

How is the world able to bear not being to itself and itself alone a universe or an earth? How is it able to bear being in the world, no more no less, having the world as an absolute measure? How is it able to bear its signifying nothing "by itself," neither I nor you nor space, but only this division of sense in all its senses? How can it stand it [*comment tenir le coup*]?

It is for this that sculpture strives to find the stance [*la tenue*]. Neither seeing nor touching, neither space nor volume, sculpture is a *techne*—of the stance, the art and mode of the body's stance. Not of how it pushes itself to the fore, but of how it appears to the world, how it presents itself.

This is why there has to be the entire space of a coming. Not the two dimensions of a simple presence, but the three dimensions whose intersection provides the fourth, the time of the infinitely slow, imminent, belated but premature coming, a coming that, although running ahead of itself, still comes from behind itself, endlessly turning around itself, bending space to this discreet rhythm.

~

The sculpture of a woman—sculpting what makes all bodies women's bodies. This does not mean modeling some raw material, drawing out neither form from the formless nor the subject from substance by throwing out the remains of the image or the full and founding idea, but hollowing out from within, mining absence to its very core, folding the mesh that encloses nothing.

Sticking skin-tight over wire mesh not a skin, but multiple skeins of pa-per, layers, strips, fragments, superpositions, and crossings of surfaces without hidden faces. This skein neither completes nor encloses a flesh (there is no flesh here, neither emaciation nor prolongation [*ni de décharnement, ni d'acharnement*]). Rather, it is the meticulous indication, place by place, space by space, moment by moment, of the indefinite ex-position that a skein is, its stance both continuous and discontinuous: a network of zones that have nothing in common except their spacing. This, their spacing, represents nothing; rather, each zone, each skein is, in turn, an origin and an end.

If one were to use a language concerned with the abstractions of under-standing and judgment, one might say that these zones were "sensible," susceptible of excitation, of information, of pleasure and pain. Here, how-ever, it is not this that is at issue, but the discreet, fleeting, and urgent touches of an almost insignificant fragility of sense.

There was no substance; there will be no subject. No turn back in on the self. No withdrawal into a violence done to the original violence. The threat is there, held and held back, but the eyes are not closed so as to hold in the representation unfolding without. These eyes do not form im-ages; they see nothing, neither inside nor out. These are eyes without rep-resentation, the absenting of vision in the birth of the look.

The mouths are not closed in order to hold discourse in. They are the absenting of speech in a kiss. The kiss does not kiss. It merely signals, without signifying. It makes the fragile, multiple sense that it always is.

Sculpted sculptures of kisses, closed, clear eyes.

~

Or else, as sculpted by a tear that hesitates and that lingers here and there—whether a tear of sorrow or of joy or of an isolated sentiment of being, one can never know for sure.

Not even a sentiment: rather, a having-a-sense-of-self, a "self-con-sciousness," if you like, but one free from any object, including its own substance or its own subject. Free from consciousness, yet still clear and distinct. Empty of any object, of any project, full of skeins of paper, of

straw and pigment, of insignificant remarks that signify this consciousness, pierced by openings that are neither wounds nor tears but an older
and more gentle violence, an incompletion of birth. A consciousness of
being, patiently amassed and impatiently gathered together.

~

Sculpture, the art of mass: the gathering of a presence, the light mas-
siveness of its immanence, the curvature of space. Mass not as a mass but
as density and as gravity, as a measure of presence.

The gathering of what is and remains dispersed, of what—at and in the
origin, shattering it—pressed forward, dissipated, and dispersed, without
there being any need for this violence or any salvation in speaking out
against it. On the contrary, it is in seeking to absolve oneself from this violent birth that ruinous violence springs forth.

Calculation of the measure and the stance needed if anything is to be
salvaged from birth, if what does not need to be saved is to be safe-
guarded. Save that "safe" here does not mean "intact, unharmed, or un-
scathed"; on the contrary, it means "nascent, touched, breached once and
for all."

*Translated by Simon Sparks*

# § 22   The Title's a Blank

A blank for a title, and perhaps that's how it begins. What? We can't say that. We can't begin by saying that it's beginning. When we say it, when we say "it's beginning," it has already begun and so already finished beginning; it has begun finishing. We can't say where it begins, or when.

But this doesn't mean that we would have to stay silent, or that the blank of the title would correspond to a religious paralysis at the entrance to a shrine. It doesn't mean that we would have to reserve or preserve the secret of this beginning and of the end of this beginning—of this end that begins in the beginning long before the beginning itself begins, of this end that begins the beginning, that broaches its opening. It doesn't mean that there would be a mysterious silence, that we would have to sit and contemplate in silence.

For there's nothing here, nothing that could take place, whether in the space-time of the world or outside of it as if in some other world beyond this one. All there is is the "there is," the taking-place itself. This taking-place is not something, but the beginning-and-end of something. It is "There is" itself and in person. Nothing and no one but the *thing itself.*

We can't say it because there's nothing to be said: nothing at all, nothing as regards the unity of substance and form, of surface and foundation, of beginning and end, and so, too, nothing as regards any part of a whole that might have absented itself from presence. We can't even say that we can't say it. Anyone who says, here and now, that we can't say it would al-

ready have had to come from somewhere else and would already have to
have said or heard said somewhere else what we can and cannot say. They
would have had to know something about this world and about another
world, about this sense and about another sense, about this saying and another saying, one that would consist in keeping silent.

Here and now, however, no one has come. It alone has come, and it begins. It finishes precisely by coming from somewhere else and by slipping
ahead into a past. The past itself has passed (it has as much finished finishing as it has finished beginning); to put it somewhat differently, nothing has come to pass. And we can't even say that nothing has "yet" come
to pass since there is no space or time for such a "not yet." There has been
neither watching nor waiting nor preparation nor formation nor promise
nor anguish. Nor has there been anything about which we could remain
silent, since there is nothing there about which we could either speak or
remain silent. There is no "there," no "over there," hidden, lost, absent.
There is no absence. Or perhaps what there is is the very presence of absence. And it is for precisely this reason that we can't say that "we can't say
that." Here, there's neither the impossibility of speaking nor the obliga-
tion to remain silent. Which means that there's neither aphasia nor ecsta-
sis nor inhumanity nor religion. There is the fact that it begins and that
alone: the beginning here-and-now without elsewhere, neither past nor
future. That through which there is a "here-and-now." There's no silencing it and no saying it, as if, before any intention to speak on my part,
there were something there, set down like an inert or formless thing simply awaiting its seizure and petrification into signification. There's no hidden sense, no machine constructed in order to express it. Here, the sense
in question is set up quite differently: like clear evidence, like the clear evidence of something that shows itself and says itself, that says itself in
showing itself.

There's nothing to say: there's the beginning and so, at the same time,
in the blank of the title, the thing and its saying and their "there is." The
"there is" as the "at the same time" of the thing and its saying. Sense as the
sense of existence. There's no "saying" this sense; all there is is the simultaneity of saying and thing. Manifestation is the simultaneity of saying
and thing: the utterance of a presentation, the presentation of an utterance.

It's not as if there is the thing on the one hand and its saying on the other. The taking-place of the thing, its beginning-and-end, is both saying and thing. It is the same "thing," but different in itself.

~

This time, then, let us say: "a blank for a title," *this time* meaning on the occasion of certain paintings by Susanna Fritscher. The occasion, the encounter, something that has neither beginning nor end, something that lies wholly in the moment, a beat between two series, between thing and saying, between place and place. The beat of an opening or of an overture in the musical sense of the term: a part in which the whole is held back, from which the beginning draws its theme, a cadence or measure held back from any sense of succession, one not measured in terms of continuity, one that has to break with continuity before it can continue.

"A blank for a title" is no more a sentence than a silence. It is certainly not a well-formed phrase, lacking as it does proper syntax and, as such, sense. For all that, however, it is not a mystery. It is not something that would harbor another sense for the initiated, for the visionary, or for the seer. It is a beginning—and how could anyone be initiated at the beginning? It is the beginning of both a saying and a thing, each one a blank for a title, a saying and a thing neither of which designate or refer to one another. Neither one of which makes sense, yet each one of which says something that makes perfect sense: Look, there is.

When there is a title, one of two things must have gone before it: either the thing-thing, in which something would have begun to propose, to indicate, or to evoke a sense; either that, or the saying-thing, in which there would be some indication or signification whence the thing could draw its momentum. Here, however, neither of these has begun; both have finished together, at the intersection of a painting and an intention [*propos*], at this intersection about which there is neither anything to paint nor anything to say, and which effects the opening of both things—or, rather, the opening of what separates them, namely, the very interplay of the intersection; it is precisely at this opening that each thing is opened for itself as with the other. It is open to the shared beat of a white blank of title.

"A blank for a title" isn't meant to function as a title so as to compensate for the lack of any title provided by Susanna Fritscher. (And we should note that this conjunction of absence and title could be read in one of two ways: either in terms of the absence *of* a title or in terms of absence *as* a title. The fact that Susanna Fritscher doesn't provide a title for any of these works could mean either that the title is being kept a secret or that the absence of a title, the blank of the title, is itself a title.)

It is neither a substitute for a title nor a title by default. It indicates (but does not indicate); it exposes (but without showing) absence itself as the beginning of the thing. Painting as the beginning of the thing. Painting comes into play where titles end, at least if the role of a title is to say what this painting is, where it comes from, where it's going, what it means … As we know, however, it's nothing like this; titles never say anything other than their own intersection with painting, which, for its part, says nothing but simply skirts around the edges of titles, touching them as it withdraws. In this sense, all titles are blank, painted blanks. And the same goes for the titles of written things.)

"A blank for a title" doesn't take the place of an absent title. It neither evokes nor mimics a sense that has been deliberately held or kept back, whether by Susanna Fritscher or by someone else. If, despite everything, it *were* to take the place of something, the only thing this could be is Susanna Fritscher's name. But nothing can take the place of a proper name since that place is, precisely, nothing. The place of a proper name is merely the space-time of a beginning, the spacing of a time, the time of a spacing, the birth of this woman.

"There is … ," then, just as easily takes her place—by which I mean the place of the woman who paints these canvases. The place of her painted gesture. The gesture through which she touches canvas and paint, touches canvas with paint, the gesture through which paint touches itself, without beginning or end, merely the beginning and end of paint, sweeping along itself, sliding smoothly over itself, through coordinating layers layered on one another.

And yet, despite all this, it does also act as a title. For a title is neither a proper nor a common name. It doesn't signify, any more than it designates. The title isn't a sign. On the contrary. The title is always a gap, a gap that belongs to the thing, the mark of a blank space between the thing and itself: its very beginning and its end, the space through which it opens itself and holds itself open. The title says nothing; rather, it indicates that there's everything—or nothing—to be said. The title does nothing but touch on the thing closed in on itself, on the closure needed in order for it to open up, in order for there to be any sense of opening. The title opens and closes with a single gesture: the overture.

~

There is something: it begins. "There is"—this is the title itself, the title of all titles and the blank of the title—"there is" belongs to both saying and thing without amounting to either. "There is" is common to saying and to thing without their having anything in common. It lies between them; it's what is exactly in between, the division of saying and thing. Their chopping-and-changing between themselves. Being in saying and saying in being, outside one another, touching one another, beginning and ending one another.

Something reaches the very limit of saying, saying nothing, bringing an end to the saying that it has begun. A thing bespeaks its own beginning and thus brings this beginning to an end, beginning to be in this end. Neither cause nor reason nor ground from which to proceed, merely a gesture, a passage, a flow sustained, smoothed, advanced, immobilized upon itself. Merely a technique, an art that, discreetly, continually, brushes against the thing, passes into it, passes through it, always at the limit, but at the limit that unfolds without limits.

We can call this *painting*. Doing so certainly helps, but it also poses a problem. For what does it mean to paint? To paint is neither to represent nor to cover a surface; rather, it is to touch on the absolute character of a *there is*. A thing agrees to exist [*consent à être là*]; it occupies its place, the place where it takes place, and makes sense only by opening this place. To paint is to agree to this agreement. It is neither to bespeak the event of this taking-place nor to hold significations in check. Rather, to paint means to agree to the division that deposes and exposes the thing.

It is the double movement of losing itself in itself and opening onto the outside, of losing itself by opening itself, of opening what loses itself to its very loss. Its loss is its opening. Still, this isn't strictly speaking a loss, since there is nothing that could be either won or gained. But to open itself to groundlessness [*s'abîmer*] is itself an opening. It opens this: the thing to itself, layer upon staggered layer, passing between them in such a way that nothing is left but the presence that conceals itself by constituting a surface. We could say that this opening appears. That it appears rather than there being appearance, and that it has already turned back in on itself, already finished beginning.

The opening opens nothing and opens onto nothing, neither density nor depth. Depth, too, is a blank. The opening opens what remains obstinately closed in the opening itself *and* what is already open, what is always already half-open. And this is why it finishes the beginning and begins the end. There is nothing playful about this; it is not simply aimless chatter. No, it is the flip side of what can be said. It is the patience of agreeing to exist.

~

Gray yields [*consent*] to white, which yields in turn to gray, each one the beginning and end of the other, each one giving itself to the other. Between them there is mixture and caesura, division, and nothing else. Yet this division divides nothing in the sense of slicing up or allocating. It is neither an exchange nor a partition. Rather, it is the division of the same among the same, difference itself, distinction as common desire, common attraction. What draws white to gray and gray to white, what draws white from gray and gray from white, is the community generated by their agreeing to differ from one another. Such difference, however, is largely imperceptible, each one being nothing but the limit of the next. Each one persists in the other, therefore, imperceptibly, indefinitely, losing itself therein.

How are we to agree to what is imperceptible [*consentir à l'insensible*]? How can we get a sense [*sens*] of what is imperceptible and, harmonizing with it, discover its rhythm? What is imperceptible should be sensible, imperceptibly sensible [*insensiblement sensible*]: neither coldness, withdrawal, nor indifference but, in some way, the act itself of sensing [*le sentir lui-même*], suspended on itself, opened onto itself. The gray-white interior of the act of sensing.

In truth, we can't speak about *gray* or *white*, any more than we can speak here about "support," "surface," "painting," "motif," or "figure." Grey and white are merely the twin poles of this flow of light through which there is something like light (*black* is a different sort of light—one that has no part in all this—the light of truth, its abyss). Gray and white are the-beginning-the-end of appearance. Between them, therefore, there is only the discontinuity of continuity, the event of being: the fact that there is only the event and that the event *is* not. Here, "gray" and "white" can't be understood as the names of colors or shades or as their combination or distillation. Color is quite simply absent. There is no color here, insofar as color is what belongs to a surface irrespective of its dimensions. More precisely, dimension is all there is. Measure and relation. And so, since it is impossible to have a surface without color, we can say there is no surface here. Rather, let's say that there is pure depth or pure dimension. Or, what amounts to much the same thing, opening and spacing, simultaneously open and closed onto itself.

Equally, from one frame of the diptych, triptych, or monochrome to the next, and between them, between each of these divisions, these statements, there is both play and relation, continuity and discontinuity, time and countertime, separation and touch, imminence and contiguity. There is *tact*—or, in German, *Takt*, rhythm and the measured beat of time.

There is measure, that is, relation and magnitude. Relation lies in affinity and separation, magnitude in closure and distance. Measure is the rhythm between shadow and light, beginning and end. Yet this measure is itself measureless. It surpasses all measure, lying clear-cut in the very movement of this surpassing, held like passing and sharing.

The measureless measure is itself agreement with "there is." Not the acceptance of everything that there is, but agreement with the fact that there is—and this latter is the measure or the rule for knowing to what we must or must not agree.

It is the measure of or the rule for what is measureless: *the fact that there is.* What there is, all things, all this has color and figure. But *what there is* is white and gray, the-beginning-the-end of everything.

~

And if the word [*le verbe*] of painting were: to agree?

Its word, that is, its verb, its act. Not its magic word or its more or less sacred name but, on the contrary, this absolute severance of the verb from the name, a severance that breaks signification, that ruins any referential constant. The referent of a name is a subject or a substance; the referent of an adjective is a quality of a substance and, because of this, remains substantial. The "referent" of a verb, however, is an action and precisely *not* a state; the most that we can say is that it is the action of maintaining a state, of persevering with being (when it isn't the action of stepping outside the being of the self, of the act of existing, of exciting). Action is always transitive. But there is no transitional word. None whatsoever. Not even the verb "to be." And perhaps above all not the verb "to be."

"To agree" does not mean to resign oneself, to submit, to go tiredly or passively along with something. Nor does it mean to enter into a "consensus." Rather, it means to admit that there is a break, the break brought about by the anguish bespoken by *you*, by the anguish that each one of us bespeaks and that each one of us dispels by doing so.

To agree to this: to its own gesture insofar as it goes without saying, insofar as it goes much further or simply goes somewhere else where no act of will would have been to force it; and yet, not abandoned—or, if abandoned, then abandoned in the very precise sense of its being abandoned to its own exactitude.

Exactitude has nothing to do with precision. Precision is a matter of reproduction, of recuperation, of approximation. Exactitude is absolute or it is nothing. It is a matter of arising, a matter of the instant.

It seems to me that we could say: we agree to exactitude. The exactitude of painting and that of writing are assuredly not the same—and there is, above all, no exactitude between them, no exactitude of one with respect to the other: there's no exact phrase that "matches" the painting, no exact painting that "matches" the phrase. All the same, we still agree [*con-sentons*] to the same exactitude (that is, by agreeing to work with it, we admit each of them together and in the same way).

We agree to exactitude since it is not something that could be either commanded or mastered; so far as exactitude is concerned, we can only agree to it (in general, the exact is the only thing to which we *can* agree). We can't approach it. We can only *be* it.

∼

Klee once said that writing and drawing were the same thing. To say this is to speak from the perspective of exactitude while still treating it as an actual proximity, as an extreme precision; it is, therefore, false. The truth of exactitude and of agreement is that they aren't the same thing and that no art is the same as any other (and such is the price of "art").

To agree to the exact: such would be, for me, here, today, painting's word—as if it expressed thus the very limit of writing, the limit of the trace of what is said [*du dire*].

In fact, this amounts to "saying"—in the sense that there should be nothing left over that is not said exactly, and that nothing exists which is not said exactly. For what is not said does not exist, and what is not said with exactitude is not said at all.

To speak with exactitude, however, is to go right up to what is said—to its end, to its beginning. It is to put the finger of what is being said on the limit of painting. As such, it means "to be quiet" or "to fall quiet," but in the exact sense in which keeping something quiet, *keeping quiet about it in painting*, is the same as saying it. Not saying it in another language, but saying it on the flip side of language. Not saying it, then, but saying everything, saying everything about it, admitting it unreservedly.

So painting, or what I am calling painting, would, from the outset, be what has slipped into writing, right up to its very limit, older than the very gesture that marks it out as such. It would be the water of writing, inky water, ink that is lost in its water, writing as the imperceptible limit of ink and water.

You have to say what you have to keep quiet. You have to say it right up to the point of imperceptibility, say it from within the imperceptible itself. And what, then, is this sense that we no longer sense? This sense that means nothing more than its own disappearance into evidence? You have to go on saying it right up to the limit, right up to its excess and to what falls blank, right up to the gray of what is said.

You have to agree to say everything because everything is said. Everything is said because everything is articulated from a "there is." But every "there is" is expressed from a blank or expresses a blank—gray-or-white. So far as everything that's thus said is concerned and hence so far as everything is concerned, the whole of what there is, there is no totality. Every "there is" is, each time, here and now, merely a particular instance of the whole, of every possible totality.

To agree or to consent: to sense with. To sense every time *with* that particular time. To stand on the threshold that separates that particular time from every other, the threshold that draws them together, that gives them a common measure. To agree to this way of being, to this *step* over the threshold. To put it somewhat differently: to agree to sense the imperceptible opening of existence, here and now.

*Translated by Simon Sparks*

# § 23   The Technique of the Present: On On Kawara

## I

Poetry, before being the name of a particular art, is the generic name of art.[1] *Techne poietike*: productive technique. This technique, this art, this calculated operation, this procedure, this artifice, produces something not with a view to something else or to a use, but with a view to its production alone, its exposition. The pro-duction of the thing brings it forth, presents and exposes it.

To expose is to move away from a simple position, which is always also a deposition, an abandonment to the contingency of a passing moment, circumstance, or point of view. What is exposed is placed under the order of absolute, immutable, and necessary presence. The word "poiesis" comes from a family that denotes ordering, arrangement, setting in position [*disposition*]. Poetry sets in position. Art is a setting in position. It sets the position of the thing according to the dictates of presence. It is technique productive of presence.

Presence is not a quality or a property of the thing. It is the act through which the thing is brought forth: *prae-est*. It is brought forth or brought before its nature as a thing, before everything that thrusts this nature into the world of its various connections: origins, relations, processes, finalities, becomings. The nature of the thing lies in its birth, as the word "nature" (*natura, nasci*) suggests, and in its unfolding within these relations. It draws its support from this movement alone, and its permanency lies in this very passing. And yet presence is the very thing that would seem to shelter the thing from any such passing. As such, it would shelter the thing from its thinghood or withdraw all thinghood from it—that is, the entire reality of the *res*—in the solitary putting forward, in this solitary advance.

This advance is that of the present. The present does not lie ahead in time since what lies ahead in relation to a past is immediately behind in relation to a future (unless the opposite is the case). In both senses, however, the present in time is nothing; it is pure time, the pure present of time, and hence its pure presence, the negativity of passing from "already no more" to "not yet," a ceaseless passing, a step untaken [*un pas non posé*], neither set up nor exposed, unexposable, merely and continually deposing all things.

The question raised by On Kawara is this: How can we expose what is unexposable? (In a sense, this is perhaps a question that the arts continually take up and pass among themselves: How can we grasp the ungraspable character of passing? How can we grasp the pure conjunction of passing and presence, of fleeing and stasis?)

The present of presence is not *in* time but ahead of time, before it. Either that, or it is inside it. Not caught in its flow but held within its core or its innermost recesses. It is pure time, time shielded from temporality, the space in which pure time opens out and is unexposed. Space does not represent time, like a line that would trace the immobile figure of a mobile process; rather, it opens time, distends it, distends the instant itself so as to set up this unpassing present that time itself is. Space is the origin of time, therefore, both its null point and the entire extension of its successive character. It is the opening of time, the simultaneity of its spacing.

On Kawara's art is a technique that produces this spacing. Spacing does not happen on its own. It is not of nature. In nature, there is only the passing of time. Time itself can be found only outside of nature. Outside of nature: in a technique, an art.

The spacing of time, or space opening time as such and as a whole, is before time, outside of time—in this "outside" that, far from being just another place (because outside all places), is the taking-place of place in general and of all such places. A place is always the curving back in or the gathering of a certain closure (with its accompanying thresholds and outlets) within absolute spacing—or, rather, a curving back in of this "within" itself. Hence, there can be no place for the pure spacing presupposed by every place. In the same way (and it amounts to much the same thing), there is no world in which the creation of the world could be said to have taken place. And so there is no place for creation. Creation does not take place. But what it is, or what it does, gives rise to every possible place and to every taking-place as such.

So how, despite all this, can we give rise to creation itself, or absolute spacing? How can time be taken out of time? What ruse, what detour, what skill is there that could be used?

On Kawara's art suggests one such technique for giving rise to spacing itself, for putting forward and exposing spacing itself in terms of the curve or contour of a place, its setting, and its local color.

The spacing of time does not present itself in time. Space-time does not open its creative nexus within time and space. In order for that to take place, there would have to be a technique: in short, a technique for re-creating the creation that has not taken place.

There has to be a technique, just as there has to be a technique for measuring the passing of time. Clocks and calendars put chronometric techniques to work. They measure the numerical order of time. What we have here, however, is a chronometry that measures time's spacing, its opening, a chronometry that overrides its yawning span. A chronomorphic poesy, let's say.

## II

On Kawara gathers the time of men, the measurers of time. A million years ago, a million years hence. Between the two, our space, the space where we are: us, here and now, *as well as* and *as* all those other heres and all those other nows, all moments and all places.

Two million years does not a history make. It is the entire span of history itself, along with its accompanying pre- and post-history. History in this sense, however, is neither the grandiose or confused movement of the destiny of peoples nor the monumental lumping together of culture and barbarity nor the adventure of events, but the simultaneous presence of each one of its millions of stories [*histoires*], present, presentified history. The Greek *historia* denotes the collection or recollection of facts. On Kawara sets up the recollection of humanity past and future, of humanity forgotten and humanity awaiting. In itself, this collection of a vast number of years is merely the logarithmic index of the enormous or monstrous number of all those who have passed and who will come to pass. The "million" is not a specific amount but the digit or code of the incommensurable in the guise of a common measure. All are present and correct, all those already past, all those not yet come, unnamed yet not anonymous, bound together in a single multiple collection: not "men" but representatives of the present.

Those who each time open space-time, those who, within nature, crack nature open, technicians of the present, makers of stelae, lyrics, and instants, all here, grasped in their striking absence, indistinguishable and unfigurable, artists, artisans, artificers.

There is nothing for us to read in this long collection, nothing about these individual histories, nothing but the exhaustive digits of a compendium that refers to no founding or revolutionary event, no feast or celebration. (Granted, it is the Western Christian calendar that is being used here; yet it serves as no more than a technical marker, its use signaling the technical dissolution of its particularly Western character, "B.C." and "A.D." having no sense other than as formal coordinates.) The only sense of solemnity here is the very idea of *formal solemnity*: what takes place each year, here, is the return of the year itself, identical and different, the solemn return of the annual.

The year presents the annular space of a cycle of life and death. Beyond this, there is no cycle, merely history, with its vast rhythmic irregularities; but even further beyond this, there is the simultaneous eternal present. There is nothing to distinguish one year from the next except a numerical difference, and nothing to present the perennial except the simultaneity, here and now, of each one of these differences. Their very sameness.

What can be read in this collection, therefore—and what *is* read, aloud, uttered by the alternating voices of a man and a woman, recorded and broadcast in the very gallery in which the work is placed—are the digits making up the number(s) of (the) years. The numbers have no real meaning. Rather, they constitute an order. What they allow us to read is the ordering of difference in identity, rather like the identity that underpins their being uttered in voices of different gender. This reading of the collection—this almost impossible reading that is nonetheless set up—is strictly ordered by its writing, by the reproduction of the traces of the digits one after another, one by one and side by side, in the heartbeat of the mechanical strokes. Poetry without letters or words, a poetry of cadenced regularity, digit by digit, moving from one line to the next as the number changes, line by line, caesura by caesura, a calculated discretion.

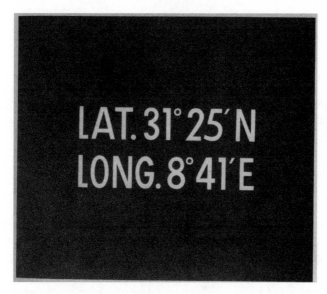

*Lat.31° 25'N, Long.8° 41'E*, by On Kawara.

## III

July 21, 1969: the date of the first moon landing. This is the date from which the timekeepers, the artists of time, open its cosmic spacing. From this point on, there is no longer a sublunary world of time and a superlunary world of pure presence. The moon is no longer the mark of the shared movement of the celestial spheres but itself merely one of the points from which the space of time opens out in all directions of the universe simultaneously, another one of those innumerable points where there is somewhere.

All art is cosmological, since the productive technique of spacing always produces the world, an ordering of the world, the world in part or as a whole, but always and each time the whole in each part. The world is only ever the infinite reference of each one of these points to all others, and what we call a work of art is, each time, a singular, monadic, and nomadic concretion of the cosmos.

On July 21, 1969, something happened in the history of painting and of poesy in general. From this point on, the skies are celestial no more. They are no longer the preserve of the light beyond all figures, nor the region of transfigurations. The skies are no longer the heavens, merely space, merely the night of space whose only possible figure is the date, *this* date, the arbitrary notation of its obscure opening up. The skies are neither ground nor form, but the universal spacing of spaces, of each point from all other points, of every opening from everything that is open.

By painting or painting over a particular space, therefore, a space identical to all spaces, a space that, as much as any other, at this moment, here and now, is the origin of all spacing, *July 21, 1969* paints the sky. Not man in space, therefore, but space in man.

## IV

What is at issue here, therefore, is the sacred, sacred painting. *Not*, however, in the sense of painting used in order to represent religious themes, but in the sense of what is properly sacred within painting itself—and, more generally, within any technique that re-produces the world. The sacred operation is a setting aside [*mise à part*], a setting apart [*mise à l'écart*] insofar as this act of partition [*écartement*] is the condition of relation or communication—or, more exactly, insofar as this break [*écart*] is the condition of the infinity of relation. (The sacred is nothing more than the ordinary condition of communication: its reserve, its threshold, its inaccessible access.)

Painting carves out a space—whence the most basic of all sacred gestures, the layout of the *templum*. The *templum* cuts out the heavens, Lucretius's *caeli lucida templa*, the *magnas caeli cavernas*.[2] The *templum* is an excavation of the heavens that defines both relations and nonrelations.

The triptych is a classical form or format of Western ecclesiastical painting. It is often placed above or before an altar. It can often be (and originally always could be) folded up and put away. It forms thus the articulation of a spacing, a space that can open onto or close around what can be seen either as part of that space or as belonging to another space altogether. It exposes the fold and the unfolding of space.

*Vietnam* is still the proper name of a time when the world had to learn a different sort of division than the one practiced by imperial domination. The principle of an empire lies outside space and time, a punctual and immobile power that extends indeterminably, virtually interminably. Empire crushes the distances over which it extends. It is a spreading rather than a spacing.

*Vietnam,* by On Kawara.

The dismantling of an empire is a dis-location that distinguishes between places. Here, Vietnam opens the present—1965—of a division of spaces that gives rise to relation. It is a matter of knowing how everything—every *one-thing,* the "one" and the "thing" inextricably linked—has its place, gives rise to its place, and places everything in equal relation to everything else.

A place is opened and delimited by the always-similar taking-place of an always-different event. Taking-place is nothing but the intersection of time by space—its opening. This opening is singular and each time produces its own *local* color—or, rather, places itself as local color. This is the topology of geographical maps. The color used here, the color of the *Vietnam* triptych, is "magenta" or "magenta red." This was the name of a battle during which an empire's troops were defeated. The battle was fought in 1859. In 1860, this deep crimson coloring was discovered and given the name of the murderous battle of the previous year. The color is the *datum* of a bloody stain.

Painting does not use colors. Rather, it produces the color of a place insofar as this place is the origin of a world. On the one hand, each place is independent of all places, every locality absolute; in that instant, it colors the totality of a world. On the other hand, however, a place is localized only by its relation to and separation from all other places. Its coordinates within the confines of the world order it.

The painting entitled *Location* paints the place of locality in general through its painting the coordinates of a particular place: Latitude 31°25' N, Longitude 8°41' E. Latitude is measured in relation to the equator, the greatest circle of the earth through the nonpolar axis. Longitude is measured in relation to an arbitrarily chosen meridian (arbitrary, at least, in the sense that the localization here is Western and, in the West, English, the imperial seat of geography) "Meridian" means "midday" or "division of the day." It is the line along which time (the particular hour) is the same from one pole of the Earth to the other. A place is the intersection of these two measures, according to space and according to time, the point at which each is shown to be devoid of all dimension, merely the crossing of two lines.

A point is nothing, nothing if not the simple exteriority of points in relation to one another. A point consists of nothing (has no "inside"); it is nothing but a relation to other points. There is no point in space, no point in time (as if such points were merely minute particles of either space or time); rather, space and time are the outside-one-another of punctuality itself. As such, puntiform space immediately opens the time that moves from one point to the next—and time opens space as the truth of its trajectory (the point that is already no longer one point and not yet another). The meeting of space and time: here-and-now.

This is in no way abstract: it is the concrete itself, what is present here as such. *Location* does not represent the coordinates of a particular point (a point, moreover, that can actually be found on a map and situated in the North African desert). It does not represent; rather, it gives these coordinates. It presents the truth of this point: its nonexistence outside of its relation to all the points of this painting *itself,* its concrete absolute. The point being pointed to here is held within a specific relation, one that can always be calculated, to the precise place where the painting itself is hung or placed. It is the concrete itself abstracted, that is, the concrete divested of everything that is not proper to it in its very concretion. Hard as a grain of sand.

(Let me just say a word or two about "conceptual art": On Kawara has often been called a conceptual artist. He himself refuses this epithet, which is, in fact, no more justified than most of these sorts of expressions: "abstract art," "minimalist art," and so on. If art can be conceptual, it is so in the sense that "to conceive" means to gather and contain within, to give rise, to give space and form to a presence. This being the case, however, art is always conceptual—and the concept itself should always end up being conceived as art.)

# V

Now this painting that brings out the spacing of time as such *also* brings out—exposes—what, precisely, *is not as such*. It is not possible to say *what* the spacing of time is, since it can be described only as negativity for itself.[3] Negativity cannot be posited *as* itself (since this would presuppose that it could be taken as something else, that it could fall under the heading of another sort of thing); negativity merely opens, it opens, excavates, or punctuates, falling under no heading, not even its own. Unexposable, absolute exposition.

The spacing of time is neither a mode of being nor an operation of or in being. It is what allows for there to be something (rather than nothing), whatever that something may be. The spacing of time, therefore, is a spacing prior to or outside of being. More exactly, it is the act of being—not in the sense of the action of a subject but in the sense of an act coextensive and cooriginary with being itself. So little is it "something," therefore, some particular thing, that not only is it *in* neither space nor time, it is neither space nor time; it is, so far as it is, more along the following lines: space and time are the names or the double name—space-time—for the necessarily double nature of what is essentially outside itself (whose essence lies in this outside-itself).

Space-time is the unity of what is outside itself in (or, rather, *outside* ...) its very unity. It is the opening of the world, creation—but creation without creator, otherwise space and time would be merely in God and thus in him lead back to a subsisting unity devoid of either space or time. Both space and time, or, rather, the space-time that they constitute, are the originary extroversion of what does not subsist in itself. Space is the condition for temporal movement [*passage*] and time the condition for spatial movement; the universal outside of the network of referrals that constitutes the inside of the world.

The present is the negation of this double movement or the pure grasping of movement as such, immobilized on itself in full flow: the instantaneous point and the punctual instant. The pure present is what is purely outside the world, much like the creation of the world, therefore. Outside the world, however, there is no outside of the world, neither the time nor the space of creation. Outside the world, there is the outside of the outside, the intimacy of the opening.

Poetic technique is geared toward presenting this present, toward "representing" it. Not, however, in the sense of a copying or a recopying, since there is nothing here that could be copied, but in the sense of a bringing forth, a putting forward. On Kawara's art—and perhaps this is true of all art—is geared toward bringing forth what remains buried, toward setting what is outside-the-world in the world.

With On Kawara, this technique is brought to bear in terms that might at first glance appear purely tautological: the date says only itself. And the tautology might well be multiplied with the apparent redundancy of several different canvases each painting the same day, each bearing the same date. In saying only itself, the date says nothing about itself. The only thing it says about itself is that *elle est peinte le jour même*. In French, we can say, with all the resources of ambiguity at our disposal, that *elle est peinte* du jour même: it paints the *day itself* or it paints the *same day*, it is painted on the *day itself* or it is painted on the *same day*.

It is thus and only thus, moreover, that the date speaks in painting, that it actually is (once again availing ourselves of the full ambiguity of the expression *le jour même*) the subject of (the) painting. It does not tell a story; it merely announces itself, puts itself forward. It is nothing other than a point in the vast network of all the world's dates—of all the dates that the world *is*. And this is why we do not read the date on the canvas. We do not interpret it. It does not tell a story. Rather, we only *hear* it. We hear a voice even though there is no recording this time to go alongside the plastic and graphic work; we hear a voice, a tone, or inflection before any recognizable word. We hear time ticking away [*le temps*]—we hear that it is the such and such of the month [*le tant*] (as in the way that we indicate a given date, the date in general, or the idea of the date: "the such and such of the month," "today's the such and such"), the *tantum quantum*, the quantity of time measured not in terms of its duration but in terms of its occurrence. Moreover, what we thus hear, before the canvas and coming from it, is not a foreign voice charged with reporting the date, with giving out information about it. Rather, it is ourselves that we hear saying the date: I see this canvas, and I utter its date, repeating thus what the canvas itself does. With the voice of a canvas, matte and flat against the wall, each one of us repeats that it's *such and such a date*.

Reference to events is not absent, if one looks to the canvas's protective box, itself occasionally exposed, and containing a single page from a newspaper from the date and place of the canvas's preparation. But the prop-

*2001 millions of years,* by On Kawara.

erly pictorial gesture consists precisely in separating the date from its use as an indication of dates and information. This tautological painting of the date makes the date what it is: a pure given, devoid of any other reference. "Date" comes from the expression *littera data, lettre donnée,* a letter signed and sealed on such and such a date. The date is the being-given of the given, or the given as such.

As such, the given is merely present: posed, deposed, be-ing-there, without past or future, without provenance or destination, without sender or recipient. The pure given as such itself suppresses the gift, reabsorbing the giving back into itself. As such, there is no longer any *given,* strictly speaking. "Date painting" effaces the date; it reinscribes it outside its giving, outside its dating. The date no longer dates; "date painting" eternalizes it. And this is why, moreover, this work indefinitely multiplies the date: the effacement is infinite since it is still a matter of the date on which the date is effaced. On the date of the painting, yes—the day itself, the same day—but also on the date of every re-exposition of the painting. Such is the logic of the present: at this precise moment, this moment effaces itself, and only thus is it a moment. The voice falls silent, sticks to the canvas, and thereby resonates. Only thus is its resonance painting. The instant is unstable. Only thus is it an instant. The present is a spacing in which presence is concealed or no longer supported, no longer given, posed, deposed, available as an object, as a thing. The present runs contrary to presence; it ruins it, supplants it, in the very movement by which it supports it.

The most that one can say is that presence is given, gives itself; it gives, is given and concealed; it gives itself and conceals itself through the very gesture of the present, through the very comings and goings of the present. But to give is precisely not to be given. To give, to give itself, is the act of a subject and might well be the exemplary act of the subject. What this presupposes, however, is that the subject draws itself from out of this side of itself in order to give itself over to what lies beyond it. In this gesture, the self absconds [se soustrait]. It is—if it can be said to "be"—nothing but the distance between this side and its beyond. This distancing "is" thus the self "itself," the present of the self and *not* its presence: the space that it needs in order to be itself, as much in order to achieve itself as to return to itself.

Here, the subject is the date. In other words, the subject of this painting is the subject. Absolutely. This has to be understood in the following way: here, the subject paints itself. Or even, if you prefer, like this: here, painting subjectivizes itself. These two propositions are correlative and reciprocal. Painting and subject are identified with one another and through one another.

(Allow me to say right away that this may or may not have anything to do with the individual subject On Kawara, with his concern or his certainty at being himself, with being a painter, with existing in general, etc. In this regard, all hypotheses are equally valid and so equally indifferent, at least regarding what is presented to us, namely painting and *not* an encounter with a particular person. It is not as if there is anyone present; here, there is nothing but the present of painting.)

The subject is present only as a painted subject. Painting can be present only as a painting of the subject. Painting is as much what presents (or what gives) the subject as the subject is what presents (or gives) painting. The present can be as such only in the spacing of the present, that is, of time itself.

# VI

Four principle traits of the various "date paintings" allow us to verify this group of interrelated propositions:

1. The act of painting itself, pigment or paste carefully brushed over, smoothed to the point of pure smoothness without ever banishing the brush strokes, confirming that the ground has indeed been covered over, bringing the ground forward as if it were surfacing, the presentation of a ground, the side of a corner in which the ground *opens the eye*: it opens itself like an eye that looks at us by opening our eyes to it. What can be seen, therefore, is painting emptied through the present of its own execution. I am painting the date on which I paint. As if each painting here were the magnification of the corners of the painting in which the painter paints the date on which the painting was completed. Equally, though, it is as if the date itself were a denuded ground, a ground that would have to be painted. To paint, in this sense, is first and foremost to affirm a surface. Why paint the walls of a room? Certainly not because this will make them look nice, but because, without paint, the walls disappear, melting into a groundless background, taking the dwelling with them. Now, there has to be a dwelling: journey, lateness, remnance, repose, and even reserve, delay. The present held back against the precipitation of time, the present drawn back from time, spaced.

2. The color of the painting, its surface vibration: the trembling, the shaking, the shudder, the quiver, or the rustle of the present, the noise and the brush of its restraint. The numbers and letters of the date are painted in white. White is color beyond colors, the color of their being present at the same time, something that also marks their disappearance, leaving behind nothing but the color of pure simultaneity.

Fundamentally, though, the ground (or the surface emptied by the date) is what is designated here by the date (what it both designates and dates, what it designates by dating), and the ground that provides thus the referent of the date, its thing, its substance, its *datum*, is a color. Precisely which color varies: navy or sky blue, green, chestnut brown or dark gray, sometimes cadmium red, the tendency always toward darker colors. Yet this darkness, this somber mood, is not a move toward obscurity; day is never wiped out by the "real blackness" of night. There is no "blackout,"[4] merely gradation, relation, and difference, coloration, flesh, complexion (*chroma* comes from *chros*, the surface of the body, skin, flesh), the emergence of a nuance, the perceptible break of an imperceptible distinction, a distinction grasped at the very moment of its detachment, of its separation at the heart of a limited but indefinitely multipliable specter. When we speak of an "imperceptible" gradation it means that we have neither felt nor grasped the passing moment, the present of the leap from one moment to the other. Each canvas, each size and color, detaches itself from all the others, opening between them a series, a rhythm, and a syncopation of presents. Difference in the identity of presents.

3. The calculation of *mimesis* or the fiction of presentation. The presence of the presence has thus to be constructed, fabricated, composed, modeled, and thus forged. The fact that this poiesis is going to grasp the ungraspable is essential. So, the painted date is immediately destabilized; it is as forged as it is true. Its veracity (the date of the day on which it was painted) has no other attestation than itself, since the painting could well have been painted on another date. Likewise, its truth (the actual day of the actual date of the actual day on which it was painted) is lost from the moment that this day and, with it, the act of painting, is over. Come midnight, this truth is no longer current, yet the painting is now ready to expose it. But this is how it becomes a truth: by conserving itself across time, the immobile repeated present of a bygone present. By exposing itself as this date—this datum, this given—it exposes the fact that the given conceals the gift absolutely. But this concealed gift is what gives itself again each time, each time there is an exposition; withdrawn into its pretence, it gives itself again. Each date announces: I am a present that has passed as the present that it speaks and that, by saying it, perhaps only pretends to have been, but that is still incontestably present as this saying and this pretence.

This is exactly what Descartes says, another great fiction writer at the pinnacle of his pretence, when he states: *ego sum, ego existo.* The certainty of the *ego sum* is coextensive with the time of its utterance (or of its being thought). Outside of this present, my being or my existence can be only a fiction. But this present is endlessly repeated, never ceasing to happen. In this instance, the certainty of the date is coextensive with its exposition. It names, from the outset, my certainty as a spectator: the fact that I see this date and that I am myself, here and now, its truth. I am not standing before an old calendar. Rather, I stand before the repetition in the present of the present of this date. I am the present of each date. "Today," the title of the series, is each time the today of the exposition.

4. The exposition as such: the position before, there before, over there before us. The date is sheltered from the passage of time and from its referential function. It coordinates nothing, allows for no situation of an act within a successive series. It exposes the simultaneity of an act with itself. "I am painting this painting," On Kawara writes on January 18, 1966. And ten days later: "I am dating here."[5]

But a date, in English, is also a meeting or an encounter. And "to date" can mean "to go out to meet" or "to encounter." The date marks the possibility of the encounter, counts it or en-counters it, as it were, indicating the place or the point orchestrated by the punctuality of such an en-countering. Here, the place is here. That is, anywhere whatsoever; anywhere that "I am dating here," that is, anywhere that a "date painting" can be shown, On Kawara is open to encounters anytime, anywhere, en-countering the "encounter" itself. The painting states: find me where I find myself, where I am, and we will meet there. You will recognize me by the fact that I am there only for the date. And I will recognize you in the same way. We will be there, you and I, simply in order to find ourselves there, simply in order to be there. (And in much the same way, a museum or a gallery is a place made to be a place.) To find ourselves there can mean both to be there *and* to find one another there, to find ourselves there. We will find ourselves through one another. Something to see that finds itself there only in order to be seen and someone to see who finds him or herself there only in order to see, for his or her look, his or her look toward the visible. This is the en-counter between seeing and vision. The en-counter between sight and its ability to have regard for its own opening, for its own wide-eyed stare, for its own ideality, then, the very form of seeing.

The form of seeing is the opening of the eye and, in it, the dilation out of the pupil. This dilation adjusts itself to the light, which allows the present of a form and its color to penetrate the opening—into this mute little mouth that opens at the very center of the iris. No form without color, no color without form. The unity of form and color marks the present of vision. Vision sees the present, but only because the present opens the eye, setting up its presentation.

The present is this setting up that exposes the thing to its vision. That is, to its desire to be open to itself. To see and to know are one and the same thing. Sanskrit *véda*, Greek *oida*, German *Wissen*. Something that is seen and known is something that is not left to its opaque thickness.

Rather, it is the thing cut through by the present that it distances from it-self, by the plane that colors and exhibits it.

It is the thing *as* this thing. The thing en-countering itself. My look is just such an en-counter. It is not the representation of the thing, and I am not the subject of a representation or of an intention (for me, in me, ab-sorbed by me, consummated, appropriated, *fulfilled*). I am the staring pre-sent of the presentation. I am the place of the en-counter. That is all that I am, and "I"—*ego*—means nothing more than this. The spacing of a point that is not the space between two points. A single, distended point: not the infinite divisibility of space but the division of the indivisible product of all division. The nondimension as distension. No intentional-ity. But the precise date of the end of all intentions, short of anything in-tended. Poetry is the technique productive of this end. For this is what we want each time to feel, this end, this overflowing of the present into any presence whatsoever. That is what we strive to create, behind the vast and perpetual flow of presence. But where, behind what, and when? There, where time opens.

*Translated by Simon Sparks*

# § 24  The Soun-Gui Experience

Soun-Gui Kim experiences the matter of time and the time of matter. She experiences [*elle expérimente*]:[1] that means she enters into things, crosses them from one side [*bord*] to the other. She moves completely from one side of things to the other. These sides are themselves varied: in front of and behind, left and right, before and after, yesterday and tomorrow, shore to shore, wall to wall, continent to continent, east to west or north to south, East to West. But these sides also form complex borders [*bords*], borders that are themselves variously woven out of these sides, these confines or extremes, mingled among those sides whose differences and crisscrossings they have also to cross, to the point of utter confusion. Equally, however, there may be only a single side, one that crosses all these limits, following and merging each one of their traces into a solitary surface like the intricate folds of a skein, involved with and unfolding into one another at one and the same time.

This "at one and the same time" is the very matter of time, what time comprises. Time comprises a two-way journey, backs and forths, comings and goings, goings and comings; equally, however, it comprises broken journeys, goings that no longer come back but keep on going to infinity, journeys that double back on themselves in a loop that is no less infinite, albeit in a different sort of a way. It comprises all the advances and withdrawals, the starts and renewals, the continuous flows and sudden splutters, the jumps, gaits, speeds, and rhythms of its movement. Through all this, it is time *itself*, utterly singular, always the same. Yet this "same" is nothing but the continual movement and change of all times at all times.

And always there is this movement, this transport, passage, transfer, overstepping, journey, trajectory, displacement. All this has to be undergone. Experience always involves a crossing, a crossing right over to the other side, a crossing that reaches the limit; and this crossing is a crossing of crossing itself, of the raw matter that constitutes the crossing of time. Time, then, is crossed. But how? Since time is what is properly endless [*sans fin*]—or, more exactly, what always ends [*qui a sa fin en chaque instant*]—it has to be slipped through, followed from one end to the other [*de bord en bord*]. This is the experience of the *always*.

~

"Always" really means "all the time." For one who is the subject of experience there is always going to be a displacement. Indeed, that subject of experience is itself a displacement and nothing more, always merging with it. Only thus can there be an experience, since no one who simply stands and watches, immobile before his or her experience as if before an object, can actually experience anything. We have to go through with experience or there will be no such thing.

(And this is why we, those of us who undergo the Soun-Gui experience or who speak of just such an experience, ought neither simply to look nor to talk nor even to think. Rather, we need ourselves to experience that experience, to embark on her crossing, without knowing to what shores, if any, we are headed. What we call "art" or "artistic practice" means first and foremost the setting to work of an experiential matter. Before being a matter of "aesthetic judgment," of beauty, of the sublime, or simply of form and sensibility, it is a matter of experience: art articulates experience. We have to allow ourselves to be articulated by it, an articulation that no doubt always involves a disarticulation. We have to remain flexible, even fragile; neither sense nor truth is in any way spoken for in advance, for discourse, too, is something that has to be crossed and transported to ends other than those of discourse. This, moreover, is how "art" begins: by giving discourse a leave of absence. Art does not explicate; it exposes.)

To undergo an experience is, then, to *be* experience. Were this not the case, we would never *undergo* anything but instead merely represent it, imagine it, talk about it. Soun-Gui Kim is the experience being discussed here under her name. In this instance, she is not an individual; no, she is the very persona of her experience. Which is why, from this point on, I shall want to speak of "experience" in order to name Soun-Gui Kim herself: the Soun-Gui experience, an experience that is the experience of the time of matter and of the matter of time.

~

Is this experience of the time of matter and the matter of time one and the same? Is it a single experience? And so is there just one crossing? Just one subject?

In a sense, yes. The time of matter is nothing other than what it is, its own substance or its own time. What is at issue, then, is the matter of the time of matter in general. Are both matters the same? Could two different matters ever be imagined? Doesn't matter designate the unity of world, where everything else would be merely different ways of crossing it, immaterial crossings of matter?

Matter "in general" is precisely not a generality or an abstraction of matter, something distinct from particular instances of matter, since the materiality of matter lies in determined particularity, in the singular consistency of all things and so of each one of those things that are singularly experienced one after another: the durability, the resistance, the equipmentality, texture, mixture, thickness, immanence of things insofar as they are things and so insofar as each one is a *particular* thing and not another. Something that is not a thing is precisely nothing at all, and what is not a *particular* thing has to be something *else*.

Experience is also a thing, or it is nothing. So, too, the words that we use to speak of it, the sense of these words, even the understanding or misunderstanding of these senses: all these are things. And so, too, the understanding of experience, the experience of understanding or of misunderstanding in which experience consists. Experience does not lead us to what is usually termed an "idea" or a "view of things." In one sense it is, no doubt, a matter of "seeing." But the view of things is itself a thing (whereas the "vision" or "notion" spoken of by philosophers and theoreticians tends to be merely a look thrown over things by a "subject," a nonthing that never undertakes the real movement through the density of things but instead skirts over them). In much the same way as the move through matter, vision is itself a thing held by matter. Held: both trapped by the impenetrability of matter *and* woven into its very fiber, squeezed from each of its movements, oozing from its every flow. Experience, what

I am here calling a movement or a journey, is matter that moves through itself, from one side to the other. And yet this, in truth, is already time itself.

~

If there is no other matter than matter as such—and here "matter" means both the unity of the world and that any "other world," assuming there is such a thing (even though there isn't), is still of this world, made of the same matter—the particular matter of time is necessarily part of matter "in general" (which, as I have already said, does not exist as such). It is that part of matter constituted by matter's movement through itself. It is that part of the return through which material density moves all the way back through itself. An immaterial return, the internal torsion from which matter is made up, through which it presents itself.

It is not a particular part of matter in the sense of being an atom, therefore. Rather, it is how every atom (every lump, bubble, mass, piece, shard, thing, call it what you will) becomes matter as such. How a particular piece of matter is made up, how it comes to be, how it comes into being. Not whence it comes, of course (since it comes from nowhere but from matter as such), but how its own particular coming or its own particular happening comes into play, how it folds and unfolds in its singular event. This, then, is the matter of time: the time of matter's coming, how matter comes to itself, how a matter is connected to and folded into itself, how it bodies forth.

In a sense, it would be the matter of matter, its active substance. If there were no time in which matter might be folded and connected, composed and gathered, opened and set inside out—and could we ever imagine such a thing?—matter would not materialize. It would remain outside itself, distinct pieces wholly separated from one another—pieces that could not even be termed "pieces" since there would be nothing other than their pure dispersal, without either beginning or end. What there would be, therefore, is a space, pure and simple. Yet this space would not even be a space; it would space nothing, lie between nothing and nothing, space nothing, hold nothing. It would not space any end or any movement toward such an end. There would be neither passage nor movement. Once there is space, once there is a *there is* (of things that take place and so make space), once there is some extension from one point to another, an extension that extends across and slides along a distance, then there is also time. Once there is space there is time; the distinction between the two is untenable.

Time is matter that spaces. Time is what is meant by the "to" of the phrase "from one point *to* another." This "to" means "up to" [*jusqu'à*], it means the movement or the passage from one point to another, from one side or from one end to another, involved in every opening of matter. Once there is a body—a grain of sand, a large rock, whatever—that body extends from one end of its extension to the other. However quick this passage may be, it still takes time.

It takes time to open and to cross space, space being what is opened in order for things happen (which is not to say that such things happen after space itself happens; rather, they are the opening of space itself). It has to take time for space to be opened. Time is what space takes from itself— from its pure immanence—in order for it to take its distance from itself and thus to take place.

It takes time for there to be anything. It always takes time, whether a nanosecond or billions of light years, a ten-minute wait or an eighteen-hour flight, the beat of a butterfly's wings or the three-day thaw of a block of ice.[2] In each case, there has to be a suspension, a "not yet" to be followed by an "already there," an "already there" that we will never have seen coming even though we were there while it did. The point here is that it is *not* a matter of "past" and "future." Such categories are relevant only to time already interpreted as social and historical. What I am concerned with here is a far more subtle conception of time; of the time of the present as it presents itself, always not yet and always already there; of time flowing like the slow thaw of the block of ice, its imperceptible yet unrelenting deformation that takes hold from the moment that the ice comes into contact with a space that is not ice: the setting in motion of a difference, without which there would be no possibility of distinction.

It takes time for things to present themselves as they are, that is, for things to be experienced, undergone, crossed from one side to the other, from their first to their final possibility. The thing, like a country, has its borders, its frontiers, its passes, its straits, its roadways, and its waterways, its valleys and its plains, its islands, its clouds.

～

But if it does indeed take time, from where should this time be taken? It is with this question alone, no doubt, that the experience of the matter of time really begins.

From where should time be taken if nothing, no thing, is given in advance of it? "Before" time would imply another time, that is, the same time already there. But before time there can be only the absence of any "before" and any "after." There can be no before and no after from which time could actually be taken.

Time is taken from nothing. It *is* nothing, and it is made from nothing. Time is "nothing" set at the heart of the thing in order for it to be able to cross itself. It is the "nothing" of presence at the heart or at the core of the fullness of the thing.

Which is why, moreover, the matter of time is neither a particular matter nor something other than matter. It is nothing other than matter coming to itself: matter to [*jusqu'à*] matter, thing to [*jusqu'à*] thing.

Time is taken from the nothing of the *up to* [*le* jusqu'à].

~

By "up to" I mean up to the other side, the other shore, the other country, the other extreme, and, more generally, up to the other pieces that are needed in order to make up a thing. From the East to the West and back to the East, for example, precisely what is needed in order for there to be a world.

There is no "world" in the sense of a vast, indistinct mass, immediately self-present, its ends seamlessly touching one another at the heart of its immanent mass, without place or direction. Were this to be the case there would be neither "space" nor "time" and so no reason for this dead matter (but we couldn't even call it dead; it would be more raw and brute) to step outside itself and come to "itself." There would be no reason for there to be a *world*.

If there is a world, then there is also a reason. But the reason in question ought not to be sought outside the world; rather, it needs to be seen as lying in the elevation of the world itself, its coming, the way in which mass (thing, matter, what there is, call it what you will) relates to itself, goes all the way to its extremities, is drawn toward itself in the same way that the atoms of a stone are drawn among themselves toward the extremity that the stone, a stone, this stone, is. Space-time is the force that draws world to itself, that opens it, breaks it open, and makes it catch hold.

In short: "world" is not an object. Rather, it is the subject of experience. Everything is oriented and occidented in a particular way; from which it follows that everything has its "all the way to" from one point to the next. In the same way, world extends from a grain of sand all the way to the cosmos, and from there it extends all the way to a village and to a lock of hair and to the very words that I am writing and that appear ... now on my computer screen: *time*. Each time is another coming or another going, another self-relation, another connection, another movement. In a sense, though, this movement is nothing. It is none of these things; rather, it is the *coming* of the thing. The thing has to come; it has to happen [*il faut que ça se passe*]; otherwise there would be nothing. And it does happen: the world keeps on opening. It did not begin "one fine day." It is always the infinite opening of time and space.

$\sim$

It is important that we don't confuse *ça passe* with *ça se passe*, "it passes by" with "it happens" or "it comes to pass."

"It passes by" refers to the thing in time: it comes and goes; it is still to come, or it is past [*passé*]; it steps outside time or disappears into it, all the while leaving time intact, like a vast, soft, empty shell. With things that come and go, we have no experience of time.

"It happens" refers to time itself. It refers to time within the thing itself: it happens within the subject, the self, the intimacy of things. Time does not pass. It is always here. No, time *is* passage. It is the "it happens." Its "always" is not immovable and its "there" is not a place. Its permanence

(and here, at this very moment and at this very fleeting of the moment itself, it is happening to your very reading, the way sense happens in the move from one letter to the next or from one word to the next, the way it happens to make sense and, in turn, the way sense happens to make sense in your head or somewhere else, and so it is also happening in all directions at the same moment)

its permanence is that of the *nothing* that is hollowed out and turned back on itself in order to become another nothing: a nothingness that is continually shifting while still remaining the nothingness that it is. As such, its place is nowhere, and that is also to say everywhere, every piece of the thing altering and never staying the same. But this nothingness drawn all the way to the other side of the thing is the force that lies behind the thing or the world.

This is neither the thawing of ice nor the falling of the drop, neither the sound of the drop oscillating in my ear nor the vapor that it exhales impalpably into the air, neither the plane flying from Seoul to Paris nor the artist walking inside this plane nor the line drawn by the artist in order to represent her return flight as an 8-shaped loop that, if turned on its side— ∞ —would resemble the mathematical sign for infinity, but what happens from one to the next, what happens incessantly between them. What happens, what never stops happening, is time, whose self-identity lies in its passing from itself to itself. It continually passes beyond itself or surpasses itself, all the while remaining within itself. Time properly is this infinite departure from itself. Its "itself" is nothing but this always-becoming-something-other-than-itself. Its self-presence, its constancy or its consistency, is this renewed absence, drawn always toward itself. This is what has to be experienced, and this is why there has to be an art, an artifice, and a simulation, an invention and installation, a manipulation, a decomposition and interweaving, a tension and a rhythm.

This opening of absence is the hollow opened for all presence—and that is also to say, at the heart of all presence. At the heart in the hollow of all such presence, with the opening of presence itself, there is time, a spacing of time.

Rather than a lack of presence, it is an excess of presence. It hollows out the space of a self-overflowing in which all presence comes to presence and presents itself.

Such is the secret of presence: it is not simply present but comes into presence, comes to presence, and comes thus to itself. Anything purely present, anything that is neither coming nor going, would not be; it would instantly crumble into dust. Presence, however, is always in the process of coming, of coming to itself and befalling itself. It rises up from its own depths to breach its surface and emerges from its surface toward the depths of other presences: their eyes, their ears, their skin.

～

And so there are images. The images are not actually copies; before anything else, they are outbursts, explosions, or outpourings of presence. They are presences that come fully charged with the time of their own presentation: rising up, taut, vibrant with the tension through which they give themselves to be seen.

In this sense, then, the image is not a matter of beauty. Rather, it is a matter of a certain tension in the look. An image draws the look, draws it in. This tension of the image is time. In time, I come before what is coming; I come right up to a thing that comes up to itself. I come, in other words, right up to the coming of the thing. What we call an "artist's work" is nothing other than the organization of this experience.

In art, an image is not a representation. It does not show something—its form, figure, and color—but shows that there is this thing. It shows the presence of the thing, its coming to presence. In truth, it is the image that brings the thing forth.

Soun-Gui's images are always images that come and go; the images on her video monitors are often frozen images of monitors that melt away as soon as they appear exposed. These images do not "reproduce." Or, rather, what they "reproduce" (a singer, an astronaut, a frog, John Cage's head) is raised not as something that has been "reproduced" (copied, imitated) but as something produced: the imitation imitates the novelty of the original. It does not "imitate" it but re-produces it.

As such, these images always have something of the beginning about them. A certain arising or emergence, a certain tension of time. In them, the thing arises (as we say of a sun or the dawn of a particular day). The thing leaves the night behind or, more accurately, is itself the night leaving itself behind, tearing itself apart or unshackling itself, transformed by the forming of its utter absence of any form, coloring its groundless darkness (a glassy and groundless darkness, the darkness of the video screen), and its division into slivers and surfaces, shards and folds.

What comes thus into view with a single stroke (for every image is a single stroke, a single line, shape, color, shadow, and volume) is the unimaginable aspect of presence: its time, the taut instant of its advent, its inauguration. An after that is not preceded by a before. A now that is not immobilized but instead wholly mobilized by this tension, by this offering of itself to a possible seeing, to another movement of coming, to a reciprocal tension of the eye that wants to imagine or to fill itself with images, to leave behind its crystalline night.

Discourse is always behind and before itself. If I talk, I presuppose that I have already done so, and presuppose, too, the infinite course of words in this and all other languages, the whole gamut and connection of significations. Yet a scream, song, or picture presupposes nothing and connects

Artwork by Soun-gui Kim.

to nothing. More accurately: they presuppose the abyss or the night from which they come and which they carry within themselves, with which they are filled, and which they overflow.

~

    The experience of time, as the experience of our time, as a contemporary experience, is the experience of the absence of myths. In myth, song or the image configures the chaos or shadow of the origin. Through such a configuration, the origin is sheltered from its own emergence, withdrawn from its being wrenched out; it is pacified, set down, and given over to a time of immobility that merely recounts the violent time of beginnings. Here, however, we have no such stories [*récit*]—we who are contemporaries of those across the whole extension of the world, from East to West, we who are no longer able to distinguish between these sides or directions.

    We are without story or, rather, without an infinite story of the finite being that has replaced the finite story of the infinite being. But an infinite narrative is no longer a narrative.

We have to absorb the full shock of the time of beginning, a time that is also that of infinite end, a time that no story has yet been able to tame, figure, or represent. "We are born out of nothing and return to it at every moment," Soun-Gui Kim once wrote. This "we" is us today, contemporaries of the world that has become the world (and no longer the earth, neither nature nor creation nor cosmos). A jolt of nothing is continually shaking us. This is the time of presence leaping ahead of itself, an always-new image, always ready to fade away; nothing imaginary but, quite the contrary, the unimaginable real. This is the time of inaudible songs that go unheard and of unimaginable images: the time in which art has unreservedly to be the technique of emergence.

The origin is no longer the object of a question that comes to be answered by way of a story. Rather, it is a matter of an experience and of an eternal return. It comes back or returns to us at each moment, and we to it, the origin of the instant itself.

Soun-Gui Kim is fond of telling a story that she learned when she was a child. An old man on a journey has to pass over the "three-year hill." Whoever falls when climbing the hill has only three years to live. The old man falls. He bemoans. Yet a young boy instructs him to fall over and over again, thus indefinitely increasing his life by three years.

Neither the origin immobilized from its very origin—like a block of ice sheltered from heat, like a view fixed in every gaze, or like a cybernetic program devoid of any uncertainty—nor the origin thrown recklessly into the flow of becoming. Neither the eternal nor the incessant, but something that is neither: time itself, the tension of originary time. Death opening onto the eternal return of birth: this is what is hardest to think, an experience that goes all the way and that can no longer even show itself as an "experience." Yet "art" "speaks" of nothing else.

∼

Either the origin is given, already there, already set up and recounted: this stone, for example, is a god or what surrounds him or his power; either it is given, then, or it is not. In which case either the stone is just a stone—a mineral aggregate—or it has to open onto the origin, and its own access to itself has to be sought in the stone.

Either way, there has to be a means of access or a technique. We have to know how to find a tension, an elasticity, a spark, a blow, a grain of salt within the rock. We have to know how to make this rock into (a) work.

To us, "a work of art" means not something "beautiful" but "something placed under the tension of an originary time." An open thing, set apart from itself and from what is given in general. A thing returned to what is not a state but a surprise, a bound, an explosion. A thing worked by a technique of opening that refers it back to the emergence of the origin. A technique of the eternal return of inaugural time.

In truth, we can no longer really call this a "work of art." It is not by chance that this expression has, so far as contemporary art is concerned, fallen out of the realm of art (it refers to what is purely decorative and to the art market). We speak of an artist's "work" as if we could designate both the work of art and its operation, the active permanence in the work of the technical *doing* [*le* faire] that opens up a way to originary time. A "work of art" is constantly at work. It constantly opens itself anew, constantly emerges, like a fountain whose hidden pump recycles its water in order for it to flow once again from its mouth or its lips.

In this way, the Soun-Gui experience is also the experience of the move through art itself, through this singular machinery that we call "art" and its modern history: a move from one side to the other, from one side right up to the point at which the "artist" makes no longer a "work of art" but something else entirely, something that still needs to be named, if it is to be named at all. This experience, which is the experience of contemporary art as a whole, is brought out by Soun-Gui as an experience of a certain fading away. Her time is, each time, the time of a dissolution, of a disappearance, of an effacement or blurring. Of a tightening of the angle or a focusing of the lens, of a sliding to the side, offscreen, or into the numerical decomposition within the video screen or within the image itself. Maps fall into shadow, photographs become blurred, screens fade, sounds die away, the image evaporates, the frog hops off ...

∽

The return of or to the origin is, of course, impossible; it is impossibility itself. Death can lead to a prenatal place only by leading us into nothing. But all this means is that what is at stake in the work of art (or what is obscurely in question with this term that is so overloaded, so eroded, exhausted with a whole heap of significations) is nothing other than a technique, or techniques, of gaining access to the impossible.

But the impossible is not arrived at in the same way that we would arrive at a place. First of all because it is the impossible, then because it is not in a place, not even in a place out of this world (since all places are essentially worldly, up to and including the outer reaches of the galaxies). It is where we are, here and now. It is a matter of reaching the proper tension of the here-and-now.

Here and now the proper tension of our time—our tension, what stretches us and raises us up, what sometimes exasperates us and exhausts us, sometimes sends the blood pounding through our veins—is the tension of the measureless infinite. Nothing forces this time under the measure of a defined rhythm. Neither gods nor heroes nor visions of the world or of destiny have been set (in) to (a) work. On the contrary, the singular style that carries us away is that of the retreat of all such figures. There is no longer any form to protect us a priori from the formlessness of the impossible or to bring us closer to it.

But this is the very experience of time. It is our territory, the voyage that demands that we go beyond every territory, demands that we begin our journey from the very point at which we thought it should be over.

*Translated by Simon Sparks*

# § 25 The Look of the Portrait

> How passionate had been our desire for thought, if it had granted us
> so clear an image of itself to look upon.
> —Plato, *Phaedrus* 250d

## The Autonomous Portrait

> The only words of Rembrandt's that we know are these: *I have done
> nothing but portraits.*
> —Matisse, *Écrits et propos sur l'art*

A portrait, according to the standard definition or description, is the representation of a person considered for him- or herself. This definition is as correct as it is straightforward. All the same, it is far from being sufficient. It defines a function or a finality, that of representing a person for him- or herself and *not* for his or her attributes or attributions, for his or her actions or for the relations in which he or she may or may not be involved. The object of the portrait is, in the strictest sense, the *absolute* subject: the subject detached from everything that does not belong to it, withdrawn from all exteriority.

(Ultimately, the question that I shall want to ask here will be nothing other than this: What is it to paint the absolute? And so: What is absolute painting?)

Clearly, however, any such finality is going to demand a whole range of clarifications. What do we mean by "person" (individual, subject, particular, *quidam*, "someone," whatever name we choose)? And what do we mean when we speak of a person "for itself," as neither character nor personality, but *for itself* without extension or restriction? As we can see, the very design of painting a portrait involves all these sorts of questions, the entire philosophy of the subject.

What is equally clear, however, is that any such definition, which addresses only the object of the portrait (of its *subject*), ignores the work that the portrait ought to be, the technique or the *art* that ought to allow for the working out of its design.[1] In view of this, then, another definition needs to be added: "The portrait is a painting organized around a figure."[2] Yet we still need to clarify precisely how such an "organization around" is able to lead properly—organically—to a "figure" that is not simply the center of attention but also understood as that of a subject being considered for itself. (To take a well-known example, Watteau's *Indifferent* is organized around a figure without actually being a portrait; at least that is what its title would suggest). The concern here, therefore, should really be with the properly pictorial marks imposed or raised by this sort of compositional design, with the traits proper to the portrait and with that of which such traits treat in painting, with what they draw from it and put on display.

The parallel between these two definitions mirrors in large part the genre of painting itself. A painting is organized around a figure insofar as this figure is itself the real end or goal of representation to the exclusion of any other stage [*représentation*] or scene, any other representational stake or value, any other evocation or signification.[3] The true portrait, then, is what art historians have tended to place within the category of the "autonomous portrait," in which the character being represented neither is caught up in any action nor bears any expression that might otherwise divert attention from his or her person. Perhaps we could say that the autonomous portrait should be the impression of—and should give the impression of being—a subject without expression.

So far as action is concerned, there is, no doubt, only one sort that is in any way admissible here: the action of painting itself, which often appears in self-portraits and sometimes in portraits of one painter by another.[4] In fact, the action of painting is one whose representation constitutes both a turning back in and a doubling of the *subject* of the painting.

As such, the portrait does not constitute simply a revelation of an identity or a "me."[5] No doubt this is always what is being *sought*, the overriding end of imitation comprising thus a revelation (an unveiling that would draw the *me* from out of the painting, something, then, that we might term an "uncanvassing"). And yet this can only ever be the case— if it ever *can* be the case, and it is precisely this faculty and this possibility that are at stake here—on the condition that it brings to light the struc-

ture of the subject: its sub-jectivity, its being-under-itself, its being-within-
and so its being-outside-, behind-, or before-itself. On the condition,
then, of its ex-position. The "unveiling" of a "me" can take place only by
acting on this exposition, putting it to work, as it were. To paint or to figure is no longer to reproduce, therefore, not even to reveal, but to produce the *exposition of the subject.* To pro-duce it: to bring it forth, to draw
it out.

The figure being portrayed ought to organize the painting, therefore,
not only in terms of balance, lines of force, or color values, but also in
such a way that the painting is absorbed into it and completed by it. What
surrounds the figure—if, indeed, it is surrounded by anything—ought to
be strictly subordinate to its pure and simple position for itself. A *self* in
and *for* itself: such is the exclusive concern of the portrait. As is well-
known, moreover, this is the exclusive concern of thinking from Descartes
(or from Augustine) right up to today (or until tomorrow). The extent to
which these two concerns are in fact *the same* is precisely what is being
asked here. Once again.[6]

It might well be, indeed it might legitimately *have* to be, that there is
nothing surrounding the figure and that the "organization" of the painting tends toward the straightforward detachment of this figure from a
monochrome ground [*fond*], which largely equates to an absence of
ground. This sort of situation is not exactly uncommon, although it is certainly never frequent. The face can emerge from the shadows but, within
a particular setting, it can also bring to the fore that aspect of shadow that
lies at the center of the look; in each case, the stakes are *visibly* the relation
between a boundary and an opening, between an orbit and a hole. Something revolves around this look. It is not enough that the painting orga-
nizes itself around a figure; this figure must itself be organized around its
look—around its vision or its clairvoyance. What does it see? What does
it have to see? What does it have to look at? Such is the central question
of my remarks here.

And yet the figure has to be detached or isolated in such a way that it
does not consume the entire canvas if the contours of the face are not to
be dissipated and the gaze turned inward, something rather different from
painting's purpose.[7] So, the figure, the whole figure and nothing but the
figure, since it is the figure as a whole and not the eye in isolation that effects the look.

Of course, there is nothing to prevent the portrait from showing the rest of the body so long as its sole function is to carry the face, so long as it remains, in short, in reserve, a resource on which the look can draw. The body is most often reduced to its upper part, with or without the hands (which doubtless have their part to play in the organization of the subject) and, except on very rare occasions, to the line formed by the shoulders. What this glimpse of the clothes tells us is that the body is not naked. Indeed, a face that hinted in that direction would displace the entire intention of the portrait. Whatever the link between a naked body and the face, nudity involves stakes that are not, or not exclusively, those of the subject, not of the "person" but of nudity for itself (albeit the nudity of the person).[8] Indeed, we could perhaps go so far as to say that the portrait marks a break with nudity (without repressing it) since it exposes another sort of nudity altogether, that of the subject.[9]

Of course, it is always possible for there to be more than one figure or for this figure to be plural. Giorgione is known for being one of the inventors and masters of the so-called "double" or "triple" portrait, and there are, in one or two very rare cases, portraits with as many as six or seven figures, occasionally even more.[10] What is most remarkable, however, is that the characteristic of a plural portrait is always the mutual avoidance of looks; the looks neither meet nor seek one another out. The characters are devoid of relation. Their common presence in the painting instead constitutes a sort of diffuseness or resonance (in musical terms, a canon or a fugue) with regard to the motif of the subject. Their looks should be without mutual regard,[11] sharing nothing but their mutual autonomy.

Whence, then, the identity of this autonomous figure? Most often from the title: *Portrait of Ugolino Martelli*, for example.[12] Sometimes the name figures in the painting itself, although this is a somewhat archaic and rare device; at other times (as we shall see a little further on with Gumpp's *Self-Portrait*) it is bound up with a specific intention. In which case, however, it tends to be accompanied by an inscription relating either to the glory and merits of the person depicted[13] or to the truth or fidelity of the representation itself,[14] to the glory of (the) painting, if you prefer, to the glory of its autonomy.

It would be possible to analyze at length all the possible variations on these identifying statements, which run from the exteriority of a name outside the painting right through to the painting's inclusion of a self-reference: ultimately, however, it is always a matter not (or, in any case, not *only*) of a painting's reference to the real person it represents, but of the general form of a self-relation, a relation that is as much that of the proper name in its nonsignificance as it is that of painting posed as truth. To put it differently, referential identity and pictorial (autonomous or self-referential) identity are asymptomatically linked to one another—unless it is from their initial identity that the portrait first proceeds.

In the first or last instance, the identity ultimately given outside the figure is merely that of *the figure itself.* And this is also why, in addition to portraits titled by a name, there are just as many portraits titled along the lines of *Portrait of a Young Girl, Portrait of an Old Man,* or simply *Old Woman* or even *Head of a Man,* and so on. Referential identity either remains extrinsic or is identified with pictorial identity. The social position of the portrait is its figural position. This, however, can be understood in either of two ways:

1. When the portrait moves in the direction of social position, when it becomes referential and descriptive (when it becomes a portrait designed for the recognition, in every sense of the word, of posterity, of the people, of the family, even of the police, as has sometimes been the case), the identity of the person lies outside it, and pictorial identity, by conforming to referential identity, is lost.[15]

2. Painting gives itself its own "social" position; it engages its own civility or sociality, and it is perhaps only through it and in it, moreover, that subjects enter into a relation between *subjects* and not of identificatory objects. In other words, the horizon of our questions is in no sense solipsistic; on the contrary, it is one in which the portrait is always the portrait of another in which, however, the value of the face as the *sense* of the other is truly given only in the portrait (in art).[16]

The identificatory image relates to its model. The portrait relates to itself alone, for it relates to the self alone: to the self as other, the sole condition for there being something like relation.

As such, the portrait attains its artistic dignity only by being, in traditional terms, a portrait of the "soul" or of interiority, not *instead of being* a portrait of external appearance, however, but *in place of* this appearance, in its place, the place of its appearance manifested on the painter's canvas. The portrait of Giovanna Tournabuoni by Ghirlandajo bears the following inscription: "Art, could you only represent [*effingere:* render and produce, express and execute, draw out and fashion] character and spirit, there would be no more beautiful painting on earth."[17] This exhortation goes for all portraits and for all painting; understood correctly, it involves more than a mere wish and more, too, than the feeling of insufficiency that a wish would evoke, since it does not call for *another* painting but states, rather, that *this* painting ought to be able to be seen as bringing into view *mores animumque*. Along with the painter's humility, perhaps, it is the assurance of his or her design that invites us to look upon a soul *in* or *on* the figure that he or she presents.

The portrait's identity is wholly contained within the portrait itself. The formal "autonomy" of the figure involves nothing less than the autonomy of the subject that is given *within* and *as* it, as the interiority of the two-dimensional canvas and so as the autonomy of painting that alone *makes up* the soul. The person "in itself" is "in" the painting. Devoid of any inside, the painting *is* the inside or the intimacy of the person. It is, in short, the subject of its subject, its support and its substance, its subjectivity and its subjectility,[18] its depth and its surface, its sameness and its alterity in a single "identity" that we call the *portrait*. (Beyond this, perhaps, we would call it *painting* in general, since no painting can ever be "soulless," as it were, and so devoid of "subject" any more than it could be devoid of "figure," *even when* it is an "abstract" or a "monochrome." We can't stop the extension of this double questioning; if every subject is a portrait, then every painting is perhaps a figure and a look.)

The subject of the portrait is the subject that the portrait itself *is*, both insofar as the portrait is the subject (the object, the motif) of such a painting and insofar as this painting is the place at which such a subject (person, soul) comes to light. Either that, or the subject of the portrait is the subject that is a subject insofar as it comports itself *to itself* ("self-present"), and it only does so to the extent that it is what comes back to itself from outside the canvas, from the inside out, maybe, the slight surface of painted canvas being nothing other than the interface or the exchange of this being-to-self.

Hegel, of course, both protested—with what was, for his time, genuine insight—against the debasement of the portrait as a genre and saw in it the true completion of painting.[19] This completion (which, for Hegel, is also the median completion of art in general: painting is the midpoint between exteriority and interiority) stems from the expression of "inner life" or "spiritual character." Hegel understands this "expression" as a translation or a reproduction of the life of Spirit through the skill of the painter; not just any painter, therefore, but the "hand of a master" (Titian, for ex-

ample). The secret of this hand—the secret of good imitation—is knowing how to produce a lively rendering of what makes up the life of Spirit.
As such, it is life *itself* that is being recognized and reproduced. In a sense,
we need add nothing to Hegel's considerations since they are more than
enough to explain the singularity of the artist. Still, they fail to measure up
to art in the truth of its execution or its exteriority. Paradoxically, the very
materiality and technique of the portrait are set aside (Hegel fails to deal
with any particular portrait) in favor of a *mimesis*, the concept of which
imposes both the difference of an original from a copy and the identity of
a pure self-expression of the life of Spirit.

　　Without wanting to pursue any further the (aporetic and/or dialectical)
question of this double self-*allo*-mimetic allocation,[20] let me recall that, in
failing to dwell on the portrait itself (in failing to wonder exactly whence
or how the "expression of Spirit" comes to be *figured*, and in failing, too,
to ask what this *life* exactly is), Hegel also fails to dwell on an essential trait
of the process of spirit (and thus of its life), the fact that it is nothing other
than self-relation mediated through a departure from the self. This is the
real cross that any dialectical thinking has to bear: either the moment of
exteriority (negativity) exists in and for itself, or it is merely negated in
turn. (Which is why, moreover, it is art that is the cross that any such
thinking has to bear.)

　　If we really want to dwell on the moment of exteriority and hold firmly
to its *autonomous* existence, the logic of a contradictory mimesis dictates
that we will also have to hold to another, more advanced logic, one that
means we will be asking no longer how the portrait comes to be the portrait of the subject but how the portrait is itself the execution of the subject. We shall be asking no longer how painting comes to represent Spirit
but how it *presents* it, how it presents what will never have been present
elsewhere. Granted, this is not going to be possible without making some
weighty decisions as to dialectics and, first and foremost, as to the claim
that exteriority is not just a moment but the very substance, support, and
surface of the subject "itself," thereby suspending the dialectical return to
the self or making of it something undreamt of by any thought of the subject, even though everything about that thought would seem to lead in
this direction: to wit, the relation of the portrait to its audience.[21]

　　With the invention of the portrait, the subject does not give itself the
pleasure of an image; instead, it assures itself of the certainty of a presence

(its "own"); it has invented itself. (Another way of putting it would be to say that pleasure and certainty here are the work of one and the same joy.)

Somewhat more profoundly—or more superficially (here, it is much the same thing)—than any imitation of the face, the portrait involves a particular relation from the outset; that it does so is the most basic trait of painting. And this is what allows us to say that painting has a particular way of *setting out* [*un* abord], that it *sets out* toward us, and that this way of setting out stems from all painting (from its essence, if you like) and is communicated to all its works and to all its genres.

The "autonomy" of the portrait shelters it from every relation to a particular setting or scene only in order to set it immediately into a relation that is simultaneously unique and exclusive *and* endlessly renewed, a relation to the subject and to the subjects to which it is presented or exposed. Exposition is neither an appendix nor an ostentation of the quality or essence or the portrait, but wholly of a piece not only with painting but even more, were this possible, with the portrait. "Interiority," as I have already said, takes place *within* "exteriority." "Exposition" is this *setting within* and *taking place* that is neither "interior" nor "exterior" but *set toward* or *in relation.* We might say that the portrait *paints exposition,* that it *puts it (in) to (the) work.* Here, however, "work" does not refer to the particular "painting" as an object or thing. Rather, it refers to the painting *as relation.* In this sense, then, it is *the subject* that is *the work of the portrait.*

The portrait paints a subject only by setting itself within a subject-relation; as such, it sets a putative subject (me, you, the painter) within a relation to the subject that is being exposed. It sets a subject within a subject-relation and so within a relation to self. The portrait is the subject of a subject that lies before (or behind) it. But how so, and whence this relation that constitutes the very being of the subject (if a subject can be said to be a being-for-(and through)-another-subject)?

It has often been said that every portrait is a self-portrait and that *ogni pittore dipinge sè.*[22] Without wanting to deal with the various ways in which this phrase (which relates, moreover, to every genre of painting) might be interpreted or with the respective merits of such interpretations, I still want to point to the fact that such a remark is indissociable from its opposite: *every self-portrait is first and foremost a portrait.* In fact, the circumstances that lead the painter to put himself in the position of model (circumstances that could well be based on pure convenience, unsatisfying though such an explanation may be) change nothing essential as regards *the portrait ≠ the representatn of a subject, but the execution of subjectivity or of being-self*

*autonomy = the putting (self to work / putting self into the work*

the real concern of the portrait, to wit: its being not the representation of a subject but the execution of subjectivity or of being-self as such. Its *autonomy* has to be understood, beyond the technical sense of the term, as the putting (in) to (the) work of the *autos* or of the *self,* of *being-to-itself.* The portrait relates to itself alone; to put it differently, it is nothing other than this relation.[23] Yet this is so only precisely insofar as it is exposed to us; it is the putting (in) to (the) work of exposition, *our* exposition, our being-before—and only thus within—ourselves.

The relation that makes up the portrait comprises three moments: the portrait resembles (me), the portrait recalls (me), the portrait looks (at me).[24]  *resembles / recalls / looks*

## Resemblance

> It gradually becomes clear that a portrait does not resemble because it looks like a face; rather resemblance begins and exists only with the portrait and in it alone; resemblance is the portrait's work, its glory or its disgrace, expressing the fact that the face is not there, that it is absent, that it only appears by way of the absence that resemblance precisely is.
>
> —Maurice Blanchot, *Friendship*

*resemblance constitutes the paradigm of representatnl of figural art*

If resemblance appears to be the overriding concern of the portrait, it ought to follow that it constitutes the paradigm of representational or "figurative" art. Everything that revolves around the figure of the portrait, that binds it to the problematic of representation itself, also all concerns this particular art.

The portrait appears dedicated to the job of resembling. So much so, indeed, that it might well be seen as the only genre of painting that has a clearly determined practical finality. And it is around just such a finality, moreover, that judgment as to its artistic dignity has been meted out. (In this context, we should bear in mind that, across the field of art, the portrait is the genre that most emphatically bears the trace of a function or a service: an *hommage* or service to truth that is never too far removed from a sense of religious service. Yet what is so remarkable about this is that the portrait is also quite distinct from the religious icon. This problem involves the whole atheological autonomy of art; I will come back to it in due course.)

It is this imperious desire to resemble a particular individual that has

left the portrait in the contrasting—if not wholly contradictory or oppo-
sitional—position of being seen as both the work of a jobbing artisan and
the pinnacle of the art of painting. (Even today, and despite the advent of
photography, quick portraits attract tourists and flaneurs alike, as if satis-
fying our need both for recognition and for seeing something emerge
manually, as it were, and not out of some sort of recording device. "It's
him, it's really him!" we cry, repeating once again that most traditional of
*doxa*, very often adding, in a phrase that seems to cry out for extended
commentary: "You'd half expect it to speak.")[25]

Yet as we already know, if the identification of the particular model is
essential to any portrait that is designed to be recognized,[26] the same cannot be said for the *art* of the portrait. So much so, indeed, that we can
quite legitimately claim that the model is wholly inessential to the portrait; more exactly, that the model is what is essentially absent, that its absence and *not* its being recognized is what matters most. Resemblance has
*nothing* to do with recognition. With the large majority of portraits that
we see, we never get to see the originals, and it is hardly by chance that the
identity of the Mona Lisa, the archetypal portrait, is still so uncertain, as
much as to its gender as to the sense or inflection of its smile (indeed, it is
precisely this uncertainty that has given it its legendary place). And we can
even admire portraits that, in their own time, were judged wholly unsat-
isfactory from the point of view of recognition.[27]

Take Johannes Gumpp's self-portrait (circa 1646). Its rather odd composition has lent it a certain notoriety. Like many self-portraits it is de-
voted less to the representation of a particular person than to the representation of the act or process of representation itself. What is being
painted is less the painter than *painting*. Painting is the subject of this
painting, in every sense of the term. It is, quite explicitly, the subject of its
own resemblance.

The painter or the painting paints the entire scene, a scene that involves
two different representations of the painter's face, the face in the mirror in
which he becomes his own model, and the face on the canvas that he is in
the process of painting.[28] The resemblance is twofold; there are two distinct resemblances. The painting shows the dissemblance of resemblances.

The image in the mirror and the one on the canvas are identical (the
portrait, like the mirror image, being reversed: have a look at the lock of

*Self-Portrait* (ca. 1646), by Johannes Gumpp. Courtesy of the Musée des Offices, Florence.

hair) except for their respective looks: the look cast by the face in the mirror looks at the painter who looks at *himself;* the look thrown by the portrait is to one side, restoring thereby the movement of the eye that the painter has to make in order to switch from the mirror to the canvas. As

such, the look of the portrait no longer looks at *itself* but looks instead at
the one who is looking at the canvas and so at the painter in the process
of painting; the "same" who becomes thus the "other." With the same
"stroke," however, it looks out on us, the painting's prospective audience.
The look of or in the mirror is fixed on the original or model, the original
or model of or in the painting looking out onto the painter/painting.[29]

Where is the real resemblance, therefore? In the mirror or in the portrait? The painting gives us the answer in the form of the two domestic
animals set furiously against one another: the dog, placed under the portrait and in the foreground, symbolizes fidelity,[30] while the cat, beneath
the mirror and further back, indicates, if not infidelity, at least a less precise or less vivid sort of fidelity. (As if to draw out the difference further,
the name "Johannes Gumpp" is written on the piece of paper placed at
the top of the portrait.) If the mirror is indeed less faithful, it is because
the formally exact resemblance that it provides (leaving aside the inversion) is still not the resemblance afforded by painting. And since it is not
a matter of redressing the mirror's inversion, the difference has to stem
from the difference in looks. The look in the mirror is only concerned
with itself, engaged as it is in nothing more than a purely technical attention. By contrast, the look of the portrait is directed elsewhere, looking
out for the look thrown its way, looking out for an undefined possibility
of attention or encounter. As such, it mobilizes, through one or two discreet traits (to say nothing of the difference in lighting), the whole face
before finally showing a person rather than the traits of a model. Faithful
resemblance consists in showing something quite different from a correspondence between traits.

Now while this sort of resemblance does indeed show the life or the
liveliness of Spirit, as Hegel puts it, it does so only by revealing itself to be
the art of painting itself. A few details underscore this (re)presentation of
art: while the mirror, flanked by a bottle whose reflections point ultimately to the purely mechanical character of reflection, reflects part of the
studio, the painting itself is accompanied not only by two of the painter's
tools (the diluting shell[31] and the flask) but also by a flute (the portrait
doesn't speak; art makes itself heard) and a rosary hung beneath it (a gesture of gentle mockery or sulfurous devotion? or a metaphor of reverent
contemplation?).

The mirror shows an object: the object of the representation. The
painting shows a subject: painting at work.

*[handwritten marginalia at top: painting's intimate presence ≠ a model / = an idea — the idea / of painting itself]*

In the portrait—in painting—there is no *object*; nothing is *thrown out* [ob-jeté] before us. In this sense, the painting is never placed *before* us. It is not "before" but "ahead" in the sense in which it is I who am behind or within the painting, in its presence. Even this, however, what we might call the painting's intimate presence, is not defined and given before the painter like an image in a mirror, like a model in the studio. It is not a model but an Idea. Yet this Idea is nothing other than the Idea of painting itself. It does not preexist painting; rather, it is carried out by painting. The "Idea" of art is only ever art itself, and it is different each time.

The opposition of representational conformity and resemblance in painting is far from unimpassioned. Not for nothing are the cat and dog set at each others' throats. They are two forms of passion snarling at one another in defiance (the only audible noise on this little stage on which it is the role of the flute to modulate the eloquent silence of art). We might say that whereas one is the narcissism of reflection,[32] the other is the passion—simultaneously more passive *and* more active—of the self's relation to the other or to the self as other. The reflection (or the double) happens only *in praesentia*. The portrait is *in absentia*; it is essentially and in every sense exposed to absence.

Gumpp's painting, however, presents something else: ultimately nothing less than the painter himself, a third resemblance that leads us to say: this one is the right one.

It is the painter himself who, in the act of painting, occupies the foreground of the canvas. It is the painter who sums it all up in the gesture of the hand armed with brush (charged with the red of the lips), doing so in such a way that the hand, along with its arm, might almost be incorporated or, indeed, incorporate itself into the painting that it is in the process of painting, as if painting itself were painting the canvas. If we leave the hand to one side, all we can see of the painter is his back and a tumble of dark hair highlighted and situated by the white collar, which captures the light. The dark back of the painter, the back of his look, as it were, the mere reflections and effects of which peer out at us, this shadow much like the one spoken of in the fable of the birth of painting, this dark mass turned toward us and laid down before our eyes as a challenge to pictorial conventions, this is what ultimately harbors resemblance in its extreme truth, exposing it as an absence. (In much the same way, Vermeer's *Painting* shows us the painter from behind while placing a mask on the table.)

*[handwritten margin notes: resemblance of portrait relates to the absence of the face, invisible as mine is to me]*

In truth, however, we are still not finished; all this could be painted by another painter who might well paint this entire scenario set before him, doing so without ever seeing the face of the first painter, who would still remain masked.[33]

This absence shows us that the painting resembles only insofar as it exposes this absence, an absence that, in turn, is nothing other than the condition under which the *subject* relates to itself and so *resembles itself.* "Resembling oneself" is nothing other than being oneself or the same as oneself. It is this very sameness that the painting paints. But this sameness is the endless referral of a look cast on the self to a look turned outside itself and to an exposition of itself. This sameness extends all the way to the unrecognizable identity of a dark back turned toward me as if it were my own and as if I were myself the surface of the painting, my face thus before that of the painter, *my face as invisible as it always is to me.* In the first or final instance, the resemblance of the portrait relates to the absence of the face, its being-before-itself.

I can "resemble myself" only in a face that is always absent from and outside of me, not like a reflection but like a portrait brought before me, always in advance of me. The portrait portrays this advance and this movement before, this keel that, in the stream of what lies without, opens the thin and quickly erased wake of a "self."

As such, the painting resembles insofar as it resembles a "resembling itself," and the portrait resembles insofar as it "resembles a portrait" (as Pontévia remarks) and so insofar as it resembles *itself,* sameness is identified with painting, in painting, and as painting.

It does not resemble an original;[34] rather, it resembles the Idea of resemblance to an original or is itself the "original" of the resemblance-to-self of a subject in general, a subject that is each and every time singular. It is in my portrait or my portraits alone that I can learn, if I need to, of my "sameness." And each one of my portraits will identify yet another resemblance.[35] In a bad portrait, the separate elements of representation are not focused into the unity of a resemblance and constitute a mere enumeration of traits. In a good portrait, resemblance mobilizes each one of those traits in order to draw them toward that absence—simultaneously "inside" and "outside," behind and before the painting—of which resemblance is both the semblance and the arrangement.

In Auguste Pellerin's portrait of Matisse (the one dating from 1917),[36] a long black swathe is drawn out from the painting that hangs behind the painter's face, spilling over its frame so as to melt into or layer onto the bedrock of the portrait itself, a black background in which even the painter's clothes will be lost in order to bring to the fore, before the frame that surrounds it like a halo,[37] the face whose oval shape explicitly sets it apart, while two black eyes open, eyes through which the ground of the portrait (that of resemblance) may be seen, but through which it also *sees itself.*

In bearing a resemblance to a particular person and to a particular side of that person, a portrait does not thereby resemble someone or something, unless it be resemblance itself or the particular "person" insofar as that person resembles him or herself. By resembling itself, it is itself, that is, an identity *for itself* and not for another thing *in itself.* Painting paints the for-itself and not the in-itself; this is clearly something very different from how painting is usually understood since painting or portraiture means, in the first instance, *drawing out* [tirer],[38] and so a drawing out of the "in-itself" (which has, properly speaking, stifled itself, been stifled by its nocturnal ground, the very identity of a "to self"). Resemblance is *drawn* from the obscure and unidentifiable identical.[39]

It is not a matter of reproducing something recognizable, therefore, any more than it is a matter of giving phenomenal appearance to something that would otherwise remain buried, "grounded," as it were (the in-itself as the "life of the mind," as "personality trait," etc.). Rather, it is a matter of drawing out the ground itself, of drawing presence not out of absence but, quite the contrary, toward the absence that brings it before "itself" and exposes it to self-relation by exposing it to a "we."

By keeping quiet about the essential silence of the plastic arts and by carrying this silence forward through the visible mark of a mouth (Gumpp's touch of red on each of the mouths and on the brush, the pinched, narrow mouth of Auguste Pellerin's Matisse),[40] the mouth of the portrait opens (and closes) onto an obscure ground: it exposes a sense that is in no way a signification, something that could be articulated, but is instead the articulation of presence or the *pre-sense of presence* itself.

# Recall

> Images of images, shadows drawn from a past "dream of shadows,"
> paintings; with them, we cross shadows and dreams—the shadow in
> which death gathers its forces, the dream in which life is condensed—
> so as to return to the magically addressed starting point: a look that is
> neither a question nor an answer but silence and a pause, a mute
> witness to what was.
>
> —Jean-Christophe Bailly, *L'Apostrophe Muette*

The role of the portrait is to *look out for* [guarder] the image in the absence of the person, regardless of whether this absence results from distance or from death. It is the presence of what is absent, a presence *in absentia* that is charged thus not only with the reproduction of characteristics but with presenting presence insofar as it is absent; with evoking it (invoking it, even) and with exposing it, with manifesting the retreat in which this presence is maintained. The portrait recalls presence in both senses of the word: it brings back from absence, and it remembers in absence. As such, then, the portrait immortalizes; it renders immortal in death.

(A more exact way of putting it might be to say that the portrait is less the immortalization of a person than the presentation of (immortal) death in (a) person. And therein would lie the essential difference between the portrait and the death mask, which presents the dead and not death as such. The mask takes the imprint of the dead (the work struck by death), while the portrait puts death itself (in) to (the) work: death at work at the very heart of life, at the very heart of the figure, in full view. Death in this sense denotes what can be addressed under the concepts of "finitude" or "division": the departure from the in-itself, ek-sistence, ex-position.)

The Roman portrait, both of ancestors and of illustrious figures, is the first moment of the portrait proper and, along with the medallion, is what provides modernity with one of the principal models for the portrait.[41] At the same time, with the formation of the Christian subject (and so of the subject per se) and of another relation to death and to absence (to an absence opened right within the *interior intimo meo*), we see the Oriental or Christian version of the Greco-Roman portrait in the portraits of Fayoum and their "mute cries."[42]

Love, death, and glory all communicate in one and the same movement of absention: they withdraw from ordinary presence, from the presence of the object, from its existence [*l'être-là*]. They put being outside itself; thrown thus, it moves toward itself. The invention of the subject consists in the invention of an infinite movement of absention, the absolute measure of the return or the turn to oneself (to the other). It is this subtraction from the presence of the object, this access to the absent character of the subject [*l'absence-sujet*], that commands the portrait and explains why love, death, and glory were the principle sponsors of the portrait before it turned to the denuded subject, portrayed for itself, and to the painter and the act of painting: painting indefinitely recalling itself to itself. What I am here terming a "recall" is the recollection to oneself of a presence that has managed to absent itself.

The act of memory that I want to evoke is not the conversion of a present that has passed on; rather, it is the step or the move back toward the always-present—and properly immemorial—ground of absence itself. This in-some-way-hypermnesiac (or amnesiac) anamnesis refers back to the region of absent presence that was once called the sacred. The portrait takes on the somber glow of this region in which presence exceeds itself as it moves more originally from itself to itself. This is the "divine" excess (in Augustine's phrase) of originary interiority as an unclosable yawning; an identity infinitely constituted "for itself," and that is also to say: "for the other."

There is nothing surprising, then, in our saying that the *princeps* document of the history of the subject (of its presence and its presentation) is a seminal literary portrait—*The Confessions*—in which a subject represents itself through the act of presenting itself to God and through the act of presenting the nonpresentable character of God as the ultimate truth of His face.[43]

This "divine" or this "sacred" is nothing other than a distancing and hollowing out through which contact with the intimate is to be made, through which the passion of its infinite interiority/exteriority—the passion of sufferance and the passion of desire—is to be broached. It is the rupture necessary to self-communication, to the communication of the self. And in this sense, then, every portrait is "sacred."

Rather more precisely: the movement from the icon to the portrait is exactly that from divine presence, offered in the face of its own absence (for which words are not lacking, since it is itself the movement of the Word and of the Spirit), to a "desacralized" figure, that is, a figure opened onto the silence of its own absent presence. So far as this presence is concerned, it is a matter of drawing out its trace in every singular face. We

*Portrait of a Young Man Against a White Curtain* (1530), by Lorenzo Lotto. Courtesy of the Kunsthistorisches Museum, Vienna.

need not, therefore, speak of the "sacred"; rather, it is simply a matter of drawing out the trace of presence, of drawing or recalling the intimate trace of its passion. Presence is *portrayed* [*on le* pour-traict] (as the original French term has it), *drawn to itself.* And this is no less true of painting.

Take Lorenzo Lotto's portrait of a young man. A first glance immediately demonstrates the "iconic" character of this image, which is presented, moreover, as an inversion of the shadowy scene of Gumpp's canvas. The cap and hair are fairly close to a sort of inverted halo against the golden background—the decorated decor—of the vast damask curtain. Everything here, as in thousands of other portraits, denotes the model's excellence and so reveals why he merits being kept and thus held present in his absence. Just what this absence entails, however, we will never know,[44] any more than we will know whether the reason behind the painting is love, death, glory, or all three—or even a wholly different reason, the model perhaps having here (as might be suggested by the absence of any name) no other function than that of being a model.

The absence of any marked social standing immediately confers on portraits of this sort what we might term a state of pure distinction. On the one hand, the resemblance is that of a well-determined individual (overdetermined, one might say, by some of the details, the mole in the middle of the forehead being only the most obvious, but there are other details on the skin and in the precise fold of the upper of the scarcely parted lips); on the other hand, it is a resemblance that cannot be identified except as a resemblance to itself. Now, in resembling itself, it principally resembles its own withdrawal into itself; this is nothing other than presence itself, its *praes-entia*, what puts it before itself and so renders it capable of coming back to itself. The withdrawal into its "interiority" is wholly up to the challenge of the precision of its physical "exteriority," each one incessantly passing into the other.

By evoking the past presence of a handsome face, simultaneously lively and reserved, almost shy or evasive (evading what, though? identification? confusion?), this figure of a young man recalls *not* an individual but the act of recalling oneself that constitutes the subject in general—an act that, for this very reason, never takes place "generally" but only in an irreducibly and endlessly singular fashion that is continually being renewed.[45]

We could say that this young man offers what is, in some way, a quasi-aggressive exhibition of his intimacy. Through his air of defiance, through the calm bravado that projects a certain tension out onto the spectator who would seek to uncover his secret, he also poses—by holding the pose that he does—the possibility that this intimacy might concern us (that it might look toward us). He *distinguishes himself*, then, in every sense of the term, but, in doing so, forces us to recall this distinction. The withdrawn, the distinguished, is a secret, the secret of intimacy; yet this intimacy is not a secret jealously guarded by the young man, held "back," as it were. He merely exposes it and draws it out.

In point of fact, there is no "back" here. "Back" means "beside"; there is no side to the "self." The only side is the visible side of the canvas, which, as we know, is devoid of depth. Intimacy is the game of a depth that belongs to no other ground than the surface on which it is played out and stretched out. Again, then, what is being stretched is the passion of a *subject* in thrall to that mode of being-itself in which it relinquishes its hold on itself while both exposing and communicating itself in an almost violent way. (As Bataille remarks, the sacred is nothing other than the communication of the passions.) In Hegelian terms, we might say that this young man is wholly in-himself-for-himself but is so only insofar as he is *for us*.

The portrait is less the recollection of a (memorable) identity than it is the recollection of an (immemorial) intimacy.[46] Identity can always be past, whereas intimacy can only ever be present. Once again, however, the portrait is less the recollection *of* this intimacy than it is a calling back *to* it. It calls us or summons us to it or toward it, leading us there; through the painting that is offered up to our look, we enter into the manner in which it is presented to the outside.

Now, if we look closely, we can see how the painter has arranged things in such a way as to draw our look. The curtain rides up on the right side of the canvas, as if the painting were revealing its ground, its "back" or flip side. In the upper right-hand corner, where the vast, luminous curtain is most visibly folded toward us, we can see, in the background, as it were, the room in which the painting is being painted. In this dark corner there shines, somewhat unusually, a lamp, an oil lamp whose flame flickers feebly while reflecting on its copper supports.

Commentators have often tended to refer this lamp—as unusual as any number of Lotto's symbolic details—to John's *lux in tenebris lucet*. To my mind, however, the allusion to the Gospel is not really necessary once we understand that, in a strictly atheological way, the light is precisely the light of the young man's intimacy. Not, however, in the sense that the painter would be suggesting or allegorizing the idea of an inner light (although it is certainly possible that that was indeed his intention), but much more in the sense that this lamp, painted straight onto the canvas, is itself the material or pictorial luminosity of the intimacy in question.

This shadowy flame doubles the young man's look, forming thus the look of the painting itself. So, far from simply leading us symbolically outside the painting and into the depths of a soul, it also brings us back to the immanence of the canvas and the painting. Or, if you prefer, it shows us that the ground of the soul takes place here and nowhere else, in this withdrawal that is thus drawn forth.

If this were not the case, what use would painting have? It would be far more useful to tell the story, whether fictional or real, of this young man and his concerns. Painting is not an allegory of the soul or of spirit. In no sense is it the imitation of an interiority that would be given to it from somewhere else, of the life of an Idea or of a person. Rather, it is the execution of the figure of just such an interiority and is so precisely insofar as it is not a matter of an interior that one might ultimately be able to see behind a particular figure. The portrait did not appear in order to recall the memory of cherished or admired lives (the portrait is not a monument and, when it is, it is already well on the way to being a portrait no longer).[47] It appears in order to recall the subject to itself, in order to bring about its infinite return to itself.

The portrait does not recall a distant present; rather, it brings absence closer, so close that its call is silent. Never was a soul or a spirit as close to itself and to us; never did it call on itself as well as on us.

The light of the ground—of this improbable ground that yawns groundless in the ground of the canvas—is the shimmer of a presence before and beyond itself, a presence that calls it*self* forth.[48]

If the portrait does indeed give rise to and hold within itself exactly such a gesture of the recollection and anticipation—this deceptive and redemptive promise—of a presence equal to its absence, it is because it provides the repository and the emissary of the collapse of the divine into absence that lies at the very heart of monotheism or, more precisely, of the monologotheism whose path the "West" will have been. Every portrait plays out in the singular the impossible portrait of God, His retreat and His attraction [*son retrait et son attrait*].[49]

In fact, monotheism is characterized less by the unity of God (as if it were a matter of a simple numerical reduction) than by the essential propriety of this unity—what basically grounds it as a unity—namely, indivisibility. The plurality of the gods constitutes their visibility, whether potential or actual, as well as their presence. The art of polytheism provides a vision of the gods,[50] while that of monotheism recalls the indivisibility of God withdrawn into His unity. Whence, as we know, the Judeo-Islamic edict against representation[51] and, most singularly, against the portrait, as well as, in a manner both parallel to and consequent on this, the enormous importance of the intra-Christian debate around images, from the Council of Nicea to the Counter-Reformation.[52]

The art of the icon[53] is the art of a negative and apophantic theology. It is an art that denies representing what it presents. The icon exposes the invisible; not by rendering it properly visible but by exposing the presence of the invisible, calling thereby for a vision other than that of sight. The invisible God is not simply situated away from our eyes; rather, He is invisible in and for Himself, and this is why it has always been possible to think of Him as being invisible to His Son, thus making the latter an "invisible image of the visible."[54] In truth, the one God is less invisible (in the sense of being hidden) than nonappearing; far from being a matter of making this nonappearance appear (this nonappearance considered as the very act of God, his *modus operandi*, so to speak), it has to be a matter of presenting its presence, which is itself absence. Equally, the iconic figure is not a visage but a face; it exposes the nonappearing face of the whole of the visible.

The portrait will have retained one fundamental trait of the icon, however: what it *draws* and *traces* is precisely this nonappearance as the birth and death of the subject. At the very point where the icon offers itself up to the adoration that cuts through it so as to move toward the ground of the divine, the portrait offers instead the sight of ground becoming surface as the proper illumination of the painting. In this way, Matisse's *Auguste Pellerin* can be said to refer simultaneously, and more dryly or with a tension far greater than that generated by Lotto's *Young Man*, to a particular person, to painting, to the form of the icon, to the overflowing of ground in the setting out of the foreground, to a subject charged with the concern and gathering of it*self.*

The portrait recalls the icon and resembles it in much the same way as the absence of presence recalls, so as to resemble, the presence of absence. It recalls, in the finite character of each, the infinite distension of the *one.*

## Look

This "look" expresses what, precisely? Its exercise: its regularity, its
particular kind of constancy . . . the ground no longer masks the
person to which it lent the alibi of a history, of a fiction, of both a
distant sense and a role. It seems that this is what the portrait
continually repeats: the fact that there is no longer any attested or
organized sense but, above all, no longer any delegation of sense.

—Jean-Louis Schefer, *Figures peintes*

The light of the portrait shines from its obscure ground. It shines from
out of the star, eclipsed for itself, that defines a subject. What visibly disappears in the portrait, what, under our very eyes, hides itself from our
eyes, plunging into them as if to infinity, is the look of the portrait.

Before anything else, then, the portrait looks; looking, it is concentrated, both sent and lost. Its "autonomy" gathers and restricts the painting, even the entire face, in the look; this look is the goal and the site of
this autonomy.[55] Painting the look does not mean imitating it; to put it
another way, in the look the painting itself becomes the look, and if every
painting ultimately becomes what it paints, it is doubtless always through
the look that this happens—by which I mean both through the look from
out of which painting emerges *and* through the look that it becomes in
the very act of painting it.[56]

Now, this look does not look at any particular object. It is always
turned elsewhere, sometimes toward the painter/spectator,[57] at other times
toward an indeterminate outside. (Lotto's young man, afflicted as he is by
a slight squint, does one thing with the left eye, the other with his right.)
At still other times, it is lost or rapt in itself, as we say, infinitely other and
the same.[58]

The look of the portrait looks at nothing, and looks at the nothing. As
it plunges headlong into the absence of the subject (mine, its own; ours,
too, by definition, common and divided), it looks at no object. To look at
nothing is, first and foremost, the intimate contradiction of the subject
(the contrariness in which an intimacy takes place). Yet the contradiction
is resolved or suspended once we understand that the look is ultimately
not a relation to the object. What we tend to call "sight" *is* perhaps just
such a relation, and in this sense the portrait sees nothing and is not there
to be seen. "Sight" belongs to the domain of objects. The look, by contrast, brings the subject to the fore. "To look at" means, first and foremost,

*to look out for* or *to look after,* to ward or *warten,* to watch or guard over. To be concerned with or to care for. By looking, I look out for and guard (myself); I am related to the world, not to the object. Only thus can I say that I "am." In seeing, I see, by way of optics; in looking I am myself at stake. I cannot look *without this look looking back at me.*[59] What the portrait presents is always this looking out for oneself—and with it, this: how the *self* looks out for itself because it loses its way. How its being-to-itself takes place only in this outside-itself, before itself, where a face unknown to it looks the world square in the face.

This has nothing to do either with phenomena or with a phenomenology. There is nothing aimed at [*visée*] here. On the contrary, there is an absenting of aim [*la visée*] and, ultimately, of vision. Equally, there is nothing here that would respond to appearance: the look of the portrait never sees anything appear unless it is precisely the nothing, the very thing that does not appear. Nothing rises out of the depths; the ground is there, right on the surface. It does not become surface; rather, like the black cap and cloak of Lotto's young man, like Gumpp's or Pellerin's clothes, it is always the ground becoming face, facing *itself.*

The portrait extracts and exposes the immobile presence, immutable and mute, eternal and instantaneous, of its ground. The ground is a look. Equally, the entire face becomes an eye, as happens in the case of the young man, his face set in dark, dark cloth. It is no longer a question of a particular visual organ; rather, is it a matter of a guarded presence, a presence that watches out both for itself and for the other. All portraits watch out and watch out for themselves; they survey themselves (their preservation or their bearing, their reserve) and look out for themselves (their demise, their passing away, and their abandonment).

But what opens this look and the way in which it looks out for itself is nothing other than the canvas as a whole, all of which can be said to look: the eye, for example, that the lamp lights up in the background of the painting. The painting looks with its entire painterly being [*son être de peinture*].

Every portrait—and so every painting—opens up from its ground to its surface, moving in front of itself, jumping ahead of itself, both in the manner of its encounter and in the manner of its distancing. This look particular to painting doubles the look of the portrait (even though every look is double: one eye on itself, one eye on the other). There are numerous ways in which the look of a particular person can be multiplied or in-

tensified while still diverted or transposed with regard to the painting itself: the lamp in the Lotto, but also the painting hung on the wall or the
touch of red on the decoration pinned to the jacket in the Matisse portrait
of Auguste Pellerin; elsewhere a pearl, a ring, the eye of an animal, a mirror, the tip of a breast, a magnifying glass, a reflection in brass, the red
mouth, or the depiction of another drawing, even another painting, in the
portrait itself, even the allegorical look of Painting, as in one of Poussin's
self-portraits: various ways in which painting is turned into the look of the
look, into what looks out for it, its protector, its sighting, and its encounter. Various ways of *drawing the eye—of drawing it to itself outside itself.*

In 1994, Miguel Barceló paints his *Double Portrait.* In doing so, he takes
up or highlights a traditional genre of the double or triple portrait that
dates back at least to Giorgione and Raphael (then to Rigaud and many
others). What immediately leaps out at us, however, is the metamorphosis of the canvas into a close-up on the look, into a sort of unique other of
the double portrait in which the two heads become eyes.

These eyes devour the real portraits that, from the outset, the title
alone, as is only right and proper, identifies as being portraits. In each of
the dark, round masses[60] we can, albeit only just, discern certain traces or
certain evanescent touches of a face—a nose and a mouth rather than
eyes—to the point that we can even hazard a guess that the portrait on the
right is looking to the right while the one on the left is looking straight
ahead. These vestigial faces, however, these two dark masses, are also nothing more than two eyes, even two open pupils, since they show no signs
of opening at their center and are themselves the opening of the painting.

Eye masses, a look that is amassed, thrown, torn, even broken, flowing
with black blood. This canvas can and should be seen as a look of death,
as the death of the look and as death in the look. But it can also and indeed *should*—without any contradiction whatsoever—be seen in the way
that the title invites: as the fullness of a double look whose entire ground
rises up to the surface, as two subjects together, as their society into which
we ourselves sink our eyes since it draws us with them, into the association
of looks turned in different directions [*en sens divers*].

Their obscure depth is nothing other than the look overflowing its own
surface: the dense color of the two portraits spills from the eyes, spills onto
the ground and blends into it. The subject heads into what surrounds it,
itself becoming the surround or the surround becoming the subject. But

what is a surround? It is what sets up the place for a look to take place, what sets a look in place. It is the convergence [*convenance*][61] of the coming and the presence of the subject, a welcoming and a gathering in order for it to come into the world.

At the same time that the subject wholly completes itself as work—if the work is the one and only place in which a subject is wholly referred back to itself, in which a substance is able to cling to itself in the same way that the colored paste clings to the canvas it impregnates—at the same time that the subject completes itself in the work, the subject-work does nothing but open onto and overflow a look that is no longer a substance but an opening, no longer a return to itself but an exposition of it.

Wittgenstein writes: "We don't see the human eye as a receiver. . . . When you see the eye, you see something go out from it. You see the blink of an eye [*Blick des Auges*]."[62]

The look, Wittgenstein's *Blick*, is the thing that leaves or takes its leave, the thing of leaving. More precisely, the look is nothing phenomenal; on the contrary, it is the *thing in itself* of a departure from the self through which alone the subject becomes a subject. Far from being a look directed toward an object, the thing in itself of the departure or opening is an opening toward a world. In truth, it is no longer even a look *upon* but a look as a whole, open not *on* but *through* the evidence of the world.

In the look of the portrait, work's closure in upon itself coincides in a quite blinding (revelatory, luminous) way with an infinite excess over this closure. It is no longer the representation of a subject placed before a world; instead, it is nothing less than the presentation of a world rising up into its own vision, into its own evidence.

The solution of the subject or the *self* is its dissolution and resolution. The problem of self-relation is exposed and untangled in a look devoid of relation, in a look that looks upon itself only to the extent that it paints itself and thereby departs from itself.

The portrait will have brought into focus the ontological problematic of the subject in the whole extent of its constitutive distension and the entire tension of its ambivalence. On the one hand—presence in itself—closure in the work, the sovereign figure, the glorification of vision and the face; on the other—presence set outside itself—the gesture and the touch of painting, the figure gone astray, the look lost in the rhythm of its own capture. And yet the two sides are, in fact, the two faces of the same canvas; not in the sense of a face to face encounter but in the sense of an internal division of *a single back-to-back face*. Only painting can formulate thus the entire structure and genesis of the subject, *the dark intimacy of the figured and colored surface*, the shadow being brought *into the painting* by the portrait.

Only painting, then, can provide the subject with his or her own words, without either voice or language that could be rendered by discourse, and without, too, this name "subject." What it designates or names is shown here to be a single *trait*: not a self-relation, not a semblance or a recollection of the self, but the trait that draws it forth by turning it back in, the singular trait of an intimate disunion, the plane of an eclipse of an encounter missed in advance since it turns immediately, with the same stroke, with the same brush stroke, into the spacing of a world with its attraction and its disquiet. "Art" is the fragile name of this other encounter.[63] And isn't a portrait first and foremost an encounter?

It is to this that our contemporary world responds, simultaneously emptying and cutting through the look of the portrait but also (and thus) exacerbating and extending it, opening it out and leading it away from the face (Picasso), leading it toward what lies furthest within the canvas (Giacometti), what torments it (Bacon) or brings it forth, hyperrealized in an acrylic-acid clarity, scrawls on it or smears it, transforming it into a white block, and what becomes thus, ever more vertiginously, a look that plunges headlong into the evasion of the look itself, the look of the painter as well as the look of the other—one plunged into the other, into the protection of the flight itself,[64] meeting in a flash of the *sub* and the *jectum*, of the support and painting.

Here, the subject is no longer, as is or would seem to be the case with the Cartesian and philosophical model in general, the self-evidence of an interiority held within itself by the suspension of the world. Increasingly, it throws off resemblance and recollection understood in terms of humanism, intentionality, and representation (from which, however, as we know, painting will continually struggle to free itself). By hollowing out the look, however, by emptying it or aggravating it at the same time as it digs deep, turning its eyes in on itself, painting intensifies this same look, even to the extent of aggravating it if needs be. This is how it portrays beyond the portrait itself.

In a sense, it never ceases to do what Hegel said that it did when he spoke of the *life of Spirit*, and in this regard all portrait painters are

Hegelian (as they were long before Hegel), right up to the demolition of the portrait itself. The whole point is to know how the "life of Spirit" is faced and defaced, how the return to self loses itself in its look.

To be lost in a look; isn't this what we mean by painting? But drawn thus outside of itself in the *act of its being painted*, the look becomes the evidence of a world that is exposed less *before* me as a spectacle than *through* me as a force that opens my eyes in the eyes of the painting, in the opening out and bedazzlement that painting certainly does not represent but that it *is* or that it *paints*, since in what we call "art," *to paint* or *to portray* mean nothing less than the sense or meaning of *being* and so of being in the world. The painted look plunges into this *in*.

*Translated by Simon Sparks*

# Sources

The texts by Jean-Luc Nancy published here have been published previously. The works are listed below in the order in which they appear in this volume.

"Making Poetry." First published as "Faire, la poésie," in *Nous avons voué notre vie à des signes*, ed. Jean-Paul Michel (Bordeaux: William Blake, 1996); reprinted in Jean-Luc Nancy, *Résistance de la poésie* (Bordeaux: William Blake, 1997).

"Taking Account of Poetry." First published as "Compter avec la poésie," *Revue de littérature générale*, special issue entitled "Le Méchanique lyrique" 1 (1995); reprinted in Jean-Luc Nancy, *Résistance de la poésie* (Bordeaux: William Blake, 1997)

"Around the Notion of Literary Communism." First published as "Autour de la notion de commaunauté littéraire," *Tumultes* 6 (May 1995).

"He Says." Written for the Tsaï Theatre's production *Celui qui ne parle pas*, staged in Grenoble (1983) and Paris (1984). First published in *L'Indépendance amoureuse* (Brussels: Cahiers du GRIF, 1985); reprinted in Jean-Luc Nancy, *Le Poids d'une pensée* (Quebec: Presses Universitaires de Grenoble / Les Éditions Le Griffon d'argile, 1991).

"Vox Clamans in Deserto." First published in English translation as "Vox Clamans in Deserto," trans. Nathalia King, *Notebooks in Cultural Analysis* 3 (1986); reprinted in Jean-Luc Nancy, *The Birth to Presence* (Stanford, Calif.: Stanford University Press, 1993). First published in French in a modified form under the same title in *Furor* 19–20 (1990); reprinted in Jean-Luc Nancy, *Le Poids d'une pensée* (Quebec: Presses Universitaires de Grenoble / Les Éditions Le Griffon d'argile, 1991).

"Paean for Aphrodite." First published as "Péan pour Aphrodite," *Poandsie* 56

(1991); reprinted in Jean-Luc Nancy, *Le Poids d'une pensée* (Quebec: Presses Universitaires de Grenoble / Les Éditions Le Griffon d'argile, 1991).

"Les Iris." First published in a bilingual edition as "Les Iris," *Yale French Studies*, special issue entitled "Michel Leris" (1991). First published in French under the same title in *Revue de l'Université de Bruxelles* 1–2 (1990); reprinted in Jean-Luc Nancy, *Le Poids d'une pensée* (Quebec: Presses Universitaires de Grenoble / Les Éditions Le Griffon d'argile, 1991).

"On Writing: Which Reveals Nothing." First published as "De l'écriture: Qu'elle ne révèle rien," *Rue Descartes* 10 (1994).

"Roger Laporte: The Page." First published as "Roger Laporte: La page," *Le Chat messager* 11 (1995).

"In Blanchot's Company." First published as "Compagnie de Blanchot," *Ralentir travaux* 7 (Winter 1996/97); reprinted, with slight revisions, in *Revue des sciences humaines* 253 (1999).

"On Blanchot." First published as "Á propos de Blanchot," *L'Oeil de boeuf* 14/15 (May 1998).

"Deguy l'An Neuf!" First published as "Deguy l'an neuf!," in *Le Poète que je cherche à être*, Cahier Michel Deguy, ed. Yves Charnet (Paris: Le Table Ronde / Belin, 1996).

"The Necessity of Sense." First published as "Necessité du sense," in *Yves Bonnefoy: Poésie, peinture, musique* (Strasbourg: Presses Universitaires de Strasbourg, 1995).

"Ja, Bès." First published in German translation as "Ja, bès," in *Und Jabès* (Stuttgart: Legeuil, 1994). First published in French as "Ja, Bès," in *Saluer Jabès* (Bordeaux: Opales, 2000).

"Robert Antelme's Two 'Phrases.'" First published as "Les deux phrases de Robert Antelme," *Lignes* 21 (1994); reprinted in *Robert Antelme. Textes inédits sur L'espèce humaine. Essais et témoignages* (Paris: Gallimard, 1996).

"Georges." First published as "Georges," *Furor* 13 (1885); reprinted in Jean-Luc Nancy, *Le Poids d'une pensée* (Quebec: Presses Universitaires de Grenoble / Les Éditions Le Griffon d'argile, 1991).

"Catalogue." First published as "Catalogue," *Avant-guerre* 1 (1980).

"Interviews." First published as "Interviews," in *François Martin: Mozart, le nègre et la dame* (Paris: Musée de Saint-Priest, 1985).

"Res Extensa." First published as "Res extensa," in *Etienne Martin* (Valence: Musée de Valance, 1992).

"Lux Lumen Splendor." First published as "Lux lumen splendor," in *Ultimes Libres: Photographies de Guerrero* (Strasbourg: Galerie Alternance, 1993).

"Held, Held Back." First published as "Tenue, Retenue," in *Lucile Bertrand: Sculptures* (Paris: L'Arbre à Lettres, 1995).

"The Title's a Blank." First published as "Il y a blanc de titre," in *Susanna Fritscher* (Paris: CREDAC-Centre d'Art d'Ivry, 1994).

"The Technique of the Present: On On Kawara." First published as *Technique du présent: Essai sur On Kawara* (Villeurbanne: Le Nouveau Musée, 1997).

"The Soun-Gui Experience." First published as "Expérience Soun-Gui," in *Soun-Gui Kim* (Les Herbins: Éditions Sock-Jon, 1997).

"The Look of the Portrait." First published as *Le Regard du portrait* (Paris: Galilée, 2000).

# Notes

CHAPTER 2

1. Edmund Husserl, *Die Krisis der europäischen Wissenschaften und die transzendentale Phänomenologie, Husserliana* VI (The Hague: Martinus Nijhoff, 1954), §73; translated by David Carr as "Philosophy as Mankind's Self-Reflection," in Edmund Husserl, *The Crisis of European Sciences and Transcendental Phenomenology* (Evanston, Ill.: Northwestern University Press, 1970), 341.

2. See Peter Fenves's suggestive analyses in *"Chatter": Language and History in Kierkegaard* (Stanford, Calif.: Stanford University Press, 1993).

CHAPTER 3

1. Jean-Luc Nancy, *La Communauté désoeuvrée* (Paris: Bourgois, 1986; nouvelle édition 1990); translated by Peter Connor as *The Inoperative Community* (Minneapolis: University of Minnesota Press, 1991). Nancy's text originally comprised three essays, the first of which, "The Inoperative Community," was published in *Alea* (1983). A few months later, Maurice Blanchot's *The Unavowable Community* afforded a remarkable response to Nancy's own text.

2. Jean-Luc Nancy, "La Comparution (De l'existence du 'communisme' à la communauté de l'"existence'"), in *La Comparution (politique à venir)* (Paris: Bourgois, 1991); translated by Tracy B. Strong as "La Comparution / The Compearance: From the Existence of 'Communism' to the Community of 'Existence,'" *Political Theory* 20, no. 3 (Aug. 1992).

3. Nancy, *La Comparution*, 99; "La Comparution / The Compearance," 392.

4. Ibid., 99; 393.

5. Ibid.

6. Nancy, *La Communauté désoeuvrée*, 198; *Inoperative Community*, 80–81.

7. Ibid., 197; 80.

8. Jacques Rancière, *Aux bords du politique* (Paris: Osiris, 1990), 107. It should be noted that many of the questions being raised here arise from exchanges with Rancière and with his most recent work, *La Mésentente* (Paris: Galilée, 1995); translated by Julie Rose as *Disagreement: Politics and Philosophy* (Minneapolis: University of Minnesota Press, 1999).

9. Maurice Merleau-Ponty, *L'Oeil et l'esprit* (Paris: Gallimard, 1964), 13.

10. This aphorism by Elias Canetti was unpublished during his lifetime but appeared in *La Republica*, Aug. 18, 1994, the day after his death.

11. Philippe Lacoue-Labarthe, *La Fiction du politique* (Paris: Bourgois, 1986); translated by Chris Turner as *Heidegger, Art and Politics: The Fiction of the Political* (Cambridge, Eng.: Blackwell, 1990).

CHAPTER 7

1. The implicit reference here is to Michel Leiris's first autobiographical volume, *L'Âge d'homme* (*Manhood*) (Paris: Gallimard, 1945).—Trans.

2. The implicit reference here is to Leiris's autobiographical volume *Le Ruban au cou d'Olympia* (Paris: Gallimard, 1981), whose title was inspired by Manet's famous painting.—Trans.

3. The implicit reference here is to Leiris's four volumes of autobiography that share the overall title *La Règle du jeu* (*The Rule of the Game*): *Biffures, Fourbis, Fibrilles,* and *Frêle Bruit.*—Trans.

CHAPTER 8

1. See Michel Foucault, "Un 'fantastique' bibliothèque," in *Dits et écrits 1954–1988,* ed. Daniel Defert and François Ewald (Paris: Gallimard, 1994), 1: 293–325.

2. Dante, *Paradiso,* trans. John D. Sinclair (Oxford: Oxford University Press, 1961). The respective references are as follows: 29.124; 33.85–93; 32.85–87.

3. See Roger Laporte, *Une Vie: Biographie* (Paris: P.O.L., 1986).

CHAPTER 9

1. Nancy is referring here to Roger Laporte's collected shorter narratives (*La Veille, Une Voix de fin silence, Pourquoi?, Fugue, Supplément, Fugue 3, Codicille, Suite,* and *Moriendo*), brought together in a single volume as *Une Vie: Biographie* (Paris: P.O.L., 1986).—Trans.

CHAPTER 10

1. Maurice Blanchot, *L'Amitié* (Paris: Gallimard, 1971), 137; translated by Elizabeth Rottenberg as *Friendship* (Stanford, Calif.: Stanford University Press,

1997), 117. Illness makes it impossible for me to write a new text for this special Blanchot issue of the *Revue des sciences humaines*. With Roger Laporte's kind approval, I am forced to make do with reprinting a text that some readers, I hope, will not have already seen. It first appeared in *Ralentir travaux* 7 (1997) in a series of papers on Blanchot brought together by Christophe Bident. As a result, I find myself at an infinite remove from what I would wish and what I ought to write on Blanchot. But being prevented from writing in this way, am I any closer to the prospect of being released from the "overlong speaking [*la trop longue parole*]" mentioned by Blanchot at the end of *Le Pas au-delà* [*The Step Not/Beyond*]? Does not being able to write about him make me any nearer to him? Perhaps so, and yet for all that I am in no way exonerated from my debt to him, nor from that other, infinite debt, for which writing is simply another name. Indeed, because it is infinite, it is no longer a debt; it is more like a game, a game that consists in eluding the insignificance revealed by, among other things, illness and suffering, in all their brutal precision. At this point, let me simply send back to Blanchot this other phrase from *Le Pas au-delà*, in which he says, "The painful mouth spoke with tranquility." Such tranquil speaking says the same as the strange exchange of community between us, in which being-with takes nothing away from being-without, indeed takes its sense from it.

2. Blanchot, *L'Amitié*, 173; *Friendship*, 150.

3. Letter from Maurice Blanchot to Elio Vittorini, February 8, 1963, in *Lignes* 11 (Sept. 1990), 278.

CHAPTER 11

1. Historical accuracy is indispensable here. The facts of the matter have now been properly established thanks to Leslie Hill, *Blanchot: Extreme Contemporary* (London: Routledge, 1997), and to Christophe Bident's biographical studies in *Maurice Blanchot: Partenaire invisible* (Seyssel: Champ Vallon, 1998).

2. Maurice Blanchot, "La Culture française vue par un Allemand," *La Revue française* 10 (March 27, 1932), 363–65, quotation from 365. The article is a discussion of E. R. Curtius's *Essai sur la France* (1932).

3. Maurice Blanchot, *L'Écriture du désastre* (Paris: Gallimard, 1980), 95; translated by Ann Smock as *The Writing of the Disaster* (Lincoln: University of Nebraska Press, 1986), 57.

CHAPTER 12

1. Nancy's title is an untranslatable pun that collapses together Michel Deguy's family name with a traditional French New Year's greeting associating the New Year with mistletoe (*le gui*, pronounced like the English word *geek* minus the *k*): *Au gui l'an neuf!* English readers might explore the possibilities of

combining Deguy's name with the traditional Guy Fawkes's Day greeting, "A penny for the guy [Deguy]." Throughout this paper, Nancy also makes considerable use, in a number of different ways, of the French word *comme*, which I have translated here, according to context, as "as" or "like," indeed sometimes both.—Trans.

2. Interview with Michel Deguy in *Le Croc'ant* 15 (Spring–Summer 1994): 73.

3. Michel Deguy, *Poèmes* (Paris: Gallimard, 1973), 51.

4. Nancy is alluding here to the title of the collection of essays on Deguy in which this paper first appeared: *Le Poète que je cherche à être* (The Poet I Seek to Be).—Trans.

5. Michel Deguy, *Aux heures d'affluence* (Paris: Seuil, 1993), 55.

6. Michel Deguy, *A ce qui n'en finit pas* (Paris: Seuil, 1995), 122. Since the original edition of the book is unpaginated, I have for convenience numbered continuously the right-hand side of the text.

7. Ibid., 1.

8. Deguy, *Aux heures d'affluence*, 128.

9. Ibid.

10. Deguy, *A ce qui n'en finit pas*, 80.

11. Interview with Deguy in *Le Croc'ant* 15: 75.

12. Hans Sahl, *Lyrik nach Auschwitz? Adorno und die Dichter* (Stuttgart: Reclam, 1995), 144.

13. As elsewhere, the implicit reference here is to Georges Bataille's *The Hatred of Poetry* of 1947, later published under the title *The Impossible*.—Trans.

14. The implicit reference here is to the opening lines of Rimbaud's *A Season in Hell.*—Trans.

15. Michel Deguy, *Gisants* (Paris: Gallimard, 1985), 20.

16. Ibid., 69.

17. Ibid., 63.

18. Deguy, *Poèmes*, 27.

19. Deguy, *A ce qui n'en finit pas*, 106.

20. Ibid., 17.

21. Deguy, *Gisants*, 47.

22. Interview with Deguy in *Le Croc'ant* 15: 75.

23. Ibid., 77.

24. Ibid.

25. Ibid.

26. Deguy, *A ce qui n'en finit pas*, p. 106.

27. I can't find the reference for this ... There had to be one at least, and M.D. cannot find it either: this is what a makeshift working life is like, no doubt ...

28. Deguy says of transcendental schematism (in a lecture in Strasbourg in June 1995) that it is "the philosopher's wailing wall," which seems to imply that the poet's job is to daub it with graffiti.

29. Deguy, *A ce qui n'en finit pas*, 22.
30. Ibid.
31. Deguy, *Gisants*, 35.
32. Deguy, *Poèmes*, 34.
33. Deguy, *A ce qui n'en finit pas*, 46.
34. Ibid., 67.
35. See for example Michel Deguy, *Brevets* (Seyssel: Champ Vallon, 1986), 22.
36. Ibid., 161.
37. Deguy, *Poèmes*, 110.
38. Ibid., 127.
39. Michel Deguy, *Arrêts fréquents* (Paris: A. M. Métailié, 1990), 110.
40. Deguy, *Gisants*, 118.
41. Deguy, *Poèmes*, 71.
42. Deguy, *Arrêts fréquents*, 62.
43. Michel Deguy, ed., *Au sujet du Shoah* (Paris: Belin, 1990), 47.
44. Deguy, *Gisants*, 95.
45. Deguy, *Brevets*, 153.
46. Deguy, *Gisants*, 30.
47. Ibid., 106.
48. Ibid., 131.
49. Deguy, *A ce qui n'en finit pas*, 128.
50. Ibid., 4.
51. Deguy, *Arrêts fréquents*, 115. [Deguy's words are based on an untranslatable pun simultaneously combining the phrase *le poème mot-dit*, literally "the poem word-spoken," and, homophonically, *le poème maudit* (as in *poète maudit*, "ill-starred poet"), literally "the ill-starred poem."—Trans.]
52. Deguy, *Gisants*, 106.
53. Interview with Deguy in *Le Croc'ant* 15: 84.
54. Deguy, *Poèmes*, 61.
55. See Philippe Lacoue-Labarthe et al., *La Politique des poètes* (Paris: Albin Michel, 1992), 63.
56. Deguy, *A ce qui n'en finit pas*, 14.
57. Deguy, *Gisants*, 96.
58. Ibid.
59. Deguy, *A ce qui n'en finit pas*, 126.
60. Ibid., 11.
61. Ibid., 127.
62. Ibid., 126.
63. Deguy, *Gisants*, 39.
64. Deguy, *A ce qui n'en finit pas*, 88.
65. Deguy, *Gisants*, 98.
66. Deguy, *A ce qui n'en finit pas*, 31.

67. Ibid., 77.
68. Ibid., 118.

CHAPTER 13

1. Yves Bonnefoy, *Poèmes* (Paris: Mercure de France, 1978), 304.
2. Ibid., 74.
3. See Michèle Finck, *Yves Bonnefoy, le simple et le sens* (Paris: Corti, 1989).
4. Yves Bonnefoy, *L'Arrière-Pays* (Geneva: Skira, 1972), 110.
5. Yves Bonnefoy, *Rue Traversière* (Paris: Mercure de France, 1977), 64.
6. Plato, *Gorgias* 502c; see, too, *Republic* 601a, and the *Apology* 22b–c.
7. Plato, *Republic* 607d.
8. Pierre Alféri, "A Henri Deluy," *Action poétique*, 131 (Summer 1993): 36.
9. See Bonnefoy, *Poèmes*, 255, 287, 288, 293, 303, etc.
10. Ibid., 312. See also 295, 296 (the word is repeated several times at the end of the line or caesura).
11. Ibid., 261.
12. The text is playing here on the two possible senses of the noun *coupe*: on the one hand "break" or "caesura," and on the other hand "cup" or "vase." The same pun is also exploited in the lines that follow.—Trans.
13. Bonnefoy, *Poèmes*, 272; see also 275.

CHAPTER 14

1. Edmond Jabès, *Le Parcours* (Paris: Gallimard, 1985), 81.
2. " . . . yes, yes—a pure yes-word, the yes-word as name, what does it mean, or how does it go? might it mean Yes?" This German passage and those below are in German in Nancy's original text.—Trans.
3. Nancy is implicitly referring here to *Frêle Bruit* (Paris: Gallimard, 1976), the fourth volume in Michel Leiris's autobiographical sequence *La Règle du jeu*, which also plays considerably on the phonetic and graphic associations of words, including the author's name.—Trans. [See also "Les Iris," Chapter 7 above.—Ed.]
4. " . . . meaning the same as *jota*, from *yod*, which is the Semitic name for the letter that, in the Bible, serves to symbolize what is small or tiny. *Jott* is the tiniest of the tiny, the last tiniest fragment of the name. The letter: as good as nothing. Mystery as less than nothing."—Trans.
5. "Or the book—beech, tree, or wood—marked with a stick: the stick that is the vertical line in runic writing. Jabès writes in Semitic runes."—Trans.
6. "The dash—the stroke of thought—of the literal name: A—B."—Trans.
7. "E.J., J.E., ever, ever and a day, ever since the beginning, ever endlessly saying yes."—Trans.

8. This passage is in English in Nancy's original text.—Trans.

9. Edmond Jabès, *Le Soupçon Le Désert* (Paris: Gallimard, 1978), 99.

10. "*Yes*: Jabès must have spoken German after all. Must have spoken this (for him) unspeakable language. Spoken aloud. Unnoticed by anybody, must have hidden the word and name so deeply in the language that either the one or the other disappears. And never returns. With every letter—jabès—says yes to the writing of this disappearing, and thus writing says yes to itself. Which is what it is also capable of doing."—Trans.

CHAPTER 15

1. "Phrases" would typically be translated as "sentences," although it also can mean "words." I have used "phrases" in order to preserve both of these senses, as well as to allow for the presence of "phrasis," which neither of the usual translations affords.—Trans.

2. Dionys Mascolo, *Autour d'un effort de mémoire. Sur une lettre de Robert Antelme* (Paris: Maurice Nadeau, 1997).

CHAPTER 17

1. Immanuel Kant, *Kritik der Urteilskraft*, in *Kants gesammelte Schriften*, ed. Königlich Preußischen Akademie der Wissenschaften (Berlin: Walter de Gruyter, 1908), 5: 330 (§53).

2. Martin Heidegger, "Der Ursprung des Kunstwerkes," in *Holzwege, Gesamtausgabe*, vol. 5 (Frankfurt am Main: Vittorio Klostermann, 1994), 43; translated by Albert Hofstadter as "The Origin of the Work of Art," in Heidegger, *Basic Writings*, ed. David Farrell Krell (London: Routledge, 1993), 181.

CHAPTER 19

1. Nancy is playing here on the two senses of the verb *demeurer*: "to live or dwell" and "to remain."—Trans.

CHAPTER 23

1. This lecture was given in January 1997 at the Nouveau Musée during On Kawara's exhibition "Whole and Parts." The text was read in the very rooms in which the exhibition itself was being held, the speaker and the public moving their way through it alongside one another. Parts I and II were read in the gallery given over to *One Million Years—Past* (1972) and *One Million Years—Future* (1982–95), Part III in the gallery of *July 21, 1969 (Today Series 1966–)*, Part IV in the *Title* (1965) gallery, which contained the *Vietnam* triptych and *Location Painting (Lat. 31°25'N / Long. 8°41'E)*, and Parts V and VI in the gallery housing

the "Today Series 1966—(30 Years Date Paintings)" (1966–95). My thanks to Jean-Claude Conésa for his active collaboration in this talk, as well as to Jean-Louis Maubant, Pascal Pique, and the whole team at the Nouveau Musée.

2. Lucretius, *De rerum natura* 1.1014 and 4.171.

3. See Hegel, *Encyclopedia*, §257ff.

4. Both "real blackness" and "blackout" are in English in the original.—Trans.

5. Both quotations are in English in the original.—Trans.

CHAPTER 24

1. The verb *expérimenter*, which derives from the same Latin root as the English "experiment," *experiri*, "to try," needs here to be understood in the original sense of its English counterpart. According to the *OED*, this sense is one of experience or of ascertainment through experience (a word derived from the same Latin root). So, too, in *Robert*, where the principle sense of *expérimenter* is given as *connaître par expérience*, "to know by experience." Equally one should note that *expérimenté* tends usually to be rendered by the adjective "experienced." Therefore, both *expérimenter* and *expériencer*, terms that Nancy seems not really to distinguish, have been translated by the English "experience." The reader should bear in mind, however, that what is involved is an active as opposed to a merely passive experience, an *engagement*, perhaps.—Trans.

2. All these have provided the "raw materials" for Soun-gui Kim's video installations.—Trans.

CHAPTER 25

The Matisse epigraph is from *Matisse: Écrits et propos sur l'art*, ed. Dominique Foucade (Paris: Hermann, 1984), 174. (My thanks to Jean-Claude Conésa.) In a note, the editor refers to the version of this remark recalled by Aragon in his own book on Matisse: "We know only these words of Rembrandt's: 'I make portraits.' In times of crisis, I have often clung to these words."

1. And we could immediately add that there can be several different arts of the portrait: pictorial, sculptural, photographic, literary, musical, even chorographic. Here, however, I have limited myself to painting, in which, moreover, there are already several sorts of portrait (self/*allo*, simple or multiple, staged or solitary ...). As will become clear, I am further limiting myself here to the latter, indicating on occasion how the other sorts of portrait highlight its particular traits. In art, everything is always plural, and it would thus be all the more interesting to ponder how the "portrait" is able to pick out its "genre" from the diversity of the arts. This is merely a suggestion.

2. Jean-Marie Pontévia, *Écrits sur l'art* (Bordeaux: William Blake, 1986), 3: 12. These masterly pages on the portrait, like those of Louis Marin, lie behind everything that follows.

3. Staying with the example of Watteau's *Indifferent*, it should be made clear that some paintings that might at first glance appear to be portraits need to be ruled out: Géricault's *Monomaniac of Envy* (Lyon) or Joseph Soumy's *Disdain* (1859, Lyon), for example, as well as all other representations or stagings of affects or passions, however discreet their expression may be. (I should add that I will refer to the date and place of the paintings cited only where the works are sufficiently little-known to make this necessary.)

4. Two cases that are divided by title alone, and not the portrait; see Paul Ricoeur's "Sur un autoportrait de Rembrandt," in *Lectures 3* (Paris: Seuil, 1994). Another and far rarer sort of action would ultimately be admissible, the sort announced in the title *Portrait of a Woman Raising a Curtain* (Jean Raoux, 1720, Lyon). Here, a woman pulls up a blue curtain that, in the foreground of the painting, falls across her; she makes herself thus appear, and we could consider this gesture as a regulated transformation of the basic gesture of painting (the fabric of the canvas drawn aside in order to become a figure, the curtain raised on a presence, etc.). Doubtless it would be possible to analyze in precisely the same vein any number of portraits of reading or writing (Holbein or Quentin Metsys's *Eurasmus*), of sculptors holding a work (Titian's *Jacopo de Strada*, Vienna), or of musicians or even painters themselves holding a score or an instrument (Sofonisba Anguissola, *Self-Portrait at the Harpsichord*, 1561, Althorp). But it goes without saying that we could extend and refine the inquiry as well as the analysis. The "autonomous" portrait has itself various types and accents.

5. This is a position that Milan Kundera, for example, has accurately and carefully developed; see his "Le geste brutal de peintre," in *Bacon: Portraits et autoportraits* (Paris: Les Belles Lettres/Archimbault, 1996).

6. Philippe Lacoue-Labarthe has already dealt with precisely this question in *Portrait de l'artiste, en général* (Paris: Christian Bourgois, 1979). This book—on Urs Lüthi's self-portraits—which Lacoue-Labarthe and François Martin followed some years later with *Retrait de l'artiste, en deux personnes* (Lyon: Éditions MEM/FRAC Rhône-Alpes, 1982), lies behind much of what is being said here, as do the studies of Pontévia and Marin. Of this question, Lacoue-Labarthe writes, among other things, that "for Baudelaire, there is something that obscurely ties these two questions to one another: that of the identity of the painting and that of the identity of the subject." This knot is the very one that I am trying to tie both anew and otherwise, having already dealt with the issue in the question of the portrait in Descartes; see Jean-Luc Nancy, *Ego Sum* (Paris: Flammarion, 1979).

7. The case of extremely large close-ups often appears contemporary, tied as it is to photography. Chuck Close, for example, with *Robert* (1974, New York), approaches the grain of the skin—of the support and of the medium; the limit of the portrait would begin to be touched upon at the point where the figure is opened through all of its pores, even though the skin of the face, along with its

other openings (nose, mouth, ears: all of the senses on offer), is obviously of importance to the arrangement of the look.

8. I cannot deal here with an analysis of nude portraits. The genre is well-represented in contemporary painting, particularly in self-portraits by women. See Frances Borzello, *Femmes au Miroir* (Paris: Thames and Hudson, 1998).

9. On the other hand, that the dress remain relatively discreet is a correlative requirement respected by all the best portraits. By this I mean that a good many official portraits, and so a considerable number of portraits from the classical period, have to be set to one side (albeit only slightly so); we are also dealing with the problem of defining truth in painting ... The so-called "court" portrait (later, the bourgeois portrait) often puts the function before the person (and we know how Goya shook off this genre ... ); it is no longer a portrait but an emblem (one accompanied by a gesture of identification).

10. In particular, of course, the *Guilds* and *Regents* of Franz Hals, Thomas de Keyser, and others. Here again, however, the line is carefully drawn between multiple portraits (group portraits or portraits of groups) and settings that involve the action of positing some camaraderie, with all its attributes and functions ... This is why I would want to say that such portraits are actually quite rare.

11. We could also add double or triple portraits of the same person, in which that person does not look at him- or herself. Rigaud's *Portrait of the Artist's Mother* (Louvre), for example. It is nonetheless possible, however, that the doubling of the same figure plunges or seems to plunge that figure's look into that of its double (Philippe de Champaigne, *Triple Portrait of Richelieu*); this is a variation, then, of the look plunged into our own ... On the other hand, it is no less certain that, in what used to be called "history" paintings, we also find looks that are either lost in vagueness or directed upon the look of the spectator, sometimes in flagrant disregard of narrative convention; the motif of the look runs throughout the whole of painting.

12. Bronzino (1537, Berlin). This, like many of the other paintings referred to here, can be found in Norbert Schneider's *L'Art du Portrait* (Cologne: Benedikt Taschen, 1994), as well as in Flavio Caroli, *L'Anima e il Volto* (Milan: Electa, 1998).

13. For example, Moroni's *Portrait of the Duke of Albuquerque* (1560, Berlin) or similar self-portraits by de Chiciro. It is a matter of displacing the practices of the medallion (in which, it is agreed, we can see one of the origins of the portrait) and of statuary. Yet we can also see how transporting the commemorative inscription into the space of the painting displaces the functions or the senses of either and (or) each.

14. Thus Holbein's *The Basel Jurist Bonifacius Amerbach* (1519, Basel), in which the figure itself declares, in the first person, that its art is not inferior to nature.

15. This is why the portrait was long considered to be an inferior, because utilitarian, genre of painting, the noble genre being that of so-called "history painting." The documents of this history can be found in Édouard Pommier's *Théories du portrait: De la Renaissance aux Lumières* (Paris: Gallimard, 1998). One of the most striking marks of this depreciation is found in the opposition, current in Italy, between *ritrarre* (to make an identity portrait, if I can put it that way) and *imitare* (to paint while correcting the real in order to perfect it). The necessity of "perfecting" or, in any case, in part redoing, embellishing, or ennobling the face that is being painted, something that has been debated throughout the entire history of the portrait, goes back as far as Aristotle, for whom good painters, "by making portraits that resemble those who are being painted, also make them more beautiful" (*Poetics* 54b8). (I am also aware of a juridical arrangement whereby Greek painters and sculptors dedicated themselves to embellishing the characters being represented; see Claudius Aelanius, *Varia Historia*, mentioned by Reinhold Hohl in *Face to Face to Cyberspace*, catalogue to the exhibition of the same name [Basel: Fondation Beyler, 1999], 10.) But this supplement of "beauty" is perhaps also what completes the spiritual or moral "resemblance," perhaps even what completes "resemblance" as a whole by disengaging the subject's "own" traits for themselves. In this regard, see the commentaries on Aristotle's remarks in Roselyne Dupont-Roc and Jean Lallot's edition of the *Poetics* (Paris: Seuil, 1980).

16. "The face of the other is his way of signifying," writes Emmanuel Levinas in *Alterité et Transcendance* (Montpellier: Fata Morgana, 1995), 172.

17. Pommier, *Théories du portrait*, 55. The translation adopted by Pommier rather displaces, and wrongly, in my view, the accent of the first sentence. It would be necessary to follow how the relation of the face to the soul or the spirit has been progressively modified alongside the history of the portrait: from "mirror of the soul," the face became a mere effect of the agitation of the passions (an idea developed by Le Brun), before the risky adventures of the "physiognomies" of the eighteenth century and the various characterologies and typologies of the nineteenth (in which the portrait gets lost in classificatory identification, something to which photography is often thought to be in thrall). See Jean-Jacques Courtine and Claudine Haroche, *Histoire du visage* (Paris: Rivages, 1984 and 1988).

18. See Jacques Derrida, "Forcener le subjectile," in *Artaud. Dessins et portraits* (Paris: Gallimard, 1986), which speaks of nothing other than an unidentifiable identity between the subject and the support of painting.

19. G. W. F. Hegel, *Asthetik*, in *Werke in zwanzig Bände*, ed. Eva Moldenhauer and Michael Karl Markus (Frankfurt am Main: Suhrkamp, 1971), vol. 13, 3.iii.1 §2c. Let me take this opportunity to recall that, in French, the word *portrait* denoted, first and foremost, the whole of painting (see Villard de Honnecourt's

*Livre de portraiture* of the thirteenth century, which contains models for all sorts of scenarios. The modern usage of the term comes into play only with Félibien).

20. This contradictory imitation obviously belongs to the problematic developed at length by Lacoue-Labarthe on the subject of an "originary" *mimesis*, something to which he had already made reference in his study of the self-portrait.

21. Since I shall want to come back later on to the look of the portrait, let us here simply pose the following question: why doesn't Hegel speak of this look when he evokes the painting of the face (of the face "shaped by the labor of Spirit" that is thus itself already an artistic work ... )? And we should remember that it is Hegel who declares elsewhere that art transforms every phenomenon into a look: "art makes each one of its works into a thousand-eyed Argus in which the inner soul and Spirit is seen at every point" (*Werke*, vol. 13, 1.iii.A §1; translated by T. M. Knox as *Aesthetics* [Oxford: Oxford University Press, 1975], 153–54). And it is Hegel, too, who never fails to mention the absence of the look in statuary. So why this singular forgetting? Without wanting to labor the point, given the brevity of the passage on the portrait, let me put forward the hypothesis that he unconsciously refuses to accord too much "spirituality" to painting in order to ensure its place on this side of music and poetry, in which the "sensible" tends to be dissolved. Moreover, although he does indeed recognize "spiritual life" in painting, in the remarks that precede and immediately follow this passage, Hegel still prefers to try to find that "spiritual life" in decidedly religious themes (Madonna and Christ, figures of whom there could precisely be no portrait, or at least no portrait that could present itself as such).

22. "Every painter paints himself," a phrase attributed to Cosimo de Medici. See Pontévia, *Écrits sur l'art*, 38.

23. Doubtless this essay touches closely on questions connected to Heidegger's idea of art as a putting (in) to (the) work of truth, something that also involves a setting to one side of the mimetic or representational conception of art, a conception whose acme the portrait might well be seen to be. (Nonetheless, Heidegger still seems to find no use whatsoever for the portrait, despite the references in the *Kantbuch* to the death mask and even to photographs of death masks; as we shall see, these have precisely nothing in common, however.) Here, I shall not embark on an analysis that still needs to be opened up.

24. These three moments are three logical or dialectical moments: the look will assume or sublate the others; in a sense, however, they also have a certain historical relevance: we could show how the accent has successively shifted from the fifteenth century to our own day; and we could presumably also find in them a certain topical or taxonomic value as regards the different genres of portraits (although I'm not claiming to speak about all forms of the portrait, simply the ones I'm looking at here). But it goes without saying that they are also three simultaneous and indivisible traits of the portrait itself.

25. The phrase articulates the desire for an integral representation while also expressing what matters to painting: the fact that its subject does not speak, *that is, the fact that its subject speaks through painting alone, and all it says is "ego sum"*... On the frequency of this phrase and on the debates surrounding the dignity of the portrait, see Pommier, *Théories du portrait*. So far as the matter of resemblance in its individual precision is concerned, we would need to trace how, in the Renaissance, it came to succeed, by opposing, the aspects of conventional typology still attached to the earliest portraits. What is remarkable about the portrait is that it cannot but be opposed to the idea of a *type* and so, in this sense, of a *model* (whether it be the model of sanctity, of divinity, of virtue or vice, of character or function, etc., whatever). Enrico Castelnuovo has drawn attention to the move from the "typical" portrait (an idea tied to the notion of the medallion) to the "authentic" portrait. A little later on, however, and there would be different *types of portraits*: the court portrait, the moral portrait, portraits "in painting" (itself another sort of portrait), etc. On this, see *Visages du grand siècle* (Paris: Somogy, 1997).

26. One could devote an entire study to the frequency and the (precisely) typical character of stories of recognition through portraits, of blinding flashes of insight before and for portraits, etc., in both historical and fictional narratives from the Renaissance to the eighteenth century. These sorts of scenes are sometimes represented, often being set way back inside a portrait such as Rubens's *Henry IV Admiring a Portrait of Maria de Medici* (Louvre). In *The Magic Flute*, Pamino exclaims, "This portrait is of an entrancing beauty."

27. The question of the portrait's and the self-portrait's reference, a question that I will have to address from several different angles, has been raised in Jean-Louis Déotté, Éric Van de Casteele, and Michel Servière's *Portrait, autoportrait* (Paris: Osiris, 1987), among other works. Let us hold on to the following powerful remarks from Michel Servière: "If we paint, paint ourselves, we do so in order to unpaint, to unmake and remake ourselves. A solitary injunction: junk, abandon the model" (ibid., 110).

28. The self-portrait with mirror is both frequent and old. The first ones of which we know are those of Marcia, who painted two miniatures (1402 and 1404). See the images and texts in Borzello, *Femmes au miroir*, 19–21.

29. "Verso il riguardante," says Roberto Contini in Caroli, *L'Anima e il Volto*, 284.

30. I owe this valuable insight to Sergio Risaliti.

31. As suggested by Contini's remarks in Caroli's *L'Anima e il Volto*. Still, I regret not knowing how to interpret the gilded chord to the left of the cat.

32. Something abundantly illustrated in "vanity" paintings, in certain "toilettes," etc. We would have to study all the associations made in painting between the portrait and the mirror and the uses of the mirror itself, as well as various connections between this theme and those of Narcissus, Sosia, and the

double in general: this entire family of motifs displays essential differences regarding the problematic of the portrait.

33. Such, in fact, would be the case with any "self-portrait." We could also
consider the more developed version of this representation of the representation
of the self in, say, Norman Rockwell's ironic *Self-Portrait* (cover of *The Post*, February 13, 1960), which features several famous self-portraits as well as the painter's
own image in the mirror and on canvas with and without eyes and/or glasses,
etc. (the painting is mentioned by Déotté, Van de Casteele, and Servière in *Portrait, Autoportrait*). We can compare this work to Rockwell's own *Mirror*, which
concentrates all the signs of narcissism. With this genre of representation, however, we leave painting behind; not because the intention is humorous but because the humor stems from a signifying excess (something from which Gumpp's
self-portrait is not wholly exempt).

34. For any portrait, whether or not it chooses to call itself one, it is wholly
impossible to decide whether or not it is painted after a single model or multiple
models, or indeed after any model at all, on the basis of the painting alone.

35. In the sixteenth century, the word "resemblance" had the sense of "portrait," in the expression *ressemblance faire sur le vif,* for example. We should also
note the fact that "resemblance" differs from "reproduction" or from "copy" with
regard to the value of approximation. It is only "semblance" that "resembles,"
that is an "allure," an "air," or an "aspect." In point of fact, all the portrait ever
does is manifest approximate allures of absence. *Resemblance turns on its own absence*: and to turn thus is, strictly speaking, the gesture of the painter's hand.

36. Auguste Pellerin was a great collector and seller of paintings.

37. The same setup is employed in the 1916 portrait.

38. Or *extracting* [traire]: "bringing out." Such is the emblematic value of the
trace or the trait. The trace or the trait is, first and foremost, what is ex-tracted
[*ex-trait*]. Painting is the extraction of the trace or the trait. The "por-" of "portray," homonymous with the French *pour,* "for," is an intensifier (like the "re-" of
"representing" or "resembling"). Just as *repraesentatio* (which follows *praesenta-
tio*) is a putting forward, a bringing to presence, so to portray is to draw forward,
to draw out, to present everything. It is to *render* present. To portray is to draw
out presence—even if the presence in question is only that of an absence.

39. Hence the pleasure taken in *mimesis,* according to Aristotle's well-known
formulation. It is not the pleasure of repetition but the pleasure of coming to
light and of extraction (although, if you prefer, the two are strictly indiscernible).

40. There is a whole typology to be drawn of mouths in portraits; a little later,
I shall want to turn to the half-open mouth of Lotto's *Young Man.* Here, for the
moment, is what Schelling has to say: "In this way, the formative arts are only
the dead word, and yet they are still *words,* still the act of speaking; the more
completely this speaking dies—as great as the utterance that turns to stone on

Niobe's lips—the more sublime is art in its own fashion." F. W. J. Schelling, *Sämmtliche Werke*, ed. K. F. A. Schelling (Stuttgart: J. G. Cotta, 1860); translated by D. W. Stott as *The Philosophy of Art* (Minneapolis: University of Minnesota Press, 1989), 101.

41. Whence the numerous profile portraits in the portrait's early years (often a device used to hide a flaw in the face, as in the case of the famous Federigo da Montefeltre, whose left profile only was painted by Piero della Francesca [Florence], since the right side was missing an eye). Whence, too, the portraits in which the figure holds a medallion. We would also need to trace the history of the progressive move to portraits of people of less elevated status (initially proscribed) and thence to unflattering portraits of elevated figures (see Goya).

42. The phrase is from the valuable book by Jean-Christophe Bailly cited above. It is interesting to note that portraits explicitly connected to death (with the skull, for example, in the various Vanities or Madeleines) are not quite so numerous, despite some truly remarkable cases in Holbein (*The Ambassadors*), Lovis Corinth, Picasso, and Barceló, and in Antonio Saura's *Self-Portrait* (1989), which, to all intents and purposes, is the self-portrait of the head of a dead man. Most of the time, however, it is as if death (infinite absence) had no need of being the theme of portraits, since its presence or substance (its subjectivity) is already marked within the portrait as a whole.

43. "Do not hide your face from me; that I die—so as not to die—but that I may see it . . . ! you, the height of form, who forms everything [*formosissime*]" (St. Augustine, *Confessions* 1.5.12). *Formosissime*: the most formed and the most beautiful, beauty being the correlate of form and form the completion of presence.

44. Of course, there have been plenty of hypotheses, although no firm conclusions. See Wendy Stedman Sheard, "Les Portraits," in *Lorenzo Lotto* (Paris: Réunion des Musées Nationaux, 1998), 44, notes and bibliography.

45. Many similar figures offer their very reserve and self-absorption in this way: Titian's *Man With Grey Eyes* (Florence), Giacometti's *Caroline* (Basel), Picasso's *Olga Koklowa* (1917, Marina Picasso Collection), Memling's *Portrait of a Man* (The Hague), *Ada in White Dress* by Alex Katz (1958, Robert Miller Gallery), Soutine's *Homage to Marie Leconte* (private collection; see Caroli, *L'Anima e il Volto*, 495): a quick list that has no other aim than to evoke the endless "et cetera" that is, in short, one of the major expressions of the portrait, if we can indeed speak here of an "expression" and not, rather better, of an inexpression in which the *recall to intimacy* is unmistakably impressed.

46. Allow me to refer to two other texts: "L'Image—le distinct," in the catalogue to the "Heaven" exhibition (Düsseldorf Kunsthalle, Summer 1999), and "L'Immémorial," in *Cet objet . . .* (Nancy: École nationale des Beaux-Arts, 1999).

47. We could easily show this in the case of court portraits.

48. To his portrait of a child, *Sigismondo Ponzone* (Cremona), Genovesino adds this inscription: "Father, you who have taken part in my formation, receive me formed anew by art."

49. Dürer, as we know, painted himself in the guise of Christ. The theology of man "in the image of God" and that of the Son as the "visible image of the visible" (Paul), the Incarnation and Transubstantiation, together constitute, in the self-deconstruction that Christianity releases onto itself, the armature of every theory of the subject and the easel of all portraiture.

50. Of course, the real movement is more complex. Monologotheism was a long time coming. When Plotinus says that Phidias represented Zeus such as he would be were he to want to appear (*Enneads* 5.8.1), we are on the verge of a transition between a divinity that moves toward presence and one that flies from it. From Plato to Plotinus, the whole of philosophy is played out around a (non)resemblance of and to the "Good."

51. That is, both the prohibition on staying with any vision whatsoever, even that of the sky and light, before that of and in God (see, for example, Deuteronomy 40:66), and the prohibition on reproducing God's formative gesture (Koran 40:66, for example); this is the figure without figure of the figuration of everything that remains out of reach. The history of Western art has constantly been stretched by the (a)theology of an arche-artistic god.

52. Didn't Pope John Paul II feel the need to remind us that God the father ought not to be represented as an old man with a beard? The questions concerning the representation of God, of the impossibility of painting a "portrait" of Christ, etc., were regulated centuries ago, by Catholicism itself, in much the same way as the constant depiction of the Spirit by a bird or by a light, and only very rarely by a human face. We might say that the portrait has taken over from Spirit, leaving the Father and the Son, like Mary, a sort of figuration without portraiture (which again underlines the importance of the declaration: a Madonna can be a portrait, and has been so more than once, but not avowedly so, not distinguished as such. It is still the case that the painting of a Madonna or a Helen or a Venus is organized somewhat differently, however slight such a difference may be, than a painting orchestrated strictly "around a figure").

53. In the wide sense in which I am here using the term, which includes a large percentage of Western figures up to Giotto.

54. As Origen says, after Paul, *Peri Archon* 1.2.6. On the move from the icon to the portrait, see the valuable history provided by Hans Belting in *Image et Culte* (Paris: Cerf, 1998).

55. It has recently been shown, by means of statistics drawn from thousands of portraits, that the vertical median axis of the painting most often passes through one of the eyes. Still, the look comes not from the eyes alone but equally from the mouth (very often central), the nostrils, and the ears, from each of the

pores and touches of paint. Giacometti: "If I have the curve of the eye, I also have its orbit; if I have the orbit, I have the root of the nose, I have the point of the nose, I have the holes of the nose, I have the mouth." See the conversation with Jacques Dupin in Ernst Scheidegger and Peter Münger's 1965 film *Alberto Giacometti*, cited in Hohl, *Face to Face to Cyberspace*.

56. We would have to analyze more closely the technical ingenuity employed in capturing the resemblance of the look, the gleam of the eye and the light that reflects in it so as to shine out of it. Vinci invented the technique of using a third point of light to complete the two-point arrangement that had been used before him to render the light of the eye. Still, it would also be necessary to consider how the look only looks with the contours of the face as a whole, of the mouth and the cheekbones, the nostrils, and the ears ... Along with the face and its whole aspect, the look puts into play the whole of sense, of the ability to be affected and to be touched. In modern times, it is more and more the openness of the eye, a black opacity or an emptying, that will have guided the (re)semblance of the look. The fact that the look is what is proper to painting, its subject, is illustrated by the technique of Bernin, who, in order to complete a bust of the king, sketched out the eye on the stone itself. (My thanks to Stefano Chiodi on this point.)

57. Giulio Paolini has reproduced another of Lotto's portraits, another *Young Man*, from the same period (Florence), giving it the title *Giovane che guarda Lorenzo Lotto* (1967, artist's collection). In 1981 the same young man, his look slightly shifted, was given the title *Contrafigura (critica del punto di vista)* (reproduced in *Giulio Paolini. Images* [Villeurbanne: Le Nouveau Musée, 1984]), and can be compared to other works by the same artist around portraits by Poussin or Ingres, for example. (My thanks to Jean-Claude Conésa.) Barceló writes: "I often work with a blind man. . . . When painting a portrait there's something that can't be avoided, the model's look. . . . With a blind man, there's a sort of *marvelous impunity* that allows me to avoid this fear of the look" (*Miguel Barceló* [Paris: Éditions du Jeu de Paume / Réunion des Musées Nationaux, 1996], 128).

58. To take just two of the numerous examples available to us, Rogier van der Weyden, *Portrait of a Woman* (circa 1460, Washington) and Renato Guttuso, *Mimise col cappello rosso* (1940, Verona). More rarely, the look is almost closed, absent, or empty (reduced to a black hole): Holbein the Younger, *Erasmus in profile* (1523, Louvre); Picasso, *Self-Portrait* (1983, private collection); Monet, *Camille sur la plage* (1870, Paris); Modigliani, *Portrait of Jeanne Hebitène*, etc.

59. It turns toward me, stares at me, and concerns me; it is my business; and, as we say, "it only has eyes for me."

60. The painting comes from an African journey (on the back, the artist has painted the words "Two papayas").

61. *Decet, decorum.*

62. Ludwig Wittgenstein, *Remarks on the Philosophy of Psychology*, ed. and trans. G. E. M. Anscobe and G. H. von Wright (Oxford: Blackwell, 1980), vol. I: §1100. [Nancy, citing Gérard Granel's translation, reads Wittgenstein's *Blick* as *regard* ("look").—Trans.]

63. Here, we would need to take up the analysis of the "encounter" in Duchamp's ready-mades. I refer to the analyses of Thierry de Duve and to the work in progress by Tomàs Maïa.

64. See Jean-Pierre Raynaud's *Self-Portrait (I)* (1980, Osaka), a sculpture that has no other "figure" than the shapes from which it is formed. On the look in Picasso, let me take the following remark from Françoise Gilot, one of thousands of available references: "When he met us, he saw in Geneviève a perfection of forms and, in me, a disquiet that echoed his own character. And, for him, this contrast became an image. . . . He said somewhere: 'I encounter beings that I painted twenty years ago.'" Cited by Rosalind Krauss, "Vivre avec Picasso," in *Je suis le cahier. Les Carnets de Picasso* (Paris: Grasset/Fasquelle, 1986), 121. On Giacometti, see Reinhold Hohl's essays "Das blickende Bildnis," in Hohl, *Face to Face to Cyberspace*; and "Giacometti ou l'autoportrait-défi," in Joëlle Moulin, *Autoportraits du XXe siècle* (Paris: Adam Biro, 1999). See, too, Jean Genet's *L'Atelier d'Alberto Giacometti* (Décines: Barbezat, 1963). Bacon declares, "with faces, you have to capture the energy that emanates from them" (quoted in Hohl, *Face to Face to Cyberspace*, 71). For examples of hyperrealist portraits, see in particular the work of Chuck Close and Franz Gertsch; see also the texts and documents in Dubuffet, ibid.

MERIDIAN

# Crossing Aesthetics

Ernst Bloch, *Literary Essays*

Jacques Derrida, *Resistances of Psychoanalysis*

Marc Froment-Meurice, *That Is to Say: Heidegger's Poetics*

Francis Ponge, *Soap*

Philippe Lacoue-Labarthe, *Typography: Mimesis, Philosophy, Politics*

Giorgio Agamben, *Homo Sacer: Sovereign Power and Bare Life*

Emmanuel Levinas, *Of God Who Comes to Mind*

Bernard Stiegler, Technics and Time, *1: The Fault of Epimetheus*

Werner Hamacher, *pleroma—Reading in Hegel*

Serge Leclaire, *Psychoanalyzing: On the Order of the Unconscious and the Practice of the Letter*

Serge Leclaire, *A Child Is Being Killed: On Primary Narcissism and the Death Drive*

Sigmund Freud, *Writings on Art and Literature*

Cornelius Castoriadis, *World in Fragments: Writings on Politics, Society, Psychoanalysis, and the Imagination*

Thomas Keenan, *Fables of Responsibility: Aberrations and Predicaments in Ethics and Politics*

Emmanuel Levinas, *Proper Names*

Alexander García Düttmann, *At Odds with AIDS: Thinking and Talking About a Virus*

Maurice Blanchot, *Friendship*

Jean-Luc Nancy, *The Muses*

Massimo Cacciari, *Posthumous People: Vienna at the Turning Point*

David E. Wellbery, *The Specular Moment: Goethe's Early Lyric and the Beginnings of Romanticism*

Edmond Jabès, *The Little Book of Unsuspected Subversion*

PHILOSOPHY / AESTHETICS

CROSSING AESTHETICS

"*Multiple Arts* is filled with inexplicit connections, surprises, and openings—a most notable contribution."

—*Henry Sussman, SUNY Buffalo*

This collection of writings by Jean-Luc Nancy, the renowned French critic and poet, delves into the history of philosophy to locate a fundamentally poetic modus operandi. The book represents a daring mixture of Nancy's philosophical essays, writings about artworks, and artwork of his own. With theoretical rigor, Nancy elaborates on the intrinsic multiplicity of art as a concept of "making" and outlines the tensions inherent in the *faire*, the "making" that characterizes the very process of production and thereby the structure of poetry in all its forms. Nancy shows that this multiplication that belongs to the very notion of art makes every single work communicate with every other, all material in the artwork appeal to some other material, and makes art the singular plural of a praxis of the finite imparting of an infinity which is actually there in every utterance. In the collection, Nancy engages with the work of, among others, François Martin, Maurice Blanchot, and On Kawara.

JEAN-LUC NANCY is Professor of Philosophy at the University of Strasbourg. Stanford has published English translations of a number of his works, including *The Muses* (1996), *The Experience of Freedom* (1993), *The Birth to Presence* (1993), *Being Singular Plural* (2000), *The Speculative Remark* (2001), and *A Finite Thinking* (2003).

Stanford University Press
www.sup.org

ISBN 0-8047-3954-4

9000

9 780804 739542

*Cover illustration: Photograph by Guerrero.*
*Cover design: Tim Roberts*